SPECIAL AND COMPENSATORY PROGRAMS

HOW TO ORDER THIS BOOK

BY PHONE: 800-233-9936 or 717-291-5609, 8AM–5PM Eastern Time

BY FAX: 717-295-4538

BY MAIL: Order Department
Technomic Publishing Company, Inc.
851 New Holland Avenue, Box 3535
Lancaster, PA 17604, U.S.A.

BY CREDIT CARD: American Express, VISA, MasterCard

BY WWW SITE: http://www.techpub.com

PERMISSION TO PHOTOCOPY–POLICY STATEMENT

Authorization to photocopy items for internal or personal use, or the internal or personal use of specific clients, is granted by Technomic Publishing Co., Inc. provided that the base fee of US $3.00 per copy, plus US $ .25 per page is paid directly to Copyright Clearance Center, 222 Rosewood Drive, Danvers, MA 01923, USA. For those organizations that have been granted a photocopy license by CCC, a separate system of payment has been arranged. The fee code for users of the Transactional Reporting Service is 1-56676/97 $5.00 + $ .25.

Special and Compensatory Programs
The ADMINISTRATOR'S ROLE

Floyd Boschee, Ed.D.
Associate Professor
Division of Educational Administration
School of Education—University of South Dakota

Bonnie M. Beyer, Ed.D.
Assistant Professor
Educational Administration/Public Administration
School of Education—The University of Michigan–Dearborn

Jeri L. Engelking, Ph.D.
Professor and Associate Dean
Division of Educational Administration
School of Education—University of South Dakota

Marlys Ann Boschee, Ed.D.
Assistant Professor
Division of Curriculum and Instruction
School of Education—University of South Dakota

TECHNOMIC PUBLISHING CO., INC.
LANCASTER · BASEL

Special and Compensatory Programs
a TECHNOMIC publication

Published in the Western Hemisphere by
Technomic Publishing Company, Inc.
851 New Holland Avenue, Box 3535
Lancaster, Pennsylvania 17604 U.S.A.

Distributed in the Rest of the World by
Technomic Publishing AG
Missionsstrasse 44
CH-4055 Basel, Switzerland

Copyright © 1997 by Technomic Publishing Company, Inc.
All rights reserved

No part of this publication may be reproduced, stored in a
retrieval system, or transmitted, in any form or by any means,
electronic, mechanical, photocopying, recording, or otherwise,
without the prior written permission of the publisher.

Printed in the United States of America
10 9 8 7 6 5 4 3 2 1

Main entry under title:
  Special and Compensatory Programs: The Administrator's Role

A Technomic Publishing Company book
Bibliography: p.
Includes index p. 271

Library of Congress Catalog Card No. 97-60882
ISBN No. 1-56676-537-4

CONTENTS

Foreword ix

Preface xi

Acknowledgements xv

Chapter 1. Special Education **1**
Historical Background 1
Legal Base 3
Funding 11
Disability Classification 16
Meetings and Hearings 24
Programs and Services 33
Inclusion 36
The School Administrator's Role 40
Review Activities 42
Endnotes 43

Chapter 2. Gifted and Talented **47**
Historical Background 48
Definition of the Gifted Child 65
Legal Base and Funding 67
Existing Programs 71
Program Implementation 73
Program Assessment 74
The School Administrator's Role 75
Review Activities 77
Endnotes 78

v

Chapter 3. Title I: Helping Disadvantaged Children Meet High Standards...... 83
    Historical Overview   83
    Legal Base   84
    Program Funding   95
    Programs   97
    The School Administrator's Role   101
    Review Activities   104
    Endnotes   105

Chapter 4. Reading Programs...... 107
    Historical Background of Reading Instruction   108
    What Research Tells Us about Reading   112
    The Basic Reading Theories and Models   113
    Reading Models   114
    The Four Approaches in Reading Instruction   116
    Preventive Programs Used in Reading Instruction   124
    Reading Recovery   125
    Early Intervention in Reading (EIR)   129
    The Boulder Project   131
    Success for All Program   133
    The Winston-Salem Project   134
    Students Achieving Independent Learning (SAIL)   135
    Implementing a Reading Program   136
    Improving Reading Skills in Secondary Schools   141
    The Impact of Early Educational Experiences   146
    The School Administrator's Role   150
    Review Activities   154
    Endnotes   155

Chapter 5. Bilingual Education...... 159
    Description and Overview   159
    Historical Background   162
    Research and Legal Base   163
    Program Funding   171
    Instructional Programs   178
    Bilingual Education   179
    English as a Second Language   180
    Instructional Approaches   180

Recommended Programs   182
Intensified Instruction and Program Innovation   183
Bicultural Programs   185
Parent Involvement and Support   185
Administrator's Role   186
Review Activities   188
Endnotes   189

Chapter 6. Vocational, Tech-Prep, and Career Education Programs 195

What are Vocational Education, Tech-Prep Education, and Career Education Programs?   195
What is the Background and Legal Base for Each Program?   197
How is Each Program Funded?   201
What Do Some Existing and Innovative Programs Look Like?   203
What Resources and Support are Necessary for Implementation and Maintenance of Each Program?   209
How Do You Assess Each Program after Implementation?   210
What Is the School Administrator's Role in the Program?   211
Summary   213
Review Activities   213
Endnotes   214

Chapter 7. Multicultural Education 217

Historical Background   218
Sample State Mandates for Multicultural Education   218
Demographic Research Base   225
Curricular Basics for Multicultural Education   229
Multicultural Education Assessment   233
Learning Style Assessment   234
Parent and Community Resources and Support   239
Benefits from Parent-School Relationships   244
Federal Government Support   245
The School Administrator's Role   248

Review Activities 249
Endnotes 250

Chapter 8. Student At-Risk Programs **257**
Characteristics of At-Risk Students 258
Research on At-Risk Students 259
Programs for Dealing with Students at Risk 260
Program Implementation and Assessment 263
Role of the School Administrator 265
Summary 266
Review Activities 266
Endnotes 267

Biographies 269

Index 271

FOREWORD

ALL children and youth are exceptional. Floyd Boschee, Bonnie Beyer, Jeri Engelking, and Marlys Ann Boschee have produced an exceptional textbook that will strengthen school leadership and help all students in special and compensatory programs in America's schools.

This comprehensive look at the vast knowledge base supporting special and compensatory education is a valuable resource for school administrators, teachers, and parents who work to help all children and youth become everything they can be. Our schools have been asked, indeed forced by social conditions, to be all things to all students. While this challenge is daunting, and in some instances impossible for schools to meet all of our children's needs, it is a goal worth our time and energy. Armed with the valuable information found in this book, students of educational administration and practicing school administrators can lead others in developing programs to meet the individual needs and readiness levels of all students.

This book is very readable and well organized. Each chapter begins with a contextual history and provides key definitions to help the reader enter a complex array of programs and content for each area of concentration. Each chapter concludes with a compelling section on the school administrator's role in promoting and leading others in each of the special and compensatory programs.

Professors and graduate students should find the review activities at the end of each chapter valuable for class discussions and debates. The authors have made each chapter manageable for a workshop topic or 3-hour graduate class. This text will facilitate discussion and reflective learning.

The authors have combined their rich practical experiences as school leaders with research expertise to produce a rare book. They have succeeded in aptly treating eight key topics: special education, gifted and talented, Title I, reading programs, bilingual education, vocational/tech prep/career education, multicultural education, and at-risk programs. Many books are written on each topic, but this book captures the essence of each area in a precise and interesting way. This practical, helpful guide is a valuable contribution to the school leadership literature that fills a void for university coursework and staff development programs for school administrators, and will serve as a handy reference book for harried school leaders. I will certainly use this book to help me and my students gain a clearer picture of the confusing array of programs and complex issues surrounding the administration of special and compensatory programs.

I recommend these authors and their wealth of knowledge to you to help you and your staff and community find better paths to help every child find success and well being.

JOHN R. HOYLE
Professor
Educational Administration
Texas A&M University

PREFACE

THE school administrator as educational leader has the responsibility for the daily instructional and management procedures of the school. Ensuring that every student in the school is taught in such a way that he or she benefits academically and socially from the school experience poses a challenging task. It is critical that the school administrator ensures that the individual needs and differences of every student in the school are recognized and accommodated in the instructional process with supporting services.

Students enter schools from a variety of backgrounds and with diverse personal experiences and expectations. Many come to school with the anticipation of learning, only to find that they are not experientially or emotionally ready to meet the demands placed on them. Some children come from home environments where cultural values are very different from those emphasized in schools. These differences can limit their chances for academic success. Others enter school motivated by great expectations for achievement and learning, yet there is a large group of students who come to school only because of societal requirements. The inability of some students to respond appropriately and achieve successfully in traditional academic programs presented in the schools is sometimes the result of inappropriate personal expectations, but more often than not it is related to the failure of the schools to provide the special programs necessary to aid academic and emotional growth. The educational leader has the task of ensuring that all students are provided with the opportunity to achieve to their highest academic potential.

In order to meet individual student needs, you will need to call upon and utilize the expertise of educational specialists; the support services of your school, district, and community; and the financial and programmatic support provided through federal and state special and compensatory programs. These resources may not always be able to provide quick and final solutions to all problems, but they will be able to add the critical dimensions of knowledge and support needed to analyze problems and provide alternatives for the challenges you face.

Special and compensatory programs have been designed and developed to meet specialized student needs in a variety of areas. They have been the result of educational research studies, changes in global economic markets, social and parent group pressures, and local education agencies striving to provide the best educational opportunities possible for the students they serve. These programs are standing recognition to the reality that special and compensatory programs are needed to meet the individual needs, to compensate for difference in readiness levels of students entering schools, and to give all students an equal educational opportunity.

School reform movements have often been the result of national studies that have been implemented following what has been perceived to be a national educational crisis. In the late 1950s, Sputnik was placed into orbit and awakened the United States in the cold war era to the need for schools across the nation to improve their math and science programs. The Eisenhower grants provided monies to help schools improve math and science education. Twenty-five years later, United States' faltering competition in international economic markets heralded the call once again for changes in how and what our students are taught. These suggestions for school improvement and reform were outlined in *A Nation at Risk*, the result of a study commissioned by the U.S. Department of Education. More recently, *America 2000: Improve America's Schools Act* has once again pointed to the fact that our nation's schools have not been meeting the needs of all students and the changing requirements of social structures and of the business and economic communities. As a result, schools and school programs are once again undergoing massive restructuring efforts to provide students with the knowledge they will need to be contributing members in a global economy in the twenty-first century; one that has quickly changed from the need for skilled employees, to a service economy, to one requiring employee technical knowledge and skills.

Special and compensatory educational programs start at birth and provide for a continuum of services throughout elementary and secondary curricula, culminating in school-to-work programs. The programs provide reinforcement in specific academic areas, such as the Elementary and Secondary Education Act's Title I emphasis on reading and math. Bilingual Education and English as a Second Language serve an important role in socializing new arrivals to the American scene and the nation's schools, providing them with the skills to verbally interact and be successful and contributing United States citizens. Migrant Education serves the needs of those families who travel across the nation, gathering the food we offer on the U.S. and world markets. Reading programs provide the support and literacy skills needed to survive on a daily basis. Gifted and Talented programs address the needs of that segment of the student population who might otherwise be lost to boredom and mediocrity without the strong emphasis on creativity, problem solving, and higher order and critical thinking skills. These students will serve the advancement of thought and knowledge so critical to the future of the nation and the world. Changes in immigration laws and the increased representation of people from around the globe has changed the face of student populations as never before in the history of the United States. The diversity of race, religion, and ethnic backgrounds within the schools, coupled with a greater awareness of gender equality and affirmative action issues, creates a multicultural community of learners well served by programs directly related to multicultural issues. Students at risk of failing to learn to their highest academic potential cut across the entire spectrum of our school populations and encompass a variety of factors requiring specialized services and programs to meet these students' needs. Medical science has increased the chances for survival of a large number of infants and children who would not have otherwise made it to school age. This, combined with the recognition of the rights of children with disabilities to be educated in the least restrictive environment with their peers without disabilities, has resulted in a variety of Special Education programs to serve these students' specialized needs. And finally, elementary Career Education and secondary Tech-Prep/School-to-Work programs introduce and then draw together the cumulated knowledge of an entire school career, assisting the student in the final transition from the school setting into the work place.

We have attempted to provide you with information to further your understanding of the delivery of appropriate educational services to all the students in your school or school district through the use of special and compensatory programs. We encourage you to use the resources available in your school, school district, and community, and through state and federal programs, and we ask you to reinforce your teachers as they individualize instruction to meet the unique needs of all students.

You are the role model for educational leadership in your school or school district. As a result of your guiding example and informed leadership, you and your faculty will have the opportunity to develop the best and most effective educational programs serving all your students.

ACKNOWLEDGEMENTS

WE would like to express our sincere appreciation to Marlene J. Lang, English instructor at the University of South Dakota, Vermillion, for editing and for her promptness and guidance. Gratitude is extended to Bonnie M. Beyer, co-author, for originating the thought about the need for a book of this nature and for developing the initial outline of the text.

We dedicate this book to all those individuals in our schools who understand how special and compensatory programs can affect the lives of young people and who toil to ensure that the impact is as positive as possible. This book is also dedicated to our children—Barbara, Brenda, Bonni, Beth Marjorie, Len, Beth Ann, James, and David—who benefited from and whose children may be served by special or compensatory programs in the future.

CHAPTER 1

Special Education

AS special education programs and services have expanded in schools throughout the nation over the past 20 years, so has the confusion among educators concerning who the handicapped are and what services are to be provided to these students. The information in this chapter is presented to assist educational leaders in understanding the role of the school administrator in the education of students who have specific learning needs.

This chapter will not deal with diagnosis techniques, teaching and learning methodologies, curriculum development, or methods of inclusion. This information can be found in detailed form in a variety of books and journals. It will not provide central office requirements related to the implementation of district-wide special education programs. What this chapter will provide is a summary of special education information and a practical guide for the building-level administrator in the implementation, support, and assessment of special education programs at the school site. It will describe the school administrator's role related to the administration of special education services for children with disabilities.

HISTORICAL BACKGROUND

Public Law 94-142, the Education for All Handicapped Children Act (EAHCA), was passed by Congress in 1975.[1] The law became effective 2 years later and opened the doors of public education to all handicapped children by providing access and services for children with disabilities within the regular education setting. EAHCA is a funding statute, making funds available from the federal government to individual states for distribution to local education agencies. In return, the federal government requires states to guarantee a free and appropriate public education to all children with disabilities. The EAHCA has been fully enforced in all fifty states, Department of Defense schools, Bureau of Indian Affairs schools, Puerto Rico, the Virgin Islands, and other United States protectorates. The passage of this act has substantially changed the duties of the regular education administrator by adding responsibilities for the management of special educational programs and services to be provided to students with disabilities.

EAHCA was amended and reauthorized in 1990, as Public Law 101-476, and renamed the Individuals with Disabilities Education Act (IDEA).[2] The definition of disability was expanded under IDEA and its amendments, and the number and type of students served was increased. In addition to IDEA, Section 504 of the Rehabilitation Act of 1973,[3] and subsequent amendments to that act, stipulate that it is the responsibility of the regular education program administrator to provide adaptive instruction and services to handicapped students with learning needs not identified or eligible under IDEA.

School administrators were faced with new challenges during the 1970s as a result of Public Law 94-142. Their primary concern was to ensure access and develop new programs and services for handicapped students within the regular education setting in public schools. During the 1980s, an emphasis was placed on improvement of services, administrative accountability, and the development of transitional services both within the school, from special education to regular education programs, and to post-school experiences. The 1990s have seen efforts by school administrators to meet the diverse needs of the growing numbers of students identified with disabilities; to include students with disabilities into regular education classrooms at an increased rate and to the fullest extent possible; to remain aware of ongoing changes in laws as they relate to program delivery and development; and to increase the collaborative involvement of parents and medical and social support groups in the services provided to students with disabilities.[4]

LEGAL BASE

One of the most challenging jobs of a school administrator is addressing the educational needs of students with disabilities. It is important that school administrators understand the legal base governing the special education programs for which they have responsibility. The components of Section 504 of the Rehabilitation Act of 1973, the Education for All Handicapped Children Act of 1975, better known as Public Law 94-142, and more recently the 1990 Individuals with Disabilities Education Act are extensive and complex. Not only is it necessary that the school administrator understand these federal regulations, the school administrator must also know and understand state laws and regulations and local district policy. In addition, it is equally important that the school leader be aware of current and sometimes conflicting court decisions, as special education laws are continually clarified as a result of these decisions.[5] A school administrator is often approached by concerned and sometimes unhappy parents along with their attorneys and/or parent advocates. In a social climate deluged by confrontation and litigation, parents are more apt to bypass personal dialogue and choose legal action to resolve their issues. While this process is available to parents by law, school administrators need to make sure that when legal advocates question placement, teaching, or services provided, they have the legal knowledge to protect their schools.[6]

As a school administrator, you do not want to be placed in a vulnerable position when parents challenge a decision that has been made regarding the education of their disabled children. Procedural violations by school personnel are cited most often as the greatest limitation in defending parental disputes. It is critical that school administrators be aware of special education laws and requirements and abide by these legal rules and regulations as part of their everyday practice. This may be easier said than done. School administrators and other school personnel must meet the needs of hundreds, and sometimes thousands, of students each day. Parents and their advocates can concentrate their time on legal issues relating to one particular child.

It is therefore imperative that school administrators know the legal framework for educating children with disabilities.[7]

The Education for All Handicapped Children Act and subsequently the Individuals with Disabilities Education Act require states to adopt goals to provide equal educational opportunities for children with disabilities and to provide a free, appropriate public education in the least restrictive environment as a condition for receiving federal funds.[8] Title 34 of the Code of Federal Regulations provides procedures that are required to ensure that the substantive requirements under IDEA are met.[9] In addition, Section 504 of the Rehabilitation Act of 1973 prohibits discrimination against handicapped individuals in any program or activity receiving federal funds.[10]

Educational equity was extended to persons with disabilities during the 1950s to 1970s as an extension of the civil rights movement. The National Association for Retarded Children (subsequently the National Association for Retarded Citizens), established in 1950, followed by the 1954 *Brown v. Board of Education* ruling against segregation,[11] set the precedent for equality in education, which was eventually extended to students with disabilities. The Elementary and Secondary Education Act was amended in 1966 by Public Law 89-750, providing federal funds to states to expand programs for children with disabilities.[12] The movement to integrate handicapped children into regular education programs was reinforced in 1967 by the *Hobson v. Hanson* decision in which it was ruled that a tracking system of student placement in educational programs was found to be discriminatory.[13] The 1970 *Diana v. State Board of Education* ruling against student discrimination practices within the public schools [14] was later supported by *Larry P. v. Riles* in 1984.[15] In both of these cases, it was found that the use of assessment and classification procedures resulting in inappropriate placement of minority students in special education classes was found to be discriminatory. That same year in *Pennsylvania Association for Retarded Citizens v. Commonwealth of Pennsylvania*, it was ruled that children with mental retardation have the right to a free and appropriate public education and parents who are dissatisfied with their children's educational placement have the right to a hearing.[16] Section 504 of Public Law 93-112, also known as the Vocational Rehabilitation Act of 1973, does not allow the exclusion of any person with a disability from vocational programs receiving federal funds and prohibits discrimination against handicapped individuals in any program or activity that receives federal funds.[17] The Education of the Handicapped Amendments of 1974 (P.L. 93-380) provide due process safeguards to students and their parents and assurances of a free and appropriate public education in the least restrictive environment to students with disabilities. These amendments provide federal funds to assist states in developing and improving special education programs and reaffirm the goal of equal educational opportunities for all children.[18] Section 111(a) of Public Law 93-516 in 1974 amended the Vocational Rehabilitation Act of 1973 to provide equal employment opportunities and services for any person with a disability.[19]

Public Law 94-142, the Education for All Handicapped Children Act, is generally regarded as a landmark in the establishment of educational equity for all school-age handicapped children in the United States. It requires that all handicapped children ages 3 through 21 years have access to a free, appropriate public education in the least restrictive environment. The 1977 *Federal Register*, supporting Public Law 94-142, requires public agencies to ensure that children with disabilities are educated with children without disabilities "to the maximum extent possible."[20] Services to the handicapped were further extended in 1983, when the Education of the Handicapped Amendments allowed states to use funds to provide services to children with disabilities from birth to 3 years of age. New programs were also created under these amendments to improve special education services at the secondary level and to provide transitional services to disabled students.[21]

The Regular Education Initiative (REI) of 1986[22] called for the restructuring of both special education and regular education to create a merger between the two groups to facilitate the provision of services to students with disabilities within the regular education setting. Further definition and expansion of special education legislation occurred in 1986 with the passage of PL 99-457, Education of the Handicapped Amendments.

These amendments extended rights and protections of PL 94-142 to children with disabilities ages 3 through 5 and created a new state grant program for infants with disabilities from birth through age 2.[23] The 1990 Americans with Disabilities Act (ADA) extended civil rights protection to persons with disabilities in employment in the private sector, all public services, public accommodations, transportation, and telecommunications.[24]

The Education for All Handicapped Children Act was renamed in 1990 with passage of Public Law 101-476 and became known as IDEA, the Individuals with Disabilities Education Act.[25] IDEA and its subsequent amendments changed legislated terminology from "handicapped children" to "children with disabilities," shifting emphasis from the disability to the child. Two new disability categories, Autism and Traumatic Brain Injury, were identified (see Figure 1.4, page 17) and the scope of the act was increased to include transition services, assistive technology devices, and assistive technology services.[26]

The effect of the act expanded the scope of the law and the responsibility of the school administrator. IDEA also nullified immunity under the Eleventh Amendment to the United States Constitution from lawsuits in federal courts for a state's failure to provide a free, appropriate public education to students with disabilities. This legislation is supported by Title 34 of the Code of Federal Regulations[27] and provides procedures to ensure that the requirements of IDEA are met.[28]

It is imperative that school administrators are aware of legal requirements for educating students with disabilities and the impact this legislation can have on the day-to-day operation of a school. The school administrator cannot afford to make mistakes or have school personnel make mistakes in the provision of educational and supportive services for a disabled child. Knowing and understanding the legal base for special education programs and services to be provided to students with disabilities will make decisions and practice that much easier. The sequence of legislation for the handicapped is shown in Figure 1.1.

1950	National Association for Retarded Citizens
1954	Brown v. The Board of Education of Topeka
1966	Elementary and Secondary Education Act Amendments
1967	Hobson v. Hanson
1970	Diana v. State Board of Education
1973	Section 504 of the Vocational Rehabilitation Act
1974	The Education of the Handicapped Amendments
1974	Vocational Rehabilitation Act Amendments
1975	Education of All Handicapped Children Act
1983	Education of the Handicapped Amendments
1984	Larry P. v. Riles
1984	Pennsylvania Association for Retarded Citizens v. Commonwealth of Pennsylvania
1986	Regular Education Initiative
1986	Education of the Handicapped Amendments
1990	Americans with Disabilities Act
1990	Individuals with Disabilities Education Act

Figure 1.1. Sequence of legislation for the handicapped.

EAHCA and IDEA

The basic tenets of EAHCA, and subsequently IDEA, are to provide a free and appropriate public education, an individualized education plan, specialized education services, related services for children with disabilities, procedural due process, non-discriminatory evaluation, and education in the least re-

---

- A free and appropriate public education
- An individualized education program
- Special education services
- Related services
- Procedural due process
- Nondiscriminatory evaluation
- Education in the least restrictive environment

Figure 1.2. Rights of children with disabilities.

strictive environment (see Figure 1.2).[29] In addition, both acts require that special education students are educated with regular education students to the maximum extent possible. These acts and subsequent amendments not only protect the rights of handicapped children, but also provide federal funding to assist states and local education agencies in the education of children with disabilities.

The following definitions related to the major components of IDEA, as listed in Figure 1.2, are presented to assist you in developing a knowledge base for special education program development and service delivery. This knowledge will be helpful when communicating with teachers, parents, students, legal advocates, community, and support service personnel. It will assist you when hiring and evaluating personnel, in staffings and hearings, and in curriculum planning and development.

Free Appropriate Public Education

The term *free appropriate education* means special education and related services that (a) have been provided at public expense, under public supervision and direction, and without charge; (b) meet the standards of the state education agency; (c) include an appropriate preschool, elementary, or secondary education in the state involved; and (d) are provided in conformity with the individualized education program required under Section 1414(a)(5) of this title.[30]

Individualized Education Program (IEP)

The term *individualized education program* means a written statement for each child with a disability developed in any meeting by a representative of the local educational agency or an intermediate educational unit who is qualified to provide, or supervise the provision of, specially designed instruction to meet the unique needs of children with disabilities, along with the teacher, the parents or guardian of the child, and whenever appropriate, the child. The IEP should include

- a statement of the student's present levels of educational performance
- a statement of annual goals, including short-term instructional objectives
- a statement of the specific special educational and related services to be provided to the child, and the extent to which the child will be able to participate in regular educational programs
- the projected date for initiation of services and anticipated duration of services
- appropriate objective criteria, evaluation procedures, and schedules for determining, on at least an annual basis, whether instructional objectives are being achieved
- a statement of the needed transition services for students beginning no later than age sixteen and annually thereafter (and, when determined appropriate for the individual, beginning at age fourteen or younger) including, when appropriate, a statement of the interagency responsibilities or linkages (or both) before the student leaves the school setting[31]

Special Education

Special education is

specially designed instruction, at no cost to parents or guardians, to meet the unique needs of a handicapped child, including classroom instruction, instruction in physical education, home instruction, and instruction in hospitals and institutions.[32]

Related Services

The term "related services" means transportation, and such developmental, corrective, and other supportive services (including speech pathology and audiology, psychological services, physical and occupational therapy, recreation, and medical and counseling services, except that such medical services shall be for diagnostic and evaluative purposes only) as may be required to assist a handicapped child to benefit from special education, and includes the early identification and assessment of handicapping conditions in children.[33]

A variety of related services are available to the school administrator within the school district as well as through cooperatives, state intermediate educational agencies, and through established school/community collaborative service agencies. In addition to the services listed in the definition of *related services* above, the school should provide any additional necessary services, by qualified individuals, related to early identification, parent counseling and training, social work services, and school health services.[34]

Procedural Due Process

EAHCA contains mandatory procedures that must be followed to ensure that appropriate educational services are extended to the parents and guardians of children with disabilities. These guarantees include that

- Parents must be given notice and an opportunity to participate in the development of a child's education program.
- Parents must be informed of all methods and procedures by which conflicts and grievances may be appealed and resolved.
- A hearing regarding a child's placement must be impartial and unbiased.
- Parents have the right to have the hearing conducted by

a person who is neither an employee of the school district or of the state department of education.[35]
- During the time of appeals, the child must remain or "stay put" in his or her "then current" placement.[36]

Non-Discriminatory Evaluation

Student assessment must be accomplished through the use of non-culturally biased materials. Parent information and inclusion in the evaluation and placement process must be done in the parent's native language. This includes parental rights and responsibilities handbooks and all correspondence and paperwork. An interpreter should be provided as necessary at all meetings and hearings to ensure that the parent or guardian is aware of everything that is being discussed and any decisions that are made as a result of a meeting or hearing.

Least Restrictive Environment

To the maximum extent appropriate, handicapped children, including children in public or private institutions or other care facilities, [should be] educated with children who are not handicapped, and that separate schooling, or other removal of handicapped children from the regular educational environment [should] occur only when the nature or severity of the handicap is such that education in regular classes with the use of supplementary aids and services cannot be achieved satisfactorily.[37]

FUNDING

Financial support of special education programs at the local level is the result of federal, state, and local funding. In addition, a school district may seek grant support for specific services and programs. Presently, federal funding is based on child count. The number of students with disabilities identified by a state determines the amount of money the state will receive to provide special education services to those students. Possible modifications to federal educational funding statutes would change federal funding based on child count to a funding block grant based on the total student population of the state. This change is being proposed to eliminate over-identification of students who may be eligible for special educational services.[38]

Each state receiving federal funds for the education of children with disabilities develops a statewide plan and sets out specific eligibility criteria for special education services to ensure that a free, appropriate public education is available to all students. State laws and regulations have been developed to implement, interpret, and often to expand upon federal regulations. These mandates contain very specific, detailed, and elaborate rules that pertain to educating a disabled child in that state. How special education funds are distributed to local education agencies differs from state to state. Therefore, it is paramount to know the terminology and follow the guidelines developed by state authorities for distribution of funds for special education programs to local education agencies.

Local distribution of funds is generally a central office issue, with each school district developing rules and regulations related to the distribution of funds to individual schools. The school administrator's role is one of identifying and reporting the number of children with disabilities within the school in need of special education services to the central office and keeping track of in-school or out-of-school placement, attendance, and services provided to those students. The amount of funding included in the building and district budget for the provision of special education services will be a direct result of the numbers, types, placement, programs offered, and attendance of students with disabilities reported to the central office and ultimately the state. In large districts, the building administrator will most likely be working with the central office administrator charged with coordinating and directing all special education services within the district. In smaller districts and single-school rural districts, the building administrator may be working directly with the business manager or superintendent in the preparation of state forms and reports to gain funding for the education of students with disabilities.

Funding Formulas

Disbursement of funds to the local education agency and then to the school is based on state statutory regulations. Each state has developed its own formula for the disbursement of special education funds. The amount of funding received will depend upon the distribution formula adopted by the state. A variety of funding formulas have been developed and utilized by individual states (see Figure 1.3). Among the possible formulas are

- *Unit cost* or *reimbursement* for each classroom unit may include the room, teacher, instructional aide, furniture, equipment, materials, utilities, maintenance, and administrative overhead.
- *Weight* is where the district receives a multiple, such as 1.5, 2.0, or 2.5, for each special education student of the amount received for each regular education student.
- *Actual cost* is when the state reimburses a local education agency a specified percentage of their total expenditure for each student (for example, 75 percent of total expenditures).

UNIT COST:	Reimbursement for cost of classroom unit.
WEIGHT:	Reimbursed a multiple per student of regular education funding.
ACTUAL COST:	Reimbursed a percentage of total expenditure for each student.
PERSONNEL COST:	Reimbursed full annual cost of teacher or aide.
FIXED SUM:	Reimbursed a specified sum per pupil.
EXCESS COST:	Reimbursed full amount over cost for regular education student.
BLOCK GRANT:	Overall grant covering special and compensatory programs.

Figure 1.3. State special education funding formulas.

- *Personnel cost* or *reimbursement* is the full annual cost of a teacher or instructional aide.
- *Fixed sum* is when the state reimburses the local education agency (LEA) a specified amount per special education pupil.
- *Excess cost* is when the state pays the difference between the total classroom cost of educating a special education student related to the cost for a regular education student.
- *Block grant* is when the state provides an overall grant to a school district to cover all expenses for all special and compensatory education programs.[39]

In general, average daily attendance rates, disability, and the placement of a child identified with disabilities may affect the amount of funding the district receives. Accordingly, it is important to identify on a daily basis whether the student is in full attendance in your school, one-half day attendance, absent, receiving homebound instruction, placed in an out-of-district facility, hospitalized, or incarcerated. The placement of a student will make a difference in the amount of funding your district will receive, whether you share the educational cost, or whether all funding will be allotted to another educational facility. It is important to follow the district and state guidelines for reporting daily attendance and placement of special education students.

Building-Level Expenditures

Development of a building budget to provide services to students with disabilities is tenuous at best. Budgets are generally based on projected enrollment figures for the coming fiscal year. However, when planning for special education students, flexibility is the key due to the numbers of students with disabilities that may move into or out of the district or special education programs during a school year, as well as the type of services the students will require. Submission of specific resource needs related to personnel, materials, space, and equipment is vitally important if disabled children are to receive appropriate educational opportunities. Full inclusion throughout the school may require new classroom arrangements for regular education teachers. This may necessitate extra and sometimes specialized desks, chairs, tables, storage space, work areas, hygiene facilities, instructional space, materials, and equipment. It may also require the hiring and training of additional regular education teachers, special education teachers, and classroom instructional aides.

It is important to know, as closely as possible, the number of students you anticipate to serve within each disability category and the specific type of services, personnel, and materials required to meet their needs. Depending upon the educational philosophy and choices of the state and local school district board of education, some separate classrooms may be required for instructional purposes. These classrooms will need to be identified and provided with the specialized personnel, space, materials, and equipment directly related to the needs of the students who will be served.

Capital Outlay

If the life expectancy of an item is more than 1 year, it is considered a capital expense. This includes permanent additions to existing land, buildings, and equipment.[40] The addition of extra instructional space, washroom facilities, physical education and therapy equipment, elevators, handrails, and ramps would fall under this category. It is the school administrator's responsibility to ensure that the school facilities and grounds are barrier free for the unimpeded movement of disabled students who may require wheelchairs and other adaptive devices to move from one area of the building and campus to another with the general student population. Regularly checking halls, stairs, elevators, bathrooms, and ramps for obstructions to free passage is important. The addition of wider doors, ramps, hand rails, elevators, electrical outlets, specialized furniture, bathroom facilities, and so forth to ensure free access and use throughout the school facilities will require careful forethought when planning the upcoming budget and school capital improvement needs. It is also important to remember when planning a projected budget that Section 504 of the Rehabilitation Act of

1973 and the Americans with Disabilities Act, though not a part of federally funded special education legislation, nevertheless do require the provision of specialized services and facilities to individuals with disabilities. These services and facilities are to provide equal access not only for students with disabilities, but for faculty and staff as well.

Legal Obligations

EAHCA and subsequently IDEA were enacted by Congress to provide a free and appropriate education to all handicapped children. Local school districts and states may be sued by students, parents, and other child advocates if this is not provided. Court decisions seem to be continually expanding the financial obligation of school districts in relation to provision of services for students with disabilities. The Handicapped Children's Protection Act of 1986 supports this by requiring the losing defendants to pay attorneys' fees and/or money damages to handicapped children.[41] The school administrator must be prepared to answer the demands and emotional concerns of parents, legal guardians, and attorneys. Since legal action is an option often used by parents and other child advocates, the school administrator must possess a knowledge base related to special education law to make sure that the best interests of both the child and the school are equally protected.[42]

The school administrator is required to plan for, provide, and maintain adequate facilities and resources to ensure that all children with disabilities are receiving the required services as described in their Individual Education Plans. Knowledge of your state funding formula and local plan for distribution of special education monies will assist you in planning for present and future needs. Keeping up to date with changing legislative mandates and decisions will assist school administrators in fulfilling their obligation.

DISABILITY CLASSIFICATION

School administrators should develop a knowledge base and understanding of the terminology most commonly used by

Disability Classification 17

special education personnel and found in federal and state statutes. This knowledge will be beneficial in facilitating correct placement, communicating with parents and child advocates, providing for resources, and making decisions related to program development and implementation. The twelve disability categories as identified in the Individuals with Disabilities Education Act[43] are provided in Figure 1.4 and are followed by a short definition of each classification to assist in the development of personal knowledge and understanding of the specific conditions that would qualify a student for special education services.

Learning Disability (LD)

Specific learning disability means a disorder in one or more of the basic psychological processes involved in understanding or in using language, spoken or written, which may manifest itself in an imperfect ability to listen, think, speak, read, write, spell, or to do mathematical calculations. The term includes such conditions as perceptual handicaps, minimal brain dysfunction, dys-

---

- Learning Disability
- Speech and Language Impairment
- Mental Retardation
- Serious Emotional Disturbance
- Multiple Disabilities
- Hearing Impaired
- Visually Impaired
- Orthopedically Impaired
- Other Health Impaired
- Deaf-Blind
- Autism
- Traumatic Brain Injury

Figure 1.4. *Disability classifications.*

lexia, and developmental aphasia. The LD term does not include children who have learning problems which are primarily the result of visual, hearing, or motor handicaps, or mental retardation, or emotional disturbance, or of environmental, cultural, or economic disadvantages.[44]

Speech and Language Impairment

Speech impairment means a communication disorder, such as stuttering, impaired articulation, a language impairment, or a voice impairment, which adversely affects a child's educational performance.[45]

Speech disorders are typically categorized into one of the following five components: articulation, voice, fluency, language, and hearing.[46]

Mentally Retarded (MR)

Mentally retarded means significantly subaverage intellectual functioning, existing concurrently with deficits in adaptive behavior and manifested during the developmental period, which adversely affects a child's educational performance.[47]

Mental retardation refers to substantial limitation in present functioning. It is characterized by significantly subaverage intellectual functioning, existing concurrently with related limitation in two or more of the following applicable adaptive skill areas: communication, self-care, home living, social skills, community use, self-direction, health and safety, functioning academics, leisure, and work.[48]

Serious Emotional Disturbance (SED)

Regulations define *serious emotional disturbance* as follows: A condition exhibiting one or more of the following characteristics over an extended period of time and to a marked degree, which adversely affects educational performance such as:
- an inability to learn, which cannot be explained by intellectual, sensory, or health factors

- an inability to build or maintain satisfactory interpersonal relationships with peers and teachers
- inappropriate types of behavior or feelings under normal circumstances
- a general pervasive mood of unhappiness or depression
- a tendency to develop physical symptoms of fears associated with personal or school problems

SED includes children who are schizophrenic or autistic.[49] SED does not include children who are socially maladjusted, unless it is determined that they are seriously emotionally disturbed.[50]

Children with serious emotional disturbance generally fall into the following three major categories and display a variety of behaviors.

- environmental conflict: aggressive disruptive characteristics such as fighting, bullying, and violating rules
- personal disturbances: anxiety disorders such as crying, statements of worry, and social withdrawal
- learning disorders: deficits in basic academic skills and overall educational achievement

It is also perceived that the educational performance of a student with serious emotional disturbance must be adversely affected for that child to be eligible for special education services.[51]

Multiple Disabilities

Multihandicapped means concomitant impairments (such as mentally retarded, blind and mentally retarded, orthopedically impaired); the combination of which causes such severe educational problems that they cannot be accommodated in special education programs solely for one of the impairments. The term does not include deaf-blind children.[52]

Assessment procedures performed by the multidisciplinary team members will aid in identifying the primary disability and any secondary disabilities.

Hearing Impaired

Individuals with hearing impairments may be classified either as deaf or hard of hearing.

Deaf means a hearing impairment which is so severe that the child is impaired in processing linguistic information through hearing, with or without amplification, [and which] adversely affects educational performance.[53]

Hard of hearing means a hearing impairment, whether permanent or fluctuating, that adversely affects a child's educational performance, but which is not included under the definition of "deaf" in this section.[54]

Visually Impaired

Visually handicapped means a visual impairment that, even with correction, adversely affects a child's educational performance. The term includes both partially seeing and blind children.[55]

The terms *visually impaired, low vision,* or *partially sighted* should be used when referring to a person with some usable sight. The term *blind* should be used for persons with no usable sight.[56]

Orthopedically Impaired

Orthopedically impaired is a severe orthopedic impairment that adversely affects a child's educational performance. The term includes impairment caused by congenital anomaly (e.g., clubfoot, bone tuberculosis, etc.), impairments caused by disease (e.g., poliomyelitis, bone tuberculosis, etc.), and impairments from other causes (e.g., cerebral palsy, amputations, and fractures or burns that cause contractures).[57]

Other Health Impairments

Other health impaired means limited strength, vitality, or alertness due to chronic or acute health problems such as a heart condition, tuberculosis, rheumatic fever, nephritis, asthma, sickle cell anemia, hemophilia, epilepsy, lead poisoning, leukemia, or disabilities that adversely affect a child's educational performance.[58]

An emergency care plan should be developed for children with specific health impairments. All personnel in contact with the student, including bus drivers and other school support staff members, should be familiar with the plan.

Deaf-Blind

Deaf-blind means concomitant hearing and visual impairments, the combination of which causes such severe communication and other developmental and educational problems that they cannot be accommodated in special education programs solely for deaf or blind children.[59]

Autism

The American Psychiatric Association lists the following characteristics of young children with autistic disorder.
  A. A total of six (or more) items from 1, 2, and 3, with at least two items from 1, and one each from 2 and 3 below.
   1. Qualitative impairment in social interaction, as manifested by at least two of the following:
      a. A marked impairment in the use of multiple or verbal behaviors such as eye-to-eye gazing, facial expressions, body postures, and gestures to regulate social interaction.
      b. Failure to develop peer relationships appropriate to developmental level.
      c. Lack of spontaneous seeking to share enjoyment, interests, or achievements of other people (e.g., by a lack of showing, bringing, or pointing out objects of interest).
      d. Lack of social or emotional reciprocity.
   2. Qualitative impairments in communication as manifested by at least one of the following:
      a. Delay in, or total lack of, the development of spoken language (not accompanied by an attempt to compensate through alternative mode of communication such as gesture or mime);
      b. In individuals with adequate speech, marked impair-

ment in the ability to initiate or sustain a conversation with others;
   c. Stereotyped and repetitive use of language or idiosyncratic language; and
   d. Lack of varied, spontaneous make-believe play or social imitative play appropriate to developmental level.
3. Restricted repetitive and stereotyped patterns of behavior, interest, and activities, as manifested by at least one of the following:
   a. Encompassing preoccupation with one or more stereotyped and restricted patterns of interest that is abnormal either in intensity or focus.
   b. Apparently inflexible adherence to specific, nonfunctional routines or rituals.
   c. Stereotyped and repetitive motor mannerisms (e.g., hand or finger flapping or twisting, or complex whole-body movements).
   d. Persistent preoccupation with parts of objects.
4. Delays or abnormal functioning in at least one of the following areas, with onset prior to age 3 years:
   a. Social interaction,
   b. Language as used in social communication, or
   c. Symbolic or imaginative play.[60]

Traumatic Brain Injury

Cognitive functions may change noticeably following a head injury. Some difficulties that the injured person may exhibit are confusion, distractibility, shortened attention span, difficulty remembering recent events, difficulty with language comprehension and expression, irritability, fatigability, impulsivity, and decreased frustration tolerance. Students who have experienced a head injury may experience social/emotional problems. These might include depression and sadness, apathy, poor motivation, sudden mood changes, self-centeredness, and loss of inhibition. Some students may also threaten self-destructive acts.[61]

ADD and ADHD

It is important to address another condition, even though it is not included within the twelve classifications provided by IDEA. The United States Department of Education issued a statement in 1991 concerning children with Attention Deficit Disorder (ADD) and Attention Deficit-Hyperactivity Disorder (ADHD).[62] Though there is currently no common definition of ADD or ADHD, according to the United States Department of Education, children with these disorders may be eligible for special education services under existing categories, such as other health impaired, serious emotional disturbance, or learning disabilities.[63] The condition must be identified by a medical doctor before any provision of services; however, a medical diagnosis is not enough to determine eligibility. You must first be able to show that the condition adversely affects the educational performance of the child for the student to be identified as eligible for services under any of these IDEA categories. If the condition has been determined to exist by a medical doctor, but the student is not found eligible for services under IDEA, the child is eligible for services under Section 504 of the Rehabilitation Act and under the provisions of the Americans with Disabilities Act. If you fail to act on any information received that a student has been medically diagnosed with ADD or ADHD, you violate Section 504 and ADA. You are required to follow up on any information you receive.[64]

The American Psychiatric Association diagnostic criteria for Attention-Deficit/Hyperactivity Disorder falls into

A. Either 1 or 2:
　1. Six (or more) of the following symptoms of inattention have persisted for at least six months to a degree that is maladaptive and inconsistent with developmental level:
　　Inattention
　　a. often fails to give close attention to details or makes careless mistakes in schoolwork, work, or other activities
　　b. often has difficulty sustaining attention in tasks or play activities
　　c. often does not seem to listen when spoken to directly
　　d. often does not follow through on instructions and fails to finish schoolwork, chores, or duties in the workplace (not due to oppositional behavior or failure to understand instructions)

e. often has difficulty organizing tasks and activities
f. often avoids, dislikes, or is reluctant to engage in tasks that require sustained mental effort (such as schoolwork or homework)
g. often loses things necessary for tasks or activities (e.g., toys, school assignments, pencils, books, or tools)
h. is often easily distracted by extraneous stimuli
i. is often forgetful in daily activities
2. Six (or more) of the following symptoms of *hyperactivity-impulsivity* have persisted for at least 6 months to a degree that is maladaptive and inconsistent with developmental level:

Hyperactivity
a. often fidgets with hands or feet or squirms in seat
b. often leaves seat in classroom or in other situations in which remaining seated is expected
c. often runs about or climbs excessively in situations in which it is inappropriate (in adolescents or adults, may be limited to subjective feelings of restlessness)
d. often has difficulty playing or engaging in leisure activities quietly
e. is often "on the go" or often acts as if "driven by a motor"
f. often talks excessively

Impulsivity
g. often blurts out answers before questions have been completed
h. often has difficulty awaiting turn
i. often interrupts or intrudes on others (e.g., butts into conversations or games)

B. Some hyperactive-impulsive or inattentive symptoms that caused impairment were present before age 7 years.
C. Some impairment from the symptoms is present in two or more settings (e.g., at school [or work] and at home).
D. There must be clear evidence of clinically significant impairment in social, academic, or occupational functioning.[65]

MEETINGS AND HEARINGS

A variety of meetings will be held during the course of the year relating to special education placement and services. They may involve initial identification, testing, placement, progress reviews, placement outside of the school or school district, due-process hearings, or liaison services. Any time there may be a change in educational placement or services for a child, it is necessary to hold a meeting of parents and educational professionals who have the expertise to determine eligibility and will be involved in providing educational services. These professionals may include the school administrator, regular education teachers, special education teachers, counselor, school psychologist, diagnostician, social worker, nurse, speech therapist, physical therapist, audiologist, parent, and student where appropriate. Other advocates, medical personnel, or representatives from outside agencies may also be part of these meetings when appropriate. The meetings that will be held most often throughout the school year will include the multidisciplinary placement conference and the annual review. Others may include emergency staffings, exit staffings, re-entry staffings, transitional services staffings, or due process hearings.

It is both important and required that the school administrator or administrative designee is in attendance at special education meetings, staffings, and hearings. The school administrator's presence will demonstrate program support for students to parents, advocates, faculty, and staff who will be involved in the educational decisions relating to children with disabilities. The school administrator's knowledge of educational law, testing procedures, handicapping conditions, and special education curriculum and services will be invaluable when making decisions regarding the identification and placement of children requiring specialized services. All too often placement decisions are deferred by the school administrator to special education personnel and psychologists or diagnosticians. The building administrator should maintain an active role in special education staffings. The building administrator is the professional who must sign for and will be held responsible for all student placement decisions.

Pre-referral Intervention

Prior to referring a student for special education testing, the school administrator, along with the regular education professionals should exhaust all avenues available to them to address a student's learning problem within the regular education program. A variety of interventions are available through the services of the regular education teacher, school counselor, school social worker, other special and compensatory programs, and the school administrator.

It is a cause for concern any time a student is not achieving to his or her highest academic potential, and individualized instruction and interventions are appropriate any time a student demonstrates a lack of comprehension of the class material being presented. A sequence of steps are appropriate in addressing these concerns, and it is the school administrator's role to ensure that these steps have been taken before a student is referred to special education for testing.[66] The steps should be progressive and might include student-teacher conferences, additional academic assistance before, during, or after school, peer tutoring, parent-teacher conferences, and referral to the school counselor, administration, or academic support services. These steps should be clearly outlined in the faculty handbook and addressed at the opening faculty meeting of the school year. Documentation of regular education interventions is essential. This information will be useful when gathering assessment material prior to making any decision related to special education placement.

Identification and Placement

When all regular education interventions have been exhausted and a student has been identified as possibly in need of special education services, a process begins that is outlined strictly under the rules and regulations of IDEA. The procedures and timelines must be rigidly adhered to at each stage of the process. It is important to watch for dates of recommendation and all subsequent meetings to remain in compliance with legal requirements.

The law requires that parents must be given written notice prior to holding any meeting at which the educational placement of the child will be discussed. This includes before conducting an initial evaluation; prior to initial placement or refusal to place; before a reevaluation; to discuss a change in the child's classification; and before changing a child's placement. The notice must be written and in the native language of the parent. In the event that other forms of communication are required, these too must be provided.

Assessment

Generally, assessment includes the child's educational history, a health status report, the classroom teacher's assessment, a social history, academic aptitude and achievement testing, and a psychological profile. Additional assessment is dependent on the reason that the child was originally referred for possible special education services. The testing is done to determine eligibility for special education services falling under one or more of the disability categories as outlined in IDEA (Figure 1.4). Student assessment is accomplished by a multidisciplinary team of professionals. Parent permission is required before the commencement of any testing. Parental involvement is also required as part of the assessment. The school must do its own testing and may not simply accept test results presented by parents from an outside source. The assessment instruments utilized by the appropriate professionals are chosen based on age appropriateness, must be free of cultural bias, and administered in the native language of the student.

Multidisciplinary Conference (MDC)

The multidisciplinary conference is a meeting of school personnel, parents/guardians, and student, when appropriate, to discuss the assessment results and to determine along with the parents or guardian whether placement or continued placement in a special education program will benefit the child's academic performance and growth. The development of the student's Individual Education Plan is part of this meeting.

Before the Multidisciplinary Conference

Ensuring that all the paperwork and procedures are in proper order is essential to the running of a multidisciplinary conference. The school administrator should make sure that school personnel maintain documentation that the parent has received and understands all notices.

School administrators may encounter instances where neither parent can attend the MDC, or a parent may refuse to attend. Where neither parent can attend, other methods of assuring parent participation are available through individual meetings and/or through telephone conferences. In the instance where a parent refuses to attend, a meeting can be held without the parent. In this case, the school district must have a record of its attempts to arrange a mutually agreed upon time and place such as

- detailed records of telephone calls made or attempted and the results of these calls
- copies of correspondence sent to the parents and any responses received
- detailed records of visits made to the parent's home or place of employment and the results of these visits[67]

Remember to document all your efforts. You must be prepared to defend yourself and the district if any issue arises regarding the school district's obligation to provide written notice prior to any conference or testing.

During the Multidisciplinary Conference

The multidisciplinary conference can become quite frustrating and emotional. It is critical to maintain control of the MDC to ensure that all participants contribute to the process. Some school administrators may elect to act as the chair of the meeting. DeWalt offers the following list of tips for the school administrator during the MDC:

- Determine whether all persons who are required for a duly constituted meeting are present.
- Have all individuals present at the meeting introduce themselves.
- Lay the ground rules at the beginning of the meeting.
- Use the meeting agenda to focus the discussion during the meeting.

- Maintain control of the meeting participants.
- Committee decisions concerning the required elements of the IEP must be made by mutual agreement of the required committee members.
- Keep the meeting objectives in mind.
- If mutual agreement is not achieved, the parent/guardian shall be offered a 10-day period.
- The MDC committee should record in writing its findings and decisions regarding the student's IEP.[68]

After the Multidisciplinary Conference

School personnel must follow through with the requirements of the student's IEP. Failure to monitor what happens after the MDC could result in costly due-process hearings and civil litigation. It is imperative that the school administrator design a process by which teachers and other school personnel review student IEPs and make progress reports as to the student's development and educational advancement.

A school administrator cannot possibly know every provision of law there is to know regarding special education. New administrators, in particular, should remain open-minded and listen to parents who voice their concerns. There is no replacement for using "common sense" and problem solving skills to resolve issues before they escalate to more serious, costly, and time-consuming ordeals. Training, preparation, and documentation are the key. The more you know, the more you will be prepared, and the more documentation you will have to show that you followed the rules. School administrators can take the lead in defending against parental challenges, but more importantly, administrators can be instrumental in preventing costly litigation.

Annual Review

An annual review is required by law and must be held each year to coincide with the anniversary of student placement into special education programs and services. The annual review is the time to assess the development and educational progress of each child with disabilities for which your school is responsible.

These conferences are generally held at the school site, but may also be held off campus at other educational facilities, hospitals, or detention sites where the student is receiving special education services. A telephone conference call or interactive television conference may be utilized for students placed outside of the local area. The review conference personnel must include the school administrator, special education teacher, parent, and student if appropriate. Any other specialists who have had interaction with the child during the school year should also be invited. If, for some reason, a specialist is unable to attend the conference it is the duty of the school administrator to present the specialist's pre-prepared annual academic assessment and progress review of the individual student.

Emergency Staffing

On occasion, it may be necessary to review the educational placement of a child before it is time for the annual review. This may be precipitated by an observable emergency situation that may include a medical trauma, dramatic change in student behavior, parental request, or severe and unexplained decrease in academic performance. All persons who would normally be involved in the multidisciplinary staffing or the annual review should be present if there will be a discussion of academic progress or consideration of any change in educational placement.

Exit Staffing

When a student has demonstrated academic progress and it is believed that the student is no longer in need of special education services to meet the requirements of a regular education teacher in a regular education classroom, a conference of those educators involved with the student's progress is convened. The purpose of this conference is to determine the appropriateness of the proposal to return the student to the regular education population and whether transition services are required to ensure maintenance and continued academic improvement. This would normally be done at the annual re-

Meetings and Hearings 31

view; however, if it appears the student is no longer in need of special education services prior to the annual review date, this conference may be called. Once again, this conference will include all those who had previously been invited to the original multidisciplinary conference and annual reviews.

Re-entry Staffing

When a student is returning to your school building from homebound instruction, or another educational, detention, or medical placement site, it is the responsibility of the receiving school to convene a re-entry staffing. This staffing, once again, should include all the educational specialists as mentioned above for other meetings, as well as the educational, social, and medical specialists from the temporary placement site. The purpose of the staffing is to determine present academic standing and appropriate transitional services that will be provided to accommodate educational, psychological, and physical needs of the student, and to ensure a successful transition back to the regular school setting. This staffing will be held in the school if it addresses a return from homebound placement services. If the student will be returning from any other facility, the staffing will be held at either the home school or the temporary placement site. Re-entry staffings related to return from out-of-state placements can be accomplished through a telephone conference call or an interactive television conference to discuss the student's progress with the outside agency's personnel. A follow-up staffing should be held at the school site not long after the student's return to review the student's transition back to the regular school setting.

Due-Process Hearing

The language of EAHCA and IDEA are very clear in stating that the parents or guardians of children with disabilities are accorded due-process rights under the Fourteenth Amendment of the United States Constitution. The law does not refer directly to the child's rights, but instead speaks of the rights of the parent or guardian. Children with disabilities are afforded due-process rights under Section 504 of the Vocational Rehabilitation Act of 1973[69] and therefore have a direct right to a free, appropriate public education and the right to invoke due process procedures if they do not feel they are receiving such an education. The student with a disability has a right to

- prior notice of any meeting or hearing
- due process in the disciplining of handicapped students
- file complaints and have an independent due-process hearing
- maintain current placement during a due-process hearing
- a due-process hearing, and judicial review/appeal to the state department of education, and court appeal
- access to all educational information gathered by the state or local education agency
- the amendment or correction of records that are misleading or false
- hearing if necessary to have records amended or corrected
- inclusion of statements in the records to counter or explain the material
- protection of information from disclosure unless authorized
- a private right of action for violations of the law
- investigation of complaints or assistance regarding violation of the law
- freedom from retaliatory action if the pupil is a complainant
- payment of damages and attorney's fees[70]

Three-Year Reevaluation

All special education students must be reevaluated every 3 years. This full assessment of progress and performance must be accomplished before the third anniversary of the student's original placement in special education programs and services and be reaccomplished every three years thereafter.

PROGRAMS AND SERVICES

As instructional leader and the one responsible for special education programs in your school, the school administrator is in the position to encourage collaborative development of programs that will serve the unique characteristics and needs of all students in the school. Encouraging special education and regular education teachers to work together in the best interests of all children will assist the teachers in overcoming instructional difficulties associated with the inclusion of children with disabilities in the least restrictive environment of the regular education classroom.

Services provided to students with disabilities must meet the specific needs of the disabled child and fall under one of the twelve classifications listed in Figure 1.3, page 13. Full inclusion would require that students with disabilities are assigned into regular education classrooms. The students would be taught by a regular education teacher with the support, as needed, of special education teachers, resource persons, and support service personnel. In large school districts, it may be possible to offer all services in each school building. If the student's IEP requires a resource room or self-contained classroom, the individual school may provide these or the district may create intra-district programs, choosing to assign students to a specific building or cluster that house specialized classrooms, teachers, materials, and resource personnel. Smaller school districts and particularly small rural schools may not have the specialists or facilities required to meet some individual students' needs. In this case, shared inter-district cooperatives, serving many schools and school districts, will be utilized to provide specialized services to students.

Individual Education Plan (IEP)

The Individual Education Plan is the heart of programs serving students with disabilities. It is a statement of individualized instruction outlining required services with goals and objectives and describing how the student's needs will be met. The plan is the direct result of collaborative planning between the school and the parent or guardian and describes the short-term objectives and long-term educational goals for the student, detailing the interventions and services needed to reach those goals. The IEP contains specific instructional methodologies including the minutes per week and year that the student will be receiving the specified instruction. Supportive services are also included in the IEP, detailing any transportation, therapy, or medical services required to ensure that the unique needs of the student are met.

Curriculum Development

Curriculum development for special education students in many ways resembles strategies utilized in outcome-based education (OBE). For example:

> The OBE approach typically requires the identification and specification of measurable student performance outcomes. These outcomes (often called "exit outcomes") are competencies that students must demonstrate before completing a particular lesson, unit, course, or school year. Outcome-based education offers a number of advantages. Prime among them is that the strategy is inclusive. Advocates firmly believe that all students can learn and will learn given the right (i.e., OBE) circumstances.[71]

Curricular development, implementation, and assessment are the essential elements of any curricular plan. The primary functions of curricular planning include the development of learning expectations, implementation of the curriculum, and assessment of student learning as it relates to the curriculum. The development of a special education curriculum plan should include "arranging alternative delivery systems, developing alternative means of assessment, communicating with parents, and communicating and collaborating within and across staffs."[72]

Specific classroom instructional techniques are developed utilizing the expertise of both special education and regular education personnel within the classroom. Inclusion of children with disabilities into the regular classroom will necessitate the sharing of information regarding a particular student, shared lesson plan development, team teaching, and team assessment. Both regular education and special education personnel should be present at multidisciplinary conferences to ensure that both have knowledge of the extent of the student's disability, the recommended individualized educational plan, and how assessment of progress will be determined.

Student support services will vary depending upon the needs of the child. These can include the school counselor, social worker, psychologist, diagnostician, medical doctor, speech and language therapist, physical therapist, audiologist, vocational therapist, or mental health worker to name only some. Outside community service agencies may also be involved to serve the best interests of the child and can be very supportive of the school and its programs. At times, it may be necessary to coordinate educational services between the school and a hospital, detention facility, specialized educational service agency, or the home. As long as a student is registered within a district, it is important to ensure that instruction will continue for the disabled child, wherever he or she may be receiving services. Caution must be practiced by the school administrator relating to programmatic decisions. It is often easier to make changes in programs than to resist the pressures and demands of parents, guardians, and professional interest groups. Program development and changes must be made to serve the educational interest and needs of all students enrolled in a school.

Instructional Support

The school administrator plays an important role as instructional leader in the development, implementation, and assessment of instructional programs. Selective staffing, training, and supervision of personnel in alignment with stated goals are essential steps in ensuring the successful implementation of an instructional program. Regularly scheduled staff development activities will aid both the regular and special education classroom teachers in the preparation and delivery of quality instructional programs that will serve the individualized needs of all students. Knowledge of a variety of instructional methodologies will provide teachers and aides with the skills necessary to meet specialized student needs. Instructional methodologies, such as grouping patterns, cooperative learning, and peer tutoring, can be introduced, explored, and practiced as part of staff development programs. Increased awareness of the importance of ample instructional time, practice time, frequent student feedback, and assessment will result in benefits to both the student and the teacher. Collaborative planning and sharing of knowledge is important to the development of successful staff development programs. Any seminar, conference attendance, workshop, or inservice program should support and add to the professional knowledge of all faculty and staff. This includes not only teachers, but also secretaries, bus drivers, food service personnel, building maintenance personnel, and any other staff members who provide support to the students.

Provision of resources in the form of space, time, materials, personnel, and equipment is vital to instructional program development. Teachers should be provided with the time and space to team together for lesson planning, classroom organization, sharing instructional methodologies and classroom management techniques, and for consultation related to student assessment. Master schedules that include common planning periods, available space for collaborative planning, and assignment of classrooms that facilitate shared planning and teaching are essential to the successful implementation of programs supporting the specialized needs of students with disabilities. The school administrator can provide further program support through the development of school-based problem-solving teams, encouraging parent involvement, and fostering community support.

INCLUSION

It is important to discuss the inclusion of children with disabilities within the regular education classroom. Following the Regular Education Initiative of 1986, there has been a strong emphasis on full inclusion of all disabled children regardless of their handicapping condition into regular education classrooms. Inclusion is nothing new. As pointed out in the earlier section on the legal base for special education services, earliest legislation mandated that handicapped children receive an appropriate education in the least restrictive environment. The question to be asked is, will all children receive an appropriate education that challenges them to their highest potential, or are any students being shortchanged? The social value of full inclusion for both the regular and special education child is valuable for everyone involved. Whether both regular and special education children are receiving an appropriate education, that challenges them to their highest academic potential, together in the least restrictive environment of the same classroom, is yet to be fully determined. There are advocates on both sides of the issue.

A good test for placement of students with disabilities in regular education classrooms has been provided by the Fifth Circuit Court in the case of *Daniel R. R. v. State Board of Education* (1989). In *Daniel R. R.*, the basic floor of service is thoroughly discussed and provides a guideline in determining appropriate educational placement of children with disabilities and educational services to be provided to both regular and special education students. This test consists of the following two questions:

1. Can education in the regular classroom, with the use of supplementary aids and services, be achieved satisfactorily for a given child?
2. Has the district mainstreamed to the maximum extent appropriate?[73]

The court further directs those who are involved in determining placement of a child with disabilities to examine the effect the handicapped child's presence has on the regular classroom environment and thus on the education that regular education students in the classroom are receiving. If there is undue disruption in the classroom, or the disabled child requires so much of the instructor's attention that the instructor will have to ignore the other students' needs in order to attend to the handicapped child, then the placement extends beyond the basic floor of services and is inappropriate. The school administrator must then ask whether the child has been mainstreamed to the maximum extent appropriate. It may be more appropriate to look at an intermediate placement for the disabled child rather than full inclusion in the regular education classroom.

IDEA does not require regular education instructors to devote all or most of their time to one handicapped child, nor does it require that regular education instructors modify the regular education program beyond recognition. Regular education instructors are not required to modify the curriculum to the extent that the handicapped child is not required to learn any of the skills normally taught in regular education.[74]

The key to successful inclusion of children with disabilities into regular education classrooms is training of regular education teachers side-by-side with special education teachers and promoting collaboration in program planning, curricular development, writing of daily lesson plans, and assessment of student progress. Staff development activities are the vehicle available to the building administrator to encourage the development of a knowledge base and the ability of special education and regular education teachers to plan collaboratively in the best interest of both regular and special education students.

If we are to be successful in responding to individual differences, hard work and dedication will be required of everyone concerned with the education of the student. Teachers must be encouraged to realize their integral leadership role in designing learning environments that will maximize success for each student. This will almost assuredly require teachers to provide alternative structures and methods of presenting instruction as well as providing alternative means for students to respond to instructional requirements.

Transition Services

Transition services are required by law when a student is leaving special education programs, changing educational facilities, or leaving educational programs and services altogether at the end of the academic year following the student's twenty-first birthday. Special education personnel in cooperation with specialists and/or regular education personnel, the school administrator, and parents or guardians determine what services are

- Full Inclusion in the Regular Education Classroom
- Full Inclusion with Special Education Aide
- Full Inclusion with Resource Team Support Services
- Resource Room Assistance
- Partially Mainstreamed with Resource Room Assignment
- Self-contained Classroom
- Homebound Instruction
- Specialized Educational Facility
- Hospitalization
- Residential Placement

Figure 1.5. Continuum of services.

REGULAR EDUCATION CLASSROOM

- Individualized instruction from regular education teacher
- Special education and regular education teacher collaboration
- Special education aide
- Resource team support services

RESOURCE ROOM

- Return as needed for individualized instruction
- Partially mainstreamed to regular education

SELF-CONTAINED CLASSROOM

- Cross-categorical placement
- Disability group placement

Figure 1.6. Continuum of service options.

necessary and will be provided by the school to effectuate a smooth transition into a new academic or life setting.

Continuum of Services

The continuum of services available to students with disabilities covers a span from the least restrictive environment (LRE) in the regular education classroom to the most restrictive in an institutionalized setting. IDEA requires that all students with disabilities receive services in the least restrictive environment. Initial consideration for student placement should begin at the level of the regular classroom setting with adapted instruction provided by the regular education teacher. If that setting is not considered appropriate by all participants at the multidisciplinary conference, then considerations for placement should follow the continuum of services listed in Figure 1.5.

When the decision is made to include a student with disabilities in the regular education classroom or with support services in the regular education setting, a variety of instructional options are available as demonstrated in Figure 1.6.

THE SCHOOL ADMINISTRATOR'S ROLE

The school administrator's role as organizational leader and manager is multifaceted and challenging as it relates to the provision of special education services for students with disabilities. Program leadership requires knowledge of the variety of special programs and services available for students with disabilities and the fostering of a vision and culture of coordinated effort directed toward service to all students. Management functions include legal, programmatic, curricular, instructional, budgetary, personnel, and environmental concerns. The systemic leadership role expands the function of the school administrator to include parental and community involvement, inter-agency collaboration, shared decision making, empowerment of others, creativity in program development, and implementation of quality services to meet the needs of all children with disabilities.

The leadership role of the school administrator in the implementation of special education programs in the 1990s and beyond reframes and redefines the expectations and role of the administrator from one of bureaucratic organizational head to one of collaborative planner and shared decision-maker. Changes in how improvement efforts are implemented are necessary to ensure quality programs, not only to be in compliance with federal legislation, but also to guarantee high quality programs and instruction for all students.

Special education can no longer be considered a central office function. The school administrator is the instructional leader and is responsible for the day-to-day management and implementation of programs serving students with disabilities. School administrators should act as role models and regularly set the example for expected behavior of school personnel. The school administrator's knowledge of and participation in all aspects of the special education program will help to set the standard for everyone involved in developing and implementing successful programs that are supported by the entire school community.

America 2000 suggests needs for educational improvement and reform in the areas of student services, school community relations, student achievement in basic skills, and school-to-work programs.[75] The tenets of school reform efforts calling for decentralization, delegation, local control, site-based management, parental involvement, and emphasis on basic skills is nothing new to special education. These tenets have been the foundation of special education programming since its inception. Those who have been involved in special education prior to the implementation of school reform mandates will have an easier time as an administrator implementing a strong special education program. For those new and acting school administrators who have not had the benefit of working with special education programs, the basic tenets of school reform will serve as a guide to leadership in program development, implementation, and assessment.

The school administrator's role in relationship to special education programs is varied and is an extension of regular educational administration (Figure 1.7). Organizational goals and common sense will help guide administrative decisions

- Program development, implementation, and assessment
- Change agent and facilitator
- Budget development and management
- Resource allocation
- Facility management
- Staffing
- Scheduling
- Collaborative planning
- Instructional leadership and supervision
- Curriculum development, implementation, and evaluation
- Staff development
- Articulation between levels and programs
- School community relations
- Promotion of awareness

Figure 1.7. The school administrator's role.

related to personnel, resources, programs, and planning. Organizational change will be ever present as students move in and out of schools, legislation is further defined, and improved instructional technology is developed. Visionary leadership, coupled with strong organizational management skills, will enable the school administrator in collaboration with faculty, staff, parents, and community to develop and deliver special education programs that will meet the specialized educational needs of children with disabilities.

REVIEW ACTIVITIES

1. Create a flow chart for your staff that illustrates the implementation of special education programs and processes in your school.
2. Develop a list of related services that your school has in operation and has access to. Use this list to begin a directory for staff reference.

3. Outline the steps of procedural due process. How does your school implement these procedures?
4. Set up a timeline for meetings and hearings. Address pre-referral intervention, identification and placement, assessment, multidisciplinary conference, annual review, exit staffing, re-entry staffing, and 3-year reevaluation.
5. How many children with disabilities do you have in your school? Identify the needed special education services for these children, and assess the funding.
6. Outline in-school and out-of-school placement, attendance, and services provided to students in need of special education services.

ENDNOTES

1 Education for All Handicapped Children Act. 1975. 20 U.S.C. Sacs. 1400 et seq.

2 Individuals with Disabilities Education Act. 1990. 20 U.S.C. Sacs. 1400 et seq.

3 Section 504 of the Vocational Rehabilitation Act of 1973. 42 U.S.C. 12131 et seq.

4 Wood, J. W. 1989. *Mainstreaming: A Practical Approach for Teachers.* Second edition. New York: Macmillan Publishing Company.

5 Johnson, T. P. 1986. *The Principal's Guide to the Educational Rights of Handicapped Students.* Reston, VA: The National Association of Secondary School Principals.

6 Osborn, A. G., Jr., P. D. Mattia, and F. X. Curran. 1993. *Effective Management of Special Education Programs: A Handbook for School Administrators.* New York: Teachers College Press.

7 DeWalt, M. K. 1995. The Principal's Role in ARD Committee Meetings: Practical Advice for Complying with the Legal Requirements. *The Eighth TASSP-Legal Digest Conference on Education Laws for Principals:* June 13, 1995; Austin, Texas (Conference Paper).

8 See note 1 sup.

9 34 C. F. R. 104.3(j)(1).

10 See note 3 sup.

11 Brown v. Board of Education of Topeka, 347 U.S. 483, 74 S.Ct. 686 (1954).

12 Elementary and Secondary Education Act, 20 U.S.C. 2701 et seq.

13 Hobson v. Hanson, 269 F.Supp. 401 (D.D.C. 1967).

14 Diana v. State Board of Education, No. 70-37 (N.D. Cal. 1970).

15 Larry P. v. Riles, 793 F.2d 969 (9th Cir. 1984).

16 Pennsylvania Association for Retarded Children v. Commonwealth of Pennsylvania, 334 F.Supp. 1257 (e.d.Pa. 1971).

17 Vocational Rehabilitation Act of 1973. 42 U.S.C. 12131 et seq.
18 Education of the Handicapped Amendments. 1977. P.L. 93-380.
19 Vocational Rehabilitation Act Amendments. P.L. 93-516 Sec. 111(a).
20 EAHCA Sec. 121a.550 (b)(1); *Federal Register.* 1977. Washington, DC: Department of Health, Education and Welfare, Office of Education. 42479.
21 EAHCA Amendments of 1986. Part H. Sec. 619.
22 Will, M. C. 1986. "Educating Children With Learning Problems: A Shared Responsibility." *Exceptional Children,* 52:411–415.
23 See note 21 sup.
24 Americans with Disabilities Act of 1990. 29 U.S.C. 794. P.L. 101-336.
25 See note 2 sup.
26 See note 4 sup.
27 See note 9 sup.
28 A variety of information sources were used to develop this summary of special education legislation including Alexander, K. and M. D. Alexander. 1992. *American Public School Law.* Third edition. St. Paul, MN: West Publishing Co.; Data Research, Inc. 1989. *Handicapped Students and Special Education.* Sixth edition. Rosemount, MN: Data Research, Inc. 1989; Education for All Handicapped Children Act. 1975, and the Individuals with Disabilities Education Act. 1990. 20 U.S.C.A. 1400 et seq.; Fischer, L. and G. P. Sorenson. *School Law for Counselors, Psychologists, and Social Workers.* Third edition. White Plains, NY: Longman Publishers, 1996; Osborn, A. G., Jr., P. D. Mattia, and F. X. Curran. *Effective Management of Special Education Programs: A Handbook for School Administrators.* New York: Teachers College Press, 1993; Shrybman J. A. *Due Process in Special Education.* Rockville, MA: Aspen Systems Corporation, 1993; and J. W. Wood. *Mainstreaming: A Practical Approach for Teachers.* Second edition. New York: Macmillan Publishing Company, 1989.
29 20 U.S.C. Sec. 1400(b).
30 20 U.S.C. Sec. 1400(18).
31 20 U.S.C. Sec. 1400(19).
32 20 U.S.C. Sec. 1400(16).
33 20 U.S.C. Sec. 1400(17).
34 *Federal Register,* 42 (163), August 23, 1977. Washington, DC: Department of Health, Education and Welfare, Office of Education.
35 20 U.S.C. Sec. 1415(c).
36 20 U.S.C. Sec. 1415 (3)(e).
37 20 U.S.C. Sec. 1412 (5)(b).
38 See note 7 sup.
39 Bernstein, C. D. 1993. "Financing the Educational Delivery System," in *Integrating General and Special Education,* J. I. Goodlad and T. C. Lovitt, eds. New York: Macmillan Publishing Company.
40 Thompson, D. C., R. C. Wood, and D. S. Honeyman. 1994. *Fiscal Leadership for Schools: Concepts and Practices.* New York: Longman.

Endnotes 45

41 Data Research, Inc. 1989. *Handicapped Students and Special Education.* Sixth edition. Rosemount, MN: Data Research, Inc.
42 Sage, D. D. and L. C. Burrello. 1994. *Leadership in Educational Reform: An Administrator's Guide to Changes in Special Education.* Baltimore, MD: Paul H. Brooks Publishing Co.
43 See note 2 sup.
44 EAHCA Sec.121a.5(b)(9); *Federal Register.* 1977. Washington, DC: Department of Health, Education and Welfare, Office of Education. 42478.
45 EAHCA Sec.121A.5(b)(10); *Federal Register.* 1977. Washington, DC: Department of Health, Education and Welfare, Office of Education. 42478–42479.
46 Hedge, M. N. 1991. *Introduction to Communication Disorders.* Austin, TX: PRO-ED.
47 EAHCA Sec. 121a.5(4); *Federal Register.* 1977. Washington, DC: Department of Health, Education and Welfare, Office of Education. 42478.
48 American Association on Mental Deficiency in *AAMR News and Notes.* (July/August 1992). 5(4), B1.
49 In 1981, the U.S. Department of Education amended EAHCA Sec. 121a.5 "handicapped children" definition to transfer the definition of autism from "seriously emotionally disturbed" to "other health impaired." In 1990, autism was designated a separate disability category under the Individuals with Disabilities Education Act.
50 EAHCA Sec. 121a.5(b)(8); *Federal Register.* 1977. Washington, DC: Department of Health, Education and Welfare, Office of Education. 42478.
51 Cullinan, D. and M. H. Epstein. 1990. "Communication and Sensorimotor Disorders," in N. G. Haring and L. McCormick, eds. *Exceptional Children and Youth,* Fifth edition. New York: Merrill/Macmillan.
52 EAHCA Sec.121a.5(b)(5); *Federal Register.* 1977. Washington, DC: Department of Health, Education and Welfare, Office of Education. 42418.
53 EAHCA Sec.121a.5(b)(1); *Federal Register.* 1977. Washington, DC: Department of Health, Education and Welfare, Office of Education. 42479.
54 EAHCA Sec.121a.5(b)(3); *Federal Register.* 1977. Washington, DC: Department of Health, Education and Welfare, Office of Education. 42479.
55 EAHCA Sec.121a.5(b)(11); *Federal Register.* 1977. Washington, DC: Department of Health, Education and Welfare, Office of Education. 42479.
56 American Federation for the Blind. 1987. *Low vision questions and answers.* New York: Author.
57 EAHCA Sec.121a.5(b)(6); *Federal Register.* 1977. Washington, DC: Department of Health, Education and Welfare, Office of Education. 42468.
58 EAHCA Sec.121a.5(b)(7); *Federal Register.* 1977. Washington, DC: Department of Health, Education and Welfare, Office of Education. 42478.
59 EAHCA Sec. 121a.5(b)(2); *Federal Register.* 1977. Washington, DC: Department of Health, Education and Welfare, Office of Education. 42479.
60 American Psychiatric Association. 1994. *Diagnostic and Statistical Manual of Mental Disorders.* Fourth edition. Washington, DC: Author, pp. 69–71.

61 Gaspard, N. J. and B. Boyce. 1984. *Effects of Minor and Major Head Injury in Children*. Framingham, MA: National Head Injury Foundation.
62 U.S. Department of Education. 1991. "To Assure the Free Appropriate Public Education of All Children with Disabilities." *Thirteenth Annual Report to Congress on the Implementation of the Individuals With Disabilities Education Act.* Washington, DC: U.S. Government Printing Office.
63 See note 4 supra.
64 Kunkel, A. 1995. Attention Deficit Hyperactivity Disorder Under IDEA and Section 504. *Michigan Council of School Attorneys Annual School Law Conference.* Grand Rapids, MI. October 26, 1995 (Conference Presentation).
65 See note 60 sup., pp. 83–84.
66 See note 6 sup.
67 See note 7 sup.
68 See note 7 sup.
69 Shrybman, J. A. 1982. *Due Process in Special Education.* Rockville, MA: Aspen Systems Corporation.
70 A variety of information sources were used in the development of this material including Data Research, Inc. *Handicapped Students and Special Education.* Sixth edition. Rosemount, MN: Data Research, Inc., 1989; EAHCA and IDEA 20 U.S.C.A. 1400 et seq.; Shrybman, J. A. *Due Process in Special Education.* Rockville, MA: Aspen Systems Corporation, 1982.
71 Sergiovanni, T. 1995. *The Principalship: A Reflective Practice Perspective.* Third edition. Boston: Allyn and Bacon, p. 169.
72 Lovitt, T. C. 1993. "Retrospect and Prospect," In *Integrating General and Special Education.* J. I. Goodlad and T. C. Lovitt, eds. New York: Macmillan, p. 270.
73 Daniel R. R. v. State Board of Education, 874 F.2d 1036 (5th Cir. 1989).
74 Horton, J. L. Inclusion—Educating Children in the Least Restrictive Environment. *The Seventh Annual TASSP—Legal Digest Conference on Education Law for Principals.* Austin, TX. June 7, 1994. (Conference Paper).
75 *Goals 2000: Educate America Act.* 1994. 20 U.S.C. 5801 et seq.

CHAPTER 2

Gifted and Talented

EXCEPTIONAL children differ from average children in mental characteristics, sensory abilities, physical characteristics, emotional behavior, or communication abilities to the extent that they require special educational services to develop their potential. The United States Department of Education estimates that 10 to 12 percent of the children in the United States have some type of disability. Another 2 to 3 percent are considered gifted. "For those children at the extremes—the commitment to individualization has been halting and incomplete."[1]

> Failure to help the [disabled] child reach his [or her] potential is a personal tragedy for him [or her] and his [or her] family; failure to help the gifted child reach his [or her] potential is a societal tragedy, the extent of which is difficult to measure, but which is surely great. How can we measure the sonata unwritten, the curative drug undiscovered, the absence of political insight? They are the difference between what we are and what we could be as a society.[2]

Who are the gifted children and youth in our society? Gifted children are those children who "do things a little earlier, a little better, a little faster, and often a little differently than most other children, translating into learning needs and learning styles which are different from those used in the regular classroom."[3] The gifted children generally exhibit high performance or capability in one or more of the following five ability areas: (1) intellectual, (2) creativity, (3) artistic, (4) leadership, and (5) academic.[4] Subsequently, gifted children need instruction at a level and pace as well as conceptual complexity commensurate with their advanced levels of ability and achievement. On the other hand, many school districts do not have programs for the gifted because educators, policy makers, parents, and the public believe in the five common myths that exist about gifted children:

1. Most gifted children come from white, middle-class, suburban families.
2. Gifted students are identified by IQ tests.
3. Gifted students can challenge themselves because they are so smart.
4. Any good teacher can teach the gifted.
5. Most gifted children are fulfilling their potential in school now.[5]

School administrators must understand that America's schools have an enormous stake in the well-being of American society. The youth of today will be summoned to write the unwritten sonata, to discover the curative drug for the unknown affliction, and to provide the political insight for a strong republic. For this to happen, we believe that educators, policy makers (at the local, state, and federal levels), parents, and the public need to pay more attention to how they can improve the educational program to create a more favorable atmosphere for gifted children. They are the difference between what we are and what we could be as a society. As former President John F. Kennedy said, "Let us think of education as a means of developing our greatest abilities, because in each child there is a private hope and dream, which, fulfilled, can be translated into benefits for everyone and greater strengths for our nation."[6]

HISTORICAL BACKGROUND

The earliest notions of gifted education occurred more than 25 centuries ago. Each culture featured the type of giftedness that it valued and rewarded.[7]

Early Notions of Gifted Education: 2000 B.C. to 500 A.D.

The Greek city-states of Sparta and Athens in Europe represent some of the earliest attempts to educate the best and brightest young people to become leaders. In Sparta, for example, newborn babies were examined for solid, well-developed body formation. Those found in excellent health were sent home to be nurtured until they were 7 years of age, and then they were sent to special military schools. The most able became military leaders for Sparta. Those babies found lacking in physical development were put to death.[8]

In the city-state of Athens, the philosopher Plato advocated that the political leaders should be selected from among the most intellectual of society so that a higher social order could be attained. Plato saw intelligence as a series of four stages that extended from total intellectual darkness to light or knowledge. The stages had to be passed through in a sequential order, and the most capable individuals progressed to higher stages of knowledge than those less able to learn. The definition of giftedness was viewed as an abstract, metaphorical description of how the mind developed. Thus, in Plato's view, gifted education included persons who (1) passed through the four stages of knowledge in a rapid manner, (2) reached the highest levels within each stage, (3) progressed through all the stages, and (4) attained a state of total understanding.[9]

Some other occurrences for the gifted that were documented during this period of time included the Chinese civil service examination. This was a test to determine which persons were best qualified for positions in government. Another event that indicated a more formal advanced form of education for the most able was when Daniel and three other boys were taken captive by the Babylonians in Jerusalem and sent to be educated in the court of King Nebuchadnezzar.[10]

The aforementioned landmarks on giftedness indicate that some efforts were made more than 25 centuries ago to educate the brightest in a special way. The accounts are of special significance when one considers that most education during this period was provided in the home.

Middle Age and Renaissance Gifted Education: 500 A.D. to 1800

The first 700 years of this period, 500 A.D. to 1800, regarding gifted education were inactive. Monastery and convent schools prepared persons to lead the church, but they did not seek out the most able in a planned way.[11] During the eighth century, Charlemagne initiated parish schools for all children so that any young person who wanted to learn would have an opportunity to become educated. Some effort was made to identify and nurture child prodigies during the Tang Dynasty (618–906) in China. These efforts continued until 1644 when the Ch'ing Dynasty came to power. Consequently, for 10 centuries, gifted education was valued and nurtured among the people of China. The most able were rewarded with scholarships for study or given government (imperial court) positions. The four concepts of gifted education during this period in China that still exist in the twentieth century are

1. Characteristics such as ability in literary arts, reasoning, capacity for memorizing, imagination, original thinking, and perceptiveness are used to identify the gifted students.
2. Differences between prodigies (children who continued to excel in adulthood) and early bloomers (children who became average as adults) must be discovered so that gifted education serves the appropriate population.
3. Gifted children are nurtured with special educational services to unlock their full potential and productivity.
4. Educational programs are made available to all children, but students with more intellectual capacity are taught in a manner that accommodates their ability.[12]

Near the end of this period in China, the Turkish Empire in Southeastern Europe, ruled by Suleiman the Magnificent (1494–1566), expanded the palace school in Constantinople that was started by Mehmet the Conqueror as a school for children from conquered Christian nations. The palace school was designed to prepare intelligent young boys for government service.[13]

Historical Background 51

On the European mainland, the Renaissance or rebirth of learning for all people began about 1200 and extended to 1700. During this period of time, many gifted individuals surfaced in literature, visual arts, music, and architecture. Dante, da Vinci, Boccaccio, and Michelangelo, whose works have been valued for several centuries, are testimony to the fact that there was an unusual amount of creativity and originality practiced. The gifted were supported by the government, churches, and patrons (wealthy individuals) for several centuries at the time of the Renaissance. For example, Johann Comenius (1592–1670) recognized students with an extreme aptitude for learning and sought money to educate brilliant students who were from poor families.[14]

During this time, the Japanese Tokugawa Society (1604–1868) separated the Samurai nobility from the common people for educational purposes. The intellectually gifted commoners and Samurai were educated in private academies. In this environment, students were promoted based on their skills and abilities rather than on their class. It was during this time period that America was settled and established as a nation. Among the new nation's leaders was Thomas Jefferson, who proposed that "promising youth" be educated at public expense in a university environment. Jefferson wanted to cultivate the talents and abilities of the young people so that the new nation would have able leadership. Even at this early time, Jefferson advocated tests that would identify the most intellectual students for an education at William and Mary College at public expense.[15]

Psychological and Scientific Movement in Gifted Education: 1800–1950

Known as the "psychological and scientific movement" in gifted education, the early part of this period was dominated by a fixed view of intelligence. It was related to scientific inquiry and Darwin's theory about the origin of man. The work, written in 1870 in *Hereditary Genius: An Inquiry Into Its Laws and Consequences* by Francis Galton,[16] related to fixed intelligence. This was the first psychological study of giftedness and stated that a person's intellectual abilities were inherited according to specific laws of genetics. Galton's contributions included the

1. Development of a method to observe and measure human traits
2. Design of statistical methods to summarize data, i.e., percentile rank for one person against the total population—traits of individuals may be distributed on a normal curve
3. Description of traits possessed by gifted children and the origins and development of genius[17]

Galton saw measures of intelligence as one's ability to make sensory discriminations. He defined giftedness as "inherited or unchanging abilities demonstrated in active mind powers."[18]

The view of fixed intelligence was affirmed by J. Mck. Cattell in his 1903 article entitled "A Statistical Study of Eminent Men."[19] Cattell indicated that one's innate characteristics determined one's mental capacity. This belief of intelligence influenced gifted education during the period from 1800 to 1950.

Through the efforts of researchers and scientists, several other ideas about the gifted surfaced. The first psychologist to suggest that some of one's intelligence may be learned was Dr. Alfred Binet. He initiated what was known as the nature/nurture controversy and challenged the "fixed" opinion of intelligence theory. In 1905, Binet demonstrated that

- People have a general aptitude for learning.
- Differences in mental functioning have educational significance for children.
- Developmental tests that sample factors of intellectual performance can be used to measure general learning ability.[20]

Binet's conviction of intelligence could be defined as global, because it involved the functions of reasoning, judgment, and comprehension. Binet's work with Simon in 1905 resulted in the development of the Binet-Simon Intelligence Test that measured a variety of behaviors, but placed emphasis on verbal skills.[21]

The efforts of Binet were followed and expanded by Lewis M. Terman. In 1916, Terman authored *The Measurement of Intelligence,* whereby he made recommendations that school curricula be designed to permit progress at a rate normal for the individual student and that teachers assign work to each student in proportion to his or her ability.[22] He also authored the *Stanford Revision of the Binet-Simon Scale* in 1916. The scale was refined by Dr. Terman in a manner that eliminated subjective biases by the observer and made it a valid instrument to use in identifying students who were gifted. The instrument could also detect various aptitudes for learning in students and established the foundation for research on high aptitude and talent. In addition, the Terman instrument was further refined when Dr. William Stern computed a ratio of mental age to chronological age and derived an intelligence quotient (IQ). The test became known as the Stanford-Binet Test of Intelligence. It reflected his global theory of intelligence and set forth the IQ as a measure of intellectual ability.[23]

Dr. Terman's work has often been referred to as the basis for gifted education in the United States. This conviction has prevailed due to the influence of his longitudinal study of about 1,500 children with IQs over 140, noted in *Genetic Studies of Genius* published in 1925. Even though Terman believed his contribution to mental measurements were more important to education, he realized that his efforts in gifted education would distinguish him as a pioneer in that field.[24] Even though Terman's study has been criticized for not including racial minorities, using procedures that eliminated lower socio-economic groups, and using the word "genius" in an unusual manner, the findings on the characteristics of gifted children were so accurate that identification procedures used in schools today may be traced to his work.

The findings of Terman's study that included 1,500 students with an average IQ of about 150 (eighty students had 170 or higher) revealed that

> Children with an IQ of 140 or higher are, in general, appreciably superior to unselected children in physique, health and social adjustment; markedly superior in moral attitudes as measured either by character tests or by trait ratings; and vastly superior

in their mastery of school subjects as shown by a three-hour battery of achievement tests. In fact, the typical child of the group had mastered the school subjects to a point about two grades beyond the one in which he was enrolled, some of them three or four grades beyond. Moreover, his ability as evidenced by achievement in the different school subjects is so general as to refute completely the traditional belief that gifted children are usually one-sided.[25]

Terman concluded that the evidence on mental development of geniuses and documentation on gifted subjects selected in childhood by mental tests suggested that "the capacity to achieve far beyond the average can be detected early in life by a well-constructed ability test that is heavily weighted with the 'g' factor."

Another psychologist who helped to perpetuate the nature/nurture challenge to the fixed intelligence view was Charles Spearman. He postulated a two-factor structure theory of intelligence in 1904. This theory was based on the supposition that a person's intellectual ability included

1. General aptitude common to all intellectual activities or a "g" factor
2. Specific aptitudes for each instructional area, i.e., math, reading, or "s" factors[26]

Spearman also believed that the "g" factor could be obtained by tests of abstract relations. Terman used this theory in his revision of the Binet-Simon Intelligence Test.

The prevailing view in this time period was that the gifted population is comprised of those students in the top 1 percent. Terman advocated this view as did Leta Hollingworth.[27] A case-history approach to follow children with very high intelligence was conducted by Hollingworth. Her book, *Children Above 180 IQ*, was published in 1942. Like Terman, Hollingworth stressed services in school for the most gifted 1 percent of the population.[28] She also supported early identification and special grouping for the gifted in large school districts. Accordingly, Hollingworth carried out several pilot programs in New York City schools and applied her beliefs. From this study, a narrow view of giftedness was confirmed whereby giftedness meant "merely the child with exceptional intelligence" and it did not refer to gifts in art, poetry, music, or other areas.[29]

A broader view of giftedness was advocated by Paul Witty. He wanted to include talent in the arts and believed the top 10 percent of the population should be served in gifted education.[30] Witty attempted to make it possible for every community and school to provide some type of educational alternatives for the gifted. He analyzed Terman's research and questioned such items as sex differences, absence of blacks, and the role of drive in gifted persons. Witty used his findings to question any narrow definitions of giftedness, especially those based on IQ alone. He was the first person to use the term *greatest resource* in reference to the gifted.

Witty's views were supported by G. Wallas in a 1926 publication entitled *The Art of Thought*. Wallas recognized the four stages in formation of original thought that comprised preparation, incubation, illumination, and verification. This publication was followed in 1938 by L. L. Thurstone's Primary Mental Abilities Test. This test represented knowledge about intellectual structure that was unknown to Spearman 34 years earlier. It was necessary to consider a multiple-factor structure theory, because all of the many factors that play a role in the relationship of various tasks must be analyzed rather than only the general and specific ones. As proposed by Thurstone, intelligence included seven primary mental abilities, which consisted of

- number factors
- verbal factors
- space relations
- memory
- reasoning
- word fluency
- perceptual speed

The factors listed above became the basis for a panorama of giftedness known as the pre-determined view of intelligence. This view prevailed for 15 years. S. L. Pressey added to this belief of giftedness by advocating acceleration of students through school. The theory for acceleration was that the gifted could be more self-fulfilled and contribute to society if they had more years of productivity beyond school.[31] This option for gifted education contributed to a continuing debate about the field of gifted education. It also created a pathway of services for many students.

In 1949, the Wechsler Intelligence Scales for Children and Adults were introduced. The basis of the test was a definition of intelligence that held IQ to be an individual's capacity to act in a purposeful manner and to think in a rational way.[32] This creation was the last contribution to the pre-determined opinion of intelligence.

The 150-year period dominated by psychologists and tests to measure one's intellectual development influenced gifted education in this era. Those contributions, however, are still evident today. Whether this period helped or hindered gifted education is questionable, but the historical imprint of the psychologists cannot be erased.

Gifted Education: 1950s

The first portion of the modern period in gifted education was lured by a 1945 publication entitled *General Education in a Free Society: A Report of the Harvard Committee*. This report emphasized that equal educational opportunity did not mean providing each student the same program, but rather to facilitate access to educational programs that were correlated to the student's talents and interests.[33] As 1950 dawned, the National Education Association's Educational Policies Commission issued *Education of the Gifted*. The publication discussed how the most intellectual children of America were being neglected and the lack of capable leaders in the sciences, arts, and professions. In the same year, J. P. Guilford set forth a challenge to members of the American Psychological Association to research creativity.[34] In spite of the three initiatives that should have produced some movement in gifted education, nothing new or of significance occurred until after the Soviet Union launched Sputnik in 1957.

The interactionist's theory of explaining the concepts of intelligence emerged in the late 1950s. The interactionist

Historical Background   57

theory proposed that intelligence resulted from a dynamic interaction between a person's inherited capabilities and the social, psychological, emotional, and educational environment in which the person was nurtured.[35] Piaget provided the foundation for the concept by proposing that individuals go through stages of continuous development of cognitive structure. He implied that a person advanced through the sensorimotor, preoperational, concrete operational, and formal operations stages while undergoing pressures from the environment. Piaget also documented the importance of pre-verbal development by revealing that experiences before formal schooling were necessary for optimal development. Others suggested that the interactionists should define giftedness as "remarkable performance in any human line of endeavor."[36] In essence, J. P. Guilford's challenge was answered by several breakthroughs in creativity, which provided a broadening of the perception of giftedness held by educators and psychologists. Publications and activities that impacted gifted education were the following:

- *Applied Imagination: Principles and Procedures of Creative Problem Solving* was authored in 1953 by A. F. Osborn. He recommended a personal interaction technique known as "brainstorming."
- *Motivation and Personality,* authored by Abraham Maslow in 1954, espoused that a creative person is self-actualized. He theorized that a basic change occurs in one's personality structure through creativity and the change that occurs leads toward fulfillment.
- *Taxonomy of Educational Objectives: The Classification of Educational Goals, Handbook I, Cognitive Domain,* authored by Benjamin Bloom in 1956, indicated that creative production is required by the learner at the highest levels.
- The journal article, "The Nature of the Creative Process," written by Irving A. Taylor in 1959, suggested that the creative process had five levels, namely, (1) expressive, (2) technical, (3) inventive, (4) innovative, and (5) emergentive.
- In 1959, J. P. Guilford authored "Traits of Creativity."

He responded to the challenge he made in 1950 by creating a three-dimensional model of intelligence called the "Structure of Intellect." Guilford identified 120 cognitive abilities in three categories entitled[37]
1. *Operations*, which describe what a person does in processing ideas.
2. *Contents* are the types of information on which operations are performed.
3. *Products* are the results or outcomes of the information processing.

Two significant events, not related to educators, psychologists, or researchers, were experienced that influenced gifted education in the 1950s. The first phenomenon that caused much discussion was the 1957 launching of Sputnik by the Soviet Union. The launching caused the leaders in the United States to see a need for upgrading educational programs in science, mathematics, and foreign languages.

The shock of the Soviet launching of Sputnik precipitated the United States Congress to pass the National Defense Education Act (NDEA) in 1958. The act was not specifically for gifted education, but it provided federal funds for enhancing public and private school programs in mathematics, foreign languages, and science.[38]

A synopsis of gifted education in the 1950s is characterized with the following:

1. Curriculum content was based upon the cognitive levels of the child.
2. Conceptions of giftedness were broadened by efforts to measure creativity and special talents.
3. Acceleration in some forms became acceptable.
4. Teacher preparation programs began to train teachers of the gifted in appropriate methods to use with this population.
5. The human potential of all socio-economic classes and racial backgrounds was recognized.
6. Governments at the federal and state levels became involved in a direct manner.

7. Social needs of gifted children began to have a place in gifted programs.[39]

Gifted Education: 1960s

The second portion of the modern period in gifted education was characterized as "a decade of turmoil."[40] The nation's leaders in education and politics were supportive of gifted education, but in practice little was done to make educational provisions for the gifted population. The students gifted in the arts, leadership, and the mechanics were neglected, and enrichment programs were considered a frill to be cast aside when budgets became tight. Even though President John F. Kennedy stressed the need to encourage the most able students to go to college, to study science and math, and to place a man on the moon, the civil rights initiatives during the Kennedy era and the war on poverty by President Lyndon Johnson placed primary emphasis on the disadvantaged. The Elementary and Secondary Education Act (ESEA) was passed in 1965 to benefit the less able students. The act did not contain provisions for serving gifted students.

The ESEA of 1965 was amended by Congress in 1969 to authorize state education departments to provide technical assistance for gifted education and award teachers of the gifted fellowships to study in the field. John Gardner's challenge in *Excellence: Can We Be Equal and Excellent Too?* to preserve and nurture the talent found in the nation's young people to a point of excellence was not to be realized in the 1960 decade.[41]

Publications on the gifted in the 1960s, but with significance for later development, were the following:

1. Jacob Getzels and Philip Jackson published research that documented a difference between creativity and the customary view of general intelligence for gifted children. The book, *Creativity and Intelligence: Explorations with Gifted Students*, provided evidence to support the beliefs of researchers and educators who wrote in the previous decade.[42]
2. E. Paul Torrance contributed *Guiding Creative Talent* in

1962. His work provided extensive definitions of creative thinking.
3. David R. Krathwohl edited a publication that classified levels of thinking/objectives in the affective domain. This book was a companion volume to Benjamin Bloom's 1956 book on the cognitive domain. Krathwohl's work is significant, because teachers of gifted students can move more quickly to higher levels of personal involvement, decision making, and commitment.
4. Arnold Toynbee wrote an article entitled "Is America Neglecting Her Creative Talents?" The purpose of the work was to arouse the nation's educators and political leaders by stating: To give a fair chance to potential creativity is a matter of life and death for any society. This is all important, because the outstanding creative ability of a fairly small percentage of the population is mankind's ultimate capital asset.

The aforementioned happenings brought the 1960s to a close, but of more importance was the fact that they helped to set the stage for the next era in gifted education.

Gifted Education: 1970s

The period of gifted education during the 1970s was political, educational, and financial in nature. The 1970s showed "a renewed interest" in gifted education. Gifted education was encouraged by Congress when Public Law 91-230 was passed. The Public Law was entitled "Provisions Related to Gifted and Talented Children" and was added to the ESEA of 1965 as section 806. Subsequently, the political climate established a positive gifted education attitude for the 1970s and beyond. For example, Congress directed the U.S. Commissioner of Education to conduct a study of gifted education and to prepare a status report by 1971.[42]

The findings, presented by Commissioner S. P. Marland in 1971, were that:

- There were a minimum of 2.5 million students in K–12 school that may be gifted.

- A small percentage of gifted students received special education services, but 57.5 percent of the schools reported no gifted students in their schools.
- Gifted education was a very low priority among school administrators and governmental leaders at the federal, state, and local levels.
- Attitudes among most school administrators and teachers was negative toward gifted children. This attitude established identification barriers.
- Gifted students who were not served were damaged psychologically and their abilities were permanently impaired.
- Twenty-one states did not serve gifted students.
- A minimum of one-third of identified gifted students received no specialized programming.[43]

The facts and figures presented stimulated Congress to take action. Congress proclaimed the report a landmark document in gifted education. This declaration attested to the intolerable status of gifted education in America and indicated that Congress was concerned with educating the nation's brightest youth.

The 1970s decade included several other significant publications and happenings in gifted education:

- In 1972, the ERIC Clearinghouse on Handicapped and Gifted Children was established to gather and disseminate information on all aspects of gifted education. The operation has been operated by the Council for Exceptional Children since its creation.[44]
- The National State Leadership Training Institute (LTI) was established in 1972 to direct changes in gifted education at the state level and develop staff development/inservice training packages for local, state, and regional education agencies.[45]
- The U.S. Office of Gifted and Talented Education was established in 1972 under jurisdiction of the Special Projects Act of Public Law 93-380. The office focused the nation's attention on the needs of gifted children and

exercised leadership in advocating for differentiated programming for the gifted at the local, state, and regional levels.[46]
- In 1975, Congress passed Public Law 94-142, the Education for All Handicapped Act. The legislation provided that all exceptional children must have a free, appropriate public education available. The act did not include any specific references to gifted education, but it has been used as a model for special education legislation in many states that includes provision for gifted education as well as all other types of handicapping conditions.[47]
- Categorical funds for gifted education were made available for the first time in 1975 under Section 404 of the Special Projects Act of Public Law 93-380. The funds were used to provide training for teachers, information to schools and parents, and for grants to state agencies and program evaluation.[48]
- A follow-up to the Marland report was published in 1978. The study reported that adequate funding was not available, training programs were not available, teachers of the gifted were insufficient in number and those teachers available had inadequate training, and there were problems with identification of the gifted and program evaluation.[49]
- Congress passed Public Law 95-561 in 1978. This act gave funds to local and state educational agencies, higher education institutions, and organizations to plan, develop, operate, and improve gifted education programs. The Gifted and Talented Children's Education Act provided for authorization of $25 million in fiscal year 1979 to $50 million in fiscal year 1983.[50]

All of the events representing educational, financial, and political entanglement listed above influenced gifted education in the 1970s. In essence, legislation to establish gifted education programs in the 50 states was popular in the 1970s. In addition to political groups advocating the establishment and funding of gifted programs, a broadened definition for gifted was developed. James Gallagher made it known that the definition was developed in the Marland Report for the purpose of assisting educators to identify students who should be served in gifted education programs. The definition was the first formal recognition at the federal level of the problems of education for children who are gifted.[51] The definition read

> Gifted and talented children are those identified by professionally qualified persons [and] who by virtue of outstanding abilities are capable of high performance. These are children who require differentiated educational programs and services beyond those normally provided by the regular school program in order to realize their contribution to self and society.
>
> Children capable of high performance include those with demonstrated achievement and/or potential ability in any of the following areas:
>
> 1. General intellectual ability
> 2. Specific academic aptitude
> 3. Creative or productive thinking
> 4. Leadership ability
> 5. Visual and performing arts
> 6. Psychomotor ability[52]

Although the definition made a contribution to the gifted education movement in America, it also had some problems in terms of how it was operationalized. Subsequently, the definition was modified by the Gifted and Talented Children's Act in 1978 to clarify that "gifted and talented children" meant children and youth at the preschool, elementary, and secondary levels. The act also omitted the category of psychomotor ability.[53] Too, the use of psychological tests (reliance on one IQ score) for identifying gifted children was replaced by a multiple identification criteria approach in 46 states during this era.

Even though progress was made during the 1970s in the area of gifted program student identification, there were many unresolved issues in the area of selecting gifted students with needs to be addressed.[54]

Gifted Education: 1980s

As the decade of the 1980s began, President Ronald Reagan initiated a new federal program. One part of that effort abolished the U.S. Office of Gifted and Talented Education and eliminated all federal support when the Education Consolidation and Improvement Act of 1981 was signed into law.[55] The Republican administration attempted to encourage leaders in business and industry to provide financial support to gifted education through the National Business Consortium for the Gifted and Talented. Secretary of Education, Terrel H. Bell, remarked that "the group we fail most is the gifted and talented. They may never reach the outer limits of their ability."[56] This comment by a Reagan cabinet member indicated that the United States was sacrificing its best investment.

Another initiative by the Reagan administration was the creation of the National Commission on Excellence in Education in 1981. The commission's report, *A Nation at Risk,*[57] considered many issues, but in making recommendations referred to the gifted and talented, in a general way, as a key group of students whose needs should be met. The report emphasized excellence in basic skills, more rigorous standards for high school graduation, additional time on learning, and increased salary, training, and responsibilities for teachers. Overall, the report did not impede gifted education, but it was supportive only in an indirect manner. Subsequently, the impact of the study was a setback in the forward movement of gifted education.[58]

Congressional efforts to establish gifted education as a priority were initiated in 1984 with the introduction of the Education for Gifted and Talented Children and Youth Improvement Act.[59] The bill (H.R. 5596) was not heard by the ninety-eighth Congress, but two bills regarding gifted education were introduced in the Senate and one in the House of Representatives at the opening of the ninety-ninth Congress. The Senate bills were (1) S. 134 to reestablish the Office of Gifted and Talented, and (2) S. 452 known as the Jacob K. Javits Gifted and Talented Children's Education Act to reestablish the Office of Gifted and Talented Education and to provide financial assistance for gifted programs. The House bill (H.R. 3263) entitled Gifted and Talented Children and Youth Act of 1985 was passed by the House and authorized $10 million in financial support in addition to creating a National Center for Research and Development on identifying and serving gifted children. Thus, efforts on the part of the national leaders continued in the 1980s, although none of them resulted in solid support for gifted education at the federal level.

The net result of gifted education through the 1980s showed the following:

- Progress was made in the previous decade, but many issues remained unresolved.
- General awareness of the needs of gifted students was not widespread.
- Gifted programs were not cost-effective, were limited to the academic needs of students, and were of a piecemeal nature.
- Evaluation of programs was limited, and available research was not used as the basis for designing new programs.
- Program models were not adaptable from one school/community to another, and most programs were staffed by teachers with inadequate training.
- Curriculum for the gifted programs tended to emphasize acceleration and gifted students doing more of the same rather than receiving differentiated programming.[60]

The events for gifted education up to the 1990s era made some progress in serving the gifted population. It is evident that the disposition of society and the prevailing attitudes of people at any time determine how the most talented citizens are treated. There was, however, a trend to include more students in gifted programs as psychologists discovered more about the human mind and body. In essence, each decade from the 1950s to the 1990s manifested a need for more efforts to meet the needs of all the gifted children and youth in America.

DEFINITION OF THE GIFTED CHILD

As noted in the historical background, "each culture appears to feature the type of giftedness that it rewards or values."[61] For example,

> The ancient Greeks produced great orators; the Romans, who followed them, produced excellent engineers. The Renaissance artists of sixteenth-century Italy, the German composers of the seventeenth century, and the English writers of the nineteenth century illustrate the emergence of talent that is specifically rewarded in a particular culture at a particular time.[62]

Although there are many renditions of a definition for gifted children, the most frequently used refer to Marland's (1972) and Javits's (1988) definitions, which are displayed in Figure 2.1. "Each has been generated at the federal level and many states have followed the essence of these federal definitions with their own statements."[63]

Even though the Marland definition is over 25 years old, a majority of the states still fashion their definition for gifted

Marland (1972) Definition	Javits (1988) Definition
Gifted and talented children are those identified by professionally qualified persons who by virtue of outstanding abilities are capable of high performance. These are children who require differential educational programs and services beyond those normally provided by the regular school program in order to realize their contribution to self and society. Children capable of high performance include those with demonstrated achievement and/or potential ability in any of the following areas: 1. General intellectual aptitude 2. Specific academic aptitude 3. Creative or productive thinking 4. Leadership ability 5. Visual and performing arts	The term gifted and talented student means children and youth who: 1. Give evidence of higher performance capability in such areas as artistic, creative, intellectual, or leadership capacity or in specific academic fields; and who 2. Require services or activities not ordinarily provided by the schools in order to develop such capabilities fully.

Figure 2.1. Definitions of the gifted child.[64]

students on this model. School administrators, teachers, school board members, parents, and community members should understand that gifted children "require differentiated educational programs."[65] The key words in the Marland definition are that gifted students have outstanding abilities and "are capable of high performance."[66]

The Javits language for the gifted child is simpler than the Marland definition. Both, however, discuss capabilities rather than achievement, and both indicate the necessity for gifted students to receive special educational services.

Model legislation proposed by the Gifted Education Policy Studies Program at the University of North Carolina at Chapel Hill defines the gifted and talented as

> Gifted and talented students (or children and youth with outstanding talent) as those students between preschool and twelfth grade who (when compared to others of their age, experience, or environment) excel consistently, or demonstrate the potential to excel consistently, in any one or more of the following areas: general intellectual ability and aptitude, creativity, leadership, or the arts.[67]

The model legislation definition proposed for the gifted and talented specifically states that "in order to achieve their potential, these students require educational experiences beyond those normally provided by the general school program."[68]

LEGAL BASE AND FUNDING

Federal dollars are made available through the Jacob K. Javits Gifted and Talented Students Education Act of 1988. The act was designed to "provide financial assistance to state and local educational agencies, institutions of higher education, and other public and private agencies and organizations that provide educational services to gifted and talented students."[69] The types of projects funded under the Javits program are

- preservice and inservice training for personnel involved in the education of gifted and talented students
- model projects and exemplary programs for the

identification and education of gifted and talented students
- projects that strengthen the capability of state educational agencies and institutions of higher education to provide leadership and assistance to local educational agencies and nonprofit private schools in identifying and educating gifted talented students
- programs for technical assistance and information dissemination[70]

The Constitution of the United States, Amendment X, states that "The powers delegated to the United States Constitution, nor prohibited by it to the States, are reserved to the States respectively, or to the people." Subsequently, the public schools of the United States are governed by statutes enacted by state legislatures; and, whether there should be a mandate to require and/or fund gifted and talented education programs is left entirely to the individual states.

The *Updated Reports on State Policies Related to the Identification of Gifted Students*,[71] illustrated in Figure 2.2, shows that

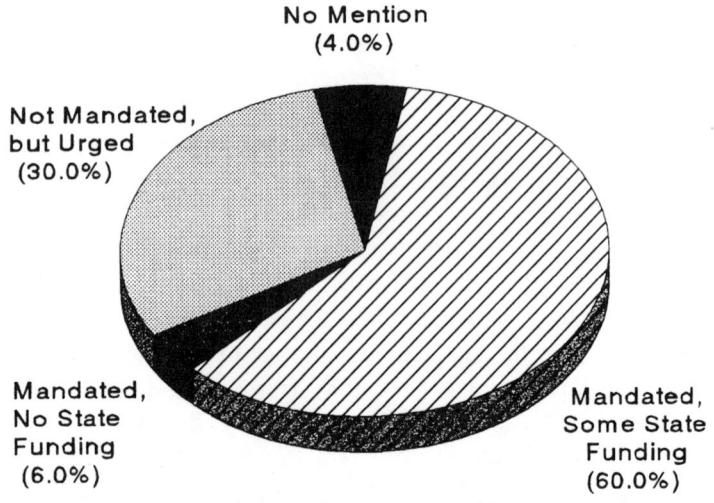

(Percent of states in each category)

Figure 2.2. *State Mandation of gifted education.*

66 percent of the states have some type of legislation mandating the identification of gifted students. Sixty percent (thirty states) of the states mandate programs for gifted students. These mandates are supported, to some degree, by state funding. However, the levels of funding that accompany these state mandates vary widely. For example, one state has a mandate for the appropriate education of gifted students that is accompanied by state funds; however, these funds are issued under a cap on the number of students that can be included. This means that, in spite of the mandate, 32,024 out of 74,468 students identified as gifted in that state are currently being served without the benefit of additional state monies. This is not an unusual example; the funding structure for most states provides only partial support for students identified as gifted.

Many states, in addition to the limited financial support for gifted students, face budget reductions that are expected to further erode the funding for programs for gifted students. Three states have a mandate in place but do not allocate state monies to fund additional services for gifted students. Fifteen states, or 30 percent of the states, have no state-level mandates for the education of the gifted. While these states may urge appropriate services for gifted students, and some may even provide state funds for this purpose, both services and funding are precariously dependent on the whim of decision makers and the condition of the budget. The recent updated report on gifted education programs (1994) shows that one state has no policies related to the education of gifted students, leaving this entirely to the discretion of the local school systems.

Samples of State Gifted and Talented Program Support[72]

The state of Wyoming does not mandate a gifted and talented program. On a voluntary basis, the state does ask each school district to do a needs assessment to meet those needs at the local level. Participating school districts may be granted a sum not to exceed $150.00 for each identified gifted and talented student, not to exceed 3 percent of the school-age population, which shall be matched by an equal amount of local funds. To apply for a grant, the school district shall submit a program plan approved by the local board to the State Department of Education. Funds shall be used to initiate or supplement services for gifted and talented students. Application for funding shall be made on forms according to a schedule set by the Department of Education. Any school district receiving state funds for gifted and talented education programs under this section shall submit to the State Department of Education

- a fiscal accounting of the expenditure of such funds
- a report of program accomplishments under program objectives
- the number of students identified and served under the program

For fiscal year beginning July 1, 1988, all grants awarded from the Public School Foundation Program account for purposes of this section shall not exceed $350,000. In the event that total grant requests by all districts applying exceed $350,000, the money shall be prorated on a per student basis.

The Wyoming Department of Education defines gifted and talented children and youth as those who are identified by professionals and other qualified individuals as having outstanding abilities and who are capable of high performance. These are children and youth whose abilities, talents, and potential require qualitatively differentiated educational programs and/or services beyond those normally provided by the regular school program in order to realize their contribution to self and society. Each school district, however, has the option to develop its own definition of gifted and talented students and its own identification procedures and programs to serve the identified population to meet individual needs.

The state of Alabama identifies gifted students as those who possess demonstrated gifted behaviors (including creative or productive thinking) and who, by reason thereof, require services not ordinarily provided by the regular school program. The local education agency must develop and implement procedures to ensure that potential gifted students are referred for special education services. The procedures include the following:

1. Consent
   - parental consent for evaluation

- parental consent for placement
- rights in gifted education

2. Evaluation
   - criteria for evaluation: The local education agency must conduct an appropriate evaluation to determine eligibility for intellectually and/or creatively gifted education services.
   - timeline: The evaluation must be conducted within 60 calendar days and, if eligible, the student must be placed in a program within 90 calendar days.
   - required evaluations: For the intellectually gifted, a vision and hearing screening, an individually administered Behavior Rating Scale for Gifted, and an individually administered evaluation of intelligence utilizing either the Wechsler Scales or Stanford-Binet must be taken by the potential enrollees.

   For the creatively gifted, a vision and hearing screening, an individually administered Behavior Rating Scale for Gifted, documentation of underachievement (if appropriate), and a score of at least two standard deviations above the mean on the Torrance Tests of Creative Thinking (either figural or verbal) must be taken by the potential enrollees.

   For environmental, cultural, and/or economic concerns, students must score at least 1.5 standard deviations above the mean on the Torrance Tests of Creative Thinking (either figural or verbal), and documentation must be submitted of disadvantage by utilizing the Environmental, Cultural, and or Economic Concerns Checklist.

The state of Connecticut reports that gifted and talented students must be identified; however, public schools are not required to provide special instructional programs. Nebraska leaves it to the local school districts to make the decision whether or not to have a gifted and talented program.

EXISTING PROGRAMS

Gifted and talented programs in the public and private schools throughout the United States have such a variance that underlying commonalities are often overlooked. Yet, in whatever way the values and interests of the local community may have shaped the approach to a gifted and talented program, most of the programs focus on three basic goals.

- Provide gifted students with an opportunity to interact with one another so they can learn and be stimulated by their intellectual peers.
- Reduce the variance within the group of instructionally relevant and challenging dimensions (e.g., past achievement) in order to make it easier for the teacher to provide instructionally relevant materials.
- Place the gifted students with an instructor who has special expertise in working with gifted students or in a relevant content area.[73]

The program options for gifted and talented students that exist in the public and private schools feature those with the least administrative adjustments by the schools to the more complex. The more common options used to modify programs for gifted education are listed below. They are organized in order from limited to extensive adaptations.

- enrichment in the classroom: A differentiated program of study for the gifted is provided by the classroom teacher without assistance from an outside resource or consultant teacher.
- consultant-teacher program: Differentiated instruction is provided within the classroom by the classroom teacher with the assistance of a specially trained consultant teacher who will provide extra materials and teach small groups of students in regular classes.
- resource room/pull-out program: Gifted students leave the classroom on a regular basis for differentiated instruction provided by a specially trained teacher.
- interest classes: Students volunteer for challenging classes on topics beyond or outside the regular curriculum (outer space, ethics, probability, etc.).
- community mentor program: Gifted students interact on

an individual basis with selected members of the community for an extended time period on a topic of special interest to the student.
- independent-study program: Differentiated instruction consists of independent-study projects supervised by a qualified teacher or mentor.
- special class: Gifted students are grouped together for most of the day and receive instruction from a specially trained teacher.
- special school: Gifted students receive differentiated instruction in a specialized school established for that purpose.
- magnet school: A school is established that focuses on specific areas (e.g., creative writing, advanced mathematics, etc.). Students with special interests are encouraged to volunteer for such programs even if they are outside the students' own neighborhood school.
- summer program: Many states have a variety of enrichment or fast-paced summer programs that can attract gifted students in art, mathematics, or general programs.[74]

All of the above mentioned programs for the gifted and talented, with the exception of the community mentor program and independent study, focus on the three basic goals for gifted education. The community mentor program and independent study do *not* provide gifted students with an opportunity to interact with one another so they can learn and be stimulated by their peers.[75]

PROGRAM IMPLEMENTATION

Regardless of what type of gifted and talented program a school district considers for those students who excel beyond the norm, three general objectives that receive broad, general agreement and acceptance among most people are that

1. Gifted children should master important conceptual systems that are at the level of their abilities in various content fields.

2. Gifted children should develop skills and strategies that enable them to become more independent, creative, and self-sufficient searchers of knowledge.
3. Gifted children should develop a joy and excitement about learning that will carry them through the drudgery and routine that is an inevitable part of learning.[76]

Although controversial, two additional objectives for gifted children would be to

- help them recognize the special responsibilities that accompany their gifts and be sensitized to the needs that society has for the productive use of those gifts; and
- make sure that they have opportunities to interact with other children of varying abilities and cultural backgrounds so that they appreciate the basic worth and value of each individual[77]

Program development and implementation for gifted children, to be successful, should focus on the objectives mentioned. Gifted students have "rapid cognitive development" and a "more extensive knowledge base" than the average students. If school administrators insist on keeping gifted education out of their schools, "children entering the first grade in [1997] will not emerge until the year [2013] if they go to college."[78]

PROGRAM ASSESSMENT

Once a gifted and talented program is developed and implemented, program assessment is essential. Accountability, which translates into some form of program assessment, is one of the watchwords of modern education. School administrators responsible for the gifted and talented program must be able to answer the question: Where is the evidence to continue to support a gifted and talented program?

Typically, goals that are not measurable and/or observable will not have an impact on a board of education or the community if there is no evidence. An example of a program objective that is measurable could be that "students in the gifted and talented program will improve by 25 percent on the Torrance

Tests of Creative Thinking within six months of the beginning of the program."[79]

The above objective clearly states how much is expected to happen, to whom, and by what specified time. It also provides the base for what instruments would be used in program evaluation. The outcomes of the program must be shown to the policy makers for continued support. Whether the gifted and talented program is in the planning stage or implemented, it is important that a form of evaluation be addressed.

THE SCHOOL ADMINISTRATOR'S ROLE

The school administrator's role, in addition to developing a sound gifted and talented program, will need to deal with the cost factor. The additional cost of programs for the gifted and talented are not high, especially when compared with the costs of other special programs. For example, special programs for children with retardation or learning disabilities spend well over 100 percent in excess of the average student, which is assumed by the local, state, and federal governments. In contrast, the cost per gifted child ranges from 16 percent to 27 percent in excess of the average student.[80] The biggest cost will be personnel and staff development.

School administrators should be cognizant of the fact that gifted and talented programs exist throughout the United States, but many are limited in scope and substance. Most gifted and talented students spend their school days without attention paid to their special learning needs. Recent studies show that

- Gifted and talented elementary school students have mastered from 35 to 50 percent of the curriculum to be offered in five basic subjects.
- Most regular classroom teachers make few, if any, provisions for talented students.
- Most of the highest-achieving students in the nation included in *Who's Who Among American High School Students* reported that they studied less than an hour a day. This suggests they get top grades without having to work hard.

- Only two cents out of every $100 spent on K–12 education in the United States supports special opportunities for gifted and talented students.

To improve education opportunities for America's top students, school administrators must take the following steps:

- *Set challenging curriculum standards.* The content standards, curriculum, and assessment practices must challenge all students, including those who are gifted and talented.
- *Provide more challenging opportunities to learn.* Communities and schools must provide more and better opportunities for top students to learn advanced material and move at their own pace. Flexibility and variety are essential. Learning opportunities for exceptional students must be available both inside and outside the school building.
- *Increase access to early childhood education.* All children, but particularly poor and minority children, must have opportunities to participate in high-quality early childhood programs that emphasize the development of their strengths rather than focus on deficiencies.
- *Increase learning opportunities for disadvantaged and minority children with outstanding talents.* These youngsters need extra support to overcome their barriers to achievement. Schools must make more high-level learning experiences available to these students.
- *Broaden the definition of gifted.* States and districts need to rethink their definitions and assessment strategies to serve a wider range of talented students. In the past 20 years, new research has challenged the view that intelligence is fixed and can be measured by one test. Today, researchers know that intelligence takes many forms and therefore requires that many criteria be used to measure it. Too, outstanding talents are present in children and youth from all cultural groups, across all economic strata, and in all areas of human endeavor.
- *Emphasize teacher development.* Teachers must receive better training in how to teach high-level curricula. They need support for providing instruction that challenges all

students significantly. This will benefit not only students with outstanding talent, but children at every academic level.
- *Match world performance.* The United States must learn from nations whose top students perform well and take steps to ensure that high-achieving American students compare favorably with their counterparts around the world.[81]
- *Don't polish the bricks and ignore the diamonds.* Public education in the United States was formed on the philosophy of equal opportunity, not "sameness." If students are denied the opportunity to excel, we have eliminated progress.

All of our students, including the most able, can learn more than we now expect. It will take a major commitment from school administrators for this to occur. The nation's school administrators have this role and responsibility.

REVIEW ACTIVITIES

1. Create a profile of a gifted child. Try to include multifaceted dimensions.
2. Discuss the values each culture and time period reflects in the identification of giftedness. What values does our society reflect in today's definition and treatment of gifted students? Project how our present educational treatment of gifted children will be viewed historically.
3. Using the definition of the gifted child, compare your school's criteria for identifying gifted children in your school.
4. Identify projects that you have in your school or could implement in your school that might qualify for federal dollars available through the Jacob K. Javits Gifted and Talented Students Education Act of 1988.
5. How do the mandates (if any) of your state compare to the samples in this chapter?
6. Identify the goals and program options for gifted and talented students in your school. What elements do they have in common with those listed in this chapter? How do these goals

and program options fulfill the vision, mission, and goals of your school?
7. What strategy does your school implement to assess the gifted and talented program in your school? Where is the evidence to continue to support a gifted and talented program? If your school provides no special education for gifted and talented students, how does that affect your overall school assessment?

ENDNOTES

1 Gallagher, J. J. 1975. *Teaching the Gifted Child.* Second edition. Boston, MA: Allyn and Bacon, Inc., p. 9.

2 Ibid.

3 Testimony to the Congress of the United States Subcommittee on Elementary, Secondary, and Vocational Education for the need of programs for the gifted by Gina Ginsberg Riggs, Executive Director of the Gifted Child Society, Inc., May 1, 1986. Gifted and Talented Children's Education Act, Committee on Education and Labor, House of Representatives. Ninety-Ninth Congress, H.R. 3263 and H.R. 2364 (Serial No. 99-142). Washington, DC: U.S. Government Printing Office, 1987:29.

4 Statement submitted to the Congress of the United States Subcommittee on Elementary, Secondary, and Vocational Education for the need of programs for the gifted by the Council for Exceptional Children and the Association for the Gifted, May 6, 1986. Gifted and Talented Children's Education Act, Committee on Education and Labor, House of Representatives. Ninety-Ninth Congress, H.R. 3263 and H.R. 2364 (Serial No. 99-142). Washington, DC: U.S. Government Printing Office, 1987:4.

5 Testimony to the Congress of the United States Subcommittee on Elementary, Secondary, and Vocational Education for the need of programs for the gifted by Gina Ginsberg Riggs, Executive Director of the Gifted Child Society, Inc., May 1, 1986. Gifted and Talented Children's Education Act, Committee on Education and Labor, House of Representatives. Ninety-Ninth Congress, H.R. 3263 and H.R. 2364 (Serial No. 99-142). Washington, DC: U.S. Government Printing Office, 1987:29–30.

6 Quote by the late and former President John F. Kennedy was taken from an American Association of School Administrators publication entitled, *How Our Investment in Education Pays Off.* 1995. Arlington, VA: American Association of School Administrators, p. 2. (AASA stock no.: 21-00431).

7 The research on the history of gifted education, 2000 B.C. to 1987, was compiled by Robert M. Geigle, a graduate student in Dr. Bruce Milne's class, EDFN 710, History of Education, at the University of South Dakota. Permission to use the research material compiled by Mr. Geigle was granted by Dr. Milne.

8 Kitano, M. and D. Kirby. 1986. *Gifted Education: A Comprehensive View.* Boston, MA: Little, Brown & Co., pp. 9–89.

9 Cited in Alexander, P. A. and J. A. Muia. 1982. *Gifted Education: A Comprehensive Roadmap.* Rockville, NY: Aspen Systems Corp., pp. 1–19.

Endnotes 79

10 Hildreth, G. 1966. *Introduction to the Gifted.* New York, NY: McGraw-Hill Book Co., pp. 41–65.
11 Kitano, M. and D. Kirby. 1986. *Gifted Education: A Comprehensive View.* Boston, MA: Little, Brown & Co., pp. 9–89.
12 Ibid.
13 Hildreth, G. 1966. *Introduction to the Gifted.* New York, NY: McGraw-Hill Book Co., pp. 41–65.
14 Kitano, M. and D. Kirby. 1986. *Gifted Education: A Comprehensive View.* Boston, MA: Little, Brown & Co., pp. 9–89.
15 Hildreth, G. 1966. *Introduction to the Gifted.* New York, NY: McGraw-Hill Book Co., pp. 41–65.
16 Cited in Clendening, C. and R. Davis. 1980. *Creating Programs for the Gifted: A Guide for Teachers, Librarians, and Students.* New York, NY: R. R. Bowker Co., pp. 3–70.
17 Cited in Hildreth, G. 1966. *Introduction to the Gifted.* New York, NY: McGraw-Hill Book Co., pp. 41–65.
18 Cited in Alexander, P. A. and J. A. Muia. 1982. *Gifted Education: A Comprehensive Roadmap.* Rockville, NY: Aspen Systems Corp., p. 3.
19 Cited in Clendening, C. and R. Davis. 1980. *Creating Programs for the Gifted: A Guide for Teachers, Librarians, and Students.* New York, NY: R. R. Bowker Co., pp. 3–70.
20 Cited in Hildreth, G. 1966. *Introduction to the Gifted.* New York, NY: McGraw-Hill Book Co., pp. 41–65.
21 Cited in Alexander, P. A. and J. A. Muia. 1982. *Gifted Education: A Comprehensive Roadmap.* Rockville, NY: Aspen Systems Corp., pp. 1–19.
22 Cited in Clendening, C. and R. Davis. 1980. *Creating Programs for the Gifted: A Guide for Teachers, Librarians, and Students.* New York, NY: R. R. Bowker Co., pp. 3–70.
23 Cited in Alexander, P. A. and J. A. Muia. 1982. *Gifted Education: A Comprehensive Roadmap.* Rockville, NY: Aspen Systems Corp., pp. 1–19.
24 Cited in Swassing, R. 1985. *Teaching Gifted Children and Adolescents.* Columbus, OH: Charles E. Merrill Publishing Co., pp. 3–24.
25 A speech given by Dr. Terman to the American Psychological Association. The speech is recorded in Terman, L. M. 1954. "The Discovery and Encouragement of Exceptional Talent," in *Psychology and Education of the Gifted.* Third edition, W. B. Barbe and J. S. Renzulli, eds. New York, NY: Irvington Publishers, pp. 20–37.
26 Cited in Alexander, P. A. and J. A. Muia. 1982. *Gifted Education: A Comprehensive Roadmap.* Rockville, NY: Aspen Systems Corp., pp. 1–19.
27 Cited in Swassing, R. 1985. *Teaching Gifted Children and Adolescents.* Columbus, OH: Charles E. Merrill Publishing Co., pp. 3–24.
28 Cited in DeHann, R. and R. Havighurst. 1961. *Educating Gifted Children.* Revised edition. Chicago, IL: The University of Chicago Press, pp. 1–37.
29 Cited in Clendening, C. and R. Davis. 1980. *Creating Programs for the Gifted: A Guide for Teachers, Librarians, and Students.* New York, NY: R. R. Bowker Co., pp. 3–70.

30 Cited in DeHann, R. and R. Havighurst. 1961. *Educating Gifted Children*. Revised edition. Chicago, IL: The University of Chicago Press, pp. 1–37.
31 Cited in Swassing, R. 1985. *Teaching Gifted Children and Adolescents*. Columbus, OH: Charles E. Merrill Publishing Co., pp. 3–24.
32 Alexander, P. A. and J. A. Muia. 1982. *Gifted Education: A Comprehensive Roadmap*. Rockville, NY: Aspen Systems Corp., pp. 1–19.
33 Cited in Clendening, C. and R. Davis. 1980. *Creating Programs for the Gifted: A Guide for Teachers, Librarians, and Students*. New York, NY: R. R. Bowker Co., pp. 3–70.
34 Ibid.
35 Alexander, P. A. and J. A. Muia. 1982. *Gifted Education: A Comprehensive Roadmap*. Rockville, NY: Aspen Systems Corp., pp. 1–19.
36 Cited in Witty, P. 1971. "The Education of the Gifted and the Creative in the U.S.A," in Psychology and Education of the Gifted, Third edition. W. B. Barbe and J. S. Renzulli, eds. New York, NY: Irvington Publishers, p. 42.
37 Cited in Clendening, C. and R. Davis. 1980. *Creating Programs for the Gifted: A Guide for Teachers, Librarians, and Students*. New York, NY: R. R. Bowker Co., pp. 3–70.
38 Ibid.
39 Fliegler, L. A. and C. E. Bish. 1961. "Summary of Research on the Academically Talented Student," in *Review of Educational Research*. R. DeHann and R. Havinghurst, eds. Washington, DC: AERA Publications, XXIX, 408–450.
40 Tannenbaum, A. 1981. "Pre-Sputnik to Post-Watergate Concern About the Gifted," in Psychology and Education of the Gifted, Third edition. W. B. Barbe and J. S. Renzulli, eds. New York, NY: Irvington Publishers, pp. 20–37.
41 Cited in Clendening, C. and R. Davis. 1980. *Creating Programs for the Gifted: A Guide for Teachers, Librarians, and Students*. New York, NY: R. R. Bowker Co., pp. 3–70.
42 Cited in Tannenbaum, A. 1981. "Pre-Sputnik to Post-Watergate Concern About the Gifted," in *Psychology and Education of the Gifted*, Third edition. W. B. Barbe and J. S. Renzulli, eds. New York, NY: Irvington Publishers, pp. 20–37.
43 Marland, S. P. 1972. *Education of the Gifted and Talented: Report to the Congress of the United States by the U.S. Commissioner of Education*. Washington, DC: U.S. Government Printing Office.
44 Clendening, C. and R. Davis. 1980. *Creating Programs for the Gifted: A Guide for Teachers, Librarians, and Students*. New York, NY: R. R. Bowker Co., pp. 3–70.
45 Ibid., and Jackson, D. 1979. "The Emerging National and State Concern," in *The Gifted and Talented: Their Education and Development: The Seventy-Eighth Yearbook of the National Society for the Study of Education*. A. Passow, ed. Chicago, IL: University of Chicago Press, pp. 45–62.

46 Clark, B. 1983. *Growing Up Gifted: Developing the Potential of Children at Home and at School.* Second edition. Columbus, OH: Charles E. Merrill Publishing Company, pp. 137–166.

47 Clendening, C. and R. Davis. 1980. *Creating Programs for the Gifted: A Guide for Teachers, Librarians, and Students.* New York, NY: R. R. Bowker Co., pp. 3–70.

48 Jackson, D. 1979. "The Emerging National and State Concern," in *The Gifted and Talented: Their Education and Development: The Seventy-Eighth Yearbook of the National Society for the Study of Education.* A. Passow, ed. Chicago, IL: University of Chicago Press, pp. 45–62.

49 Clark, B. 1983. *Growing Up Gifted: Developing the Potential of Children at Home and at School.* Second edition. Columbus, OH: Charles E. Merrill Publishing Company, pp. 137–166, and Clendening, C. and R. Davis. 1980. *Creating Programs for the Gifted: A Guide for Teachers, Librarians, and Students.* New York, NY: R. R. Bowker Co., pp. 3–70.

50 Stein, M. 1986. *Gifted, Talented, and Creative Young People: A Guide to Theory, Teaching, and Research.* New York, NY: Garland Publishing Company, pp. xi–18.

51 Gallagher, J. J. 1979. "Issues in Education for the Gifted," in *Gifted and Talented: The Seventy-Eighth Yearbook of the National Society for the Study of Education.* A. H. Passow, ed. Chicago, IL: National Society for the Study of Education, pp. 28–44.

52 Gallagher, J. J. 1975. *Teaching the Gifted Child.* Second edition. Boston, MA: Allyn and Bacon, p. 10.

53 Cassidy, J. and N. Johnson. 1986. "Federal and State Definitions of Giftedness: Then and Now," *The Gifted Child Today,* 9(6):15–21.

54 Renzulli, J. 1980. "Will the Gifted Child Movement Be Alive and Well in 1990?" *Gifted Child Quarterly,* 24:3–9, and Delisle, J. 1980. "Education of the Gifted: Coming and Going," *Roeper Review,* 2(4):11–14.

55 Stuller, J. 1986, August. "Making the Most of Our Gifted Children," *American Legion Magazine,* pp. 24-25, and Delisle, J. 1980. "Education of the Gifted: Coming and Going," *Roeper Review,* 2(4):11–14, and Clark, B. 1983. *Growing Up Gifted: Developing the Potential of Children at Home and at School.* Second edition. Columbus, OH: Charles E. Merrill Publishing Company, pp. 137–166.

56 Cited in Stuller, J. 1986, August. "Making the Most of Our Gifted Children," *American Legion Magazine,* p. 52.

57 National Commission on Excellence in Education. 1993. *A Nation At Risk: The Imperative for Education Reform.* Washington, DC: U.S. Government Printing Office.

58 Kitano, M. and D. Kirby. 1986. *Gifted Education: A Comprehensive View.* Boston, MA: Little, Brown & Co., pp. 9–89.

59 Kitano, M. and D. Kirby. 1986. *Gifted Education: A Comprehensive View.* Boston, MA: Little, Brown & Co., pp. 9–89.

60 Frehill, M. 1961. *Gifted Children: Their Psychology and Education.* New York, NY: the Macmillan Company, pp. 83–130; Renzulli, J. 1980. "Will the Gifted Child Movement Be Alive and Well in 1990?" *Gifted Child*

Quarterly, 24:3–9; and Delisle, J. 1980. "Education of the Gifted: Coming and Going," *Roeper Review,* 2(4):11–14.
61 Gallagher, J. J. and S. A. Gallagher. 1994. *Teaching the Gifted Child.* Fourth edition. Boston, MA: Allyn and Bacon, Inc., p. 5.
62 Ibid.
63 Ibid.
64 Sources are from "Education of the Gifted and Talented" (Report to Congress of the United States by the U.S. Commissioner of Education) by S. P. Marland, 1972, Washington, DC: U.S. Government Printing Office; and from Jacob K. Javits Gifted and Talented Students Education Act (Title IV, Part B of P.L. 100-297).
65 Gallagher, J. J. and S. A. Gallagher. 1994. *Teaching the Gifted Child.* Fourth edition. Boston, MA: Allyn and Bacon, Inc., p. 5.
66 Ibid.
67 Foster, A. H., J. J. Gallagher, and M. R. Coleman. 1994, February. "Model Legislation—Bill Form," *Model Legislation: Gifted and Talented,* Chapel Hill, NC: Gifted Education Policy Studies Program, p. 3.
68 Ibid.
69 Gallagher, J. J. and S. A. Gallagher. 1994. *Teaching the Gifted Child.* Fourth edition. Boston, MA: Allyn and Bacon, Inc., p. 382.
70 Ibid.
71 Coleman, M. R., J. J. Gallagher, and A. H. Foster. 1994, April. *Updated Reports on State Policies Related to the Identification of Gifted Students.* Chapel Hill, NC: Gifted Education Policy Studies Program, pp. 8–25.
72 A survey of the fifty states was made to determine the status of gifted and talented programs. The sample states, Wyoming, Alabama, Connecticut, and Nebraska, illustrate how different the programs and mandates are across the United States.
73 Gallagher, J. J. and S. A. Gallagher. 1994. *Teaching the Gifted Child.* Fourth edition. Boston, MA: Allyn and Bacon, Inc., pp. 355–356.
74 Ibid., p. 356.
75 Ibid., p. 355.
76 Ibid., pp. 79–80.
77 Ibid., p. 80.
78 Ibid., p. 87.
79 Ibid., p. 376.
80 Ibid., p. 375.
81 Ross, O. P. 1993, October. *National Excellence: A Case for Developing America's Talent.* Washington, DC: U.S. Department of Education.

CHAPTER 3

Title I: Helping Disadvantaged Children Meet High Standards

TITLE I of the Elementary and Secondary Education Act is the largest federally funded elementary and secondary compensatory education program in the nation. It evolved from the Elementary and Secondary Education Act of 1965,[1] which was enacted as part of President Lyndon B. Johnson's War on Poverty. The program provides for supplementary academic assistance and compensatory services for economically disadvantaged children. These services extend to all children of poverty, including children of migrant families, the delinquent, and the homeless, and emphasizes academic skills in reading and mathematics.

Lack of exposing economically disadvantaged children to educational opportunities in the years prior to their entrance into school places children of poverty at risk of academic failure in regular education programs unless they receive additional instructional support. The purpose of Title I is to provide supplemental educational services in the basic skill areas of mathematics and reading. Educational activities and services are provided to children and their parents prior to the child's entrance into first grade as part of Title I. Supplementary educational services are provided as an addition to the regular educational program by trained Title I teachers upon entrance into elementary school.

HISTORICAL OVERVIEW

During the years following the original implementation of

Title I of the Elementary and Secondary Education Act of 1965, a controversy persisted regarding states' use of federal Title I monies. Many educational agencies had been using federal money to supplant rather than supplement state educational funds. Not surprisingly, the original legislation underwent significant revision in 1978 to clarify intent of the law and eliminate improper use of federal funds.[2] The program was extended in 1988, by the Hawkins-Stafford Elementary and Secondary School Improvements Act and renamed Chapter 1. Necessary revisions to the act were made, targeting specific areas for improved use of funds, stressing parental involvement and administrative rules, and extending Chapter 1 funds to increase the development of preschool and secondary school programs.[3] Regulations governing the Elementary and Secondary Education Act (ESEA) and its amendments were rewritten and approved on October 20, 1994. The new act entitled Improving America's Schools Act of 1994: Reauthorizing the Elementary and Secondary Education Act of 1965[4] has extended the funding of compensatory educational programs for economically disadvantaged students from July 1, 1995, through June 20, 2000. Congress has renamed the section of the act providing compensatory programs for economically disadvantaged children, Title I—Helping Disadvantaged Children Meet High Standards (hereafter referred to as Title I).

LEGAL BASE

Improving America's Schools Act of 1994

Title I: Helping Disadvantaged Children Meet High Standards is written in four parts.

1. Part A—improving basic programs operated by local education agencies (LEAs)
2. Part B—even start family literacy programs
3. Part C—education of migratory children
4. Part D—prevention and intervention programs for children and youth who are neglected, delinquent, or at-risk of dropping out.

Part A addresses the improvement of basic programs operated by local education agencies. These include appropriations, state and local school improvement plans, assessment, attendance centers, targeted assistance schools, school choice, parental involvement, professional development, participation of children enrolled in private schools, and coordination requirements among others. Part B outlines state and local even start family literacy programs, the use of federal funds, program elements, eligible participants, evaluation, and construction guidelines. Part C emphasizes education of migratory children including state allocations, application and service guidelines, peer review, comprehensive needs assessment, service-delivery, authorized activities, bypass regulations, and coordination of migrant education activities. Part D addresses prevention and intervention programs for children and youth who are neglected, delinquent, or at risk of dropping out. Particularly, state and local agency programs and plans are discussed including institution-wide projects, 3-year programs or projects, program requirements for correctional facilities, innovative elementary school transition projects, and coordination of federal, state, and local administration. Migrant education is addressed once again under Part G, Subpart 3 of Title X of the same Improving America's Schools Act of 1994. This section outlines programs for recent immigrants, students of migrant parents, and older Americans.

Four sections under Part A are of particular interest to state and local education agencies (SEAs and LEAs). Sections 1111 through 1114, as summarized in this chapter, detail the obligations of SEAs and LEAs regarding identification, funding, program planning and development, program evaluation, student assessment, and parental involvement. They contain substantial changes to past Chapter 1 program rules and requirements. Of particular interest to school administrators is the coordination of Title I with Goals 2000: Educate America Act and the required collaborative development of detailed program improvement plans at both the state and local education agency levels.

Section 1111—State Requirements

Section 1111 requires states to develop an educational improvement plan in order to receive Title I, Part A funds. The plan must be coordinated with the state's Goals 2000 plan and any other plan that the state may decide to submit under ESEA. In an effort to reduce time and paperwork for state agencies, the United States Department of Education allows for the submission of consolidated state plans.

The program improvement plan must demonstrate that the state has developed or adopted challenging content standards and student performance standards in the basic skills content areas for disadvantaged children. Along with these content and student performance standards, the state must also demonstrate that it has developed or adopted a set of annual student assessments in at least reading and mathematics. These assessments will be the primary means of determining the yearly performance of each school district and individual school. The assessment plan must describe two levels of high performance (i.e., proficient and advanced). If the state intends to include an additional performance category, such as partially proficient, it must describe how that performance level will be assessed.

Adequate yearly progress in student academic performance must be featured in a manner that will demonstrate substantial yearly improvement toward the state goal that all children will meet specified state content and performance standards. The Title I reauthorization affords flexibility to states that have developed assessment systems that support their own systemic education reform efforts, even though these assessment systems may be inconsistent with national evaluation standards.[5] The plan must assure that it will notify school districts and the public of the standards and assessments it has developed and adopted. The new Title I regulations contain less prescriptive national standards, enabling states to request an exception to the generally applicable national evaluation standards, in order to use their own assessment systems to evaluate the effectiveness of their Title I programs.[6]

The state plan must include the development and implementation of a system of school support teams and describe how the state will use the teams to help each school district and campus affected by the state plan to develop the capacity to comply with the requirements of the new Title I legislation. In addition, the plan must provide assurances that the state will work with educational service centers or other local educational consortia or institutions to provide technical assistance to school districts and campuses. This relates particularly to professional development and school improvement requirements in the legislation. The state plan must be easy for the LEAs to implement, providing the least restrictive and least burdensome compliance regulations possible for school districts and individual schools. A committee of practitioners must be involved in the development of the state plan, and this committee will monitor the plan's implementation. Any state activities funded under Title I are to be coordinated, as appropriate, with school-to-work programs, vocational education, cooperative education, mentoring programs, and apprenticeship programs involving business, labor, and industry.[7]

Section 1112—School District Requirements

Local school district plans must be submitted to and approved by the state. The plan must be developed in consultation with teachers (including vocational education teachers) pupil service personnel, and parents. This cooperatively developed plan must be coordinated with Goals 2000 and any other ESEA district plans. For the convenience of the local school district, a consolidated plan may be submitted to the state. The plan should describe any additional student assessment or performance indicators, other than those required by the state, that will be used by the local district to determine student success in meeting state content and performance standards. A description of additional diagnostic information the school district may utilize must be included along with the LEA plan to the state, including any evaluative feedback that will be utilized to determine program improvement needs. Assurances that the district will fulfill its school improvement responsibilities under Section 1116 of Part A of Title I must be included, along with a description of any corrective actions that may be necessary to bring the district up to required standards.

The state is required to notify local school districts about the opportunity to operate schoolwide Title I programs under Section 1111. In support of this requirement, the school district plan must describe how it will notify eligible schools and parents of the opportunity to become school-wide programs. If an entire attendance area is targeted as a Title I school, the plan must describe the poverty criteria that has been used to select the attendance area for participation as a school-wide program. The school district must provide assurances to the state that it will work in consultation with individual campuses to develop school-wide program plans or targeted assistance school plans. These assurances must include district-level provision of technical assistance and support to these school-wide Title I programs. The plan must also assure that the district will coordinate efforts, to the extent feasible and necessary, with other agencies providing services to children, youth, and families. This includes a description of how the district will coordinate services provided under Title I, Part A with other supplementary services such as Even Start, Head Start, other preschool programs, vocational education programs, and school-to-work transition programs. Where appropriate, it must describe how the district will use Title I funds to support preschool programs.

The general nature of the programs to be conducted by each campus and how these programs will be implemented is an integral part of the plan. The district must describe how it will coordinate services provided under Title I, Part A with services to children with limited English proficiency, children with disabilities, migratory and formerly migratory children, neglected and delinquent youth, youth in at-risk situations, homeless children, and immigrant children. Coordination of programs and services should be directed toward increased program effectiveness, the elimination of duplication, and reduced fragmentation of instruction.[8] The district must describe and include in the plan how migrant children and formerly migrant children are selected to receive services on the same basis as other children and how students in targeted assistance schools will be identified as eligible for services. It must also assure the state that the local school district will provide services to private school children in accordance with Part A, Section 1120 of Title I.

Assurances must be made in the program improvement plan that the district will take into account educational research that indicates Title I services may be most effective if focused on students in the earliest grades. If the district chooses to use Title I funds to provide early childhood development services to children below the age of compulsory school attendance, the plan must assure that beginning in the 1997–98 school year, the district will comply with the performance standards established under the Head Start Act.[9]

Section 1113—Definition of Eligible School Attendance Areas

Eligible school attendance areas are those where the percentage of children from low-income families is at least as high as the percentage of low-income families in the district.[10] School districts may identify as eligible any school attendance area or any school in which at least 35 percent of the children are from low-income families. Title I funds may be used in a school that is not an eligible school based on an attendance area, if the percentage of children from low-income families enrolled in the school is equal to or greater than the district-wide percentage. If all eligible schools cannot be served, schools where 75 percent or more of the enrolled students meet low-income criteria must be ranked without regard to grade span and served from highest to lowest percentile ranking. If funds remain after serving these schools, the remaining schools in the district may be ranked either by grade span or for the entire school district according to the percentage of children from low-income families. Schools may be passed over for Title I services by a school district only if the following criteria are true:

1. The school meets comparability requirements under Title I.
2. The school is receiving supplementary state or local funds that are being used according to the requirements for school-wide programs or targeted assistance programs.
3. The funds expended from other sources equal or exceed the amount that would be provided under Title I.

Criteria for eligibility (see Figure 3.1) is of particular impor-

> The following criteria may be used by districts as a measure of poverty to determine student eligibility for Title I services:
> 1. the number of children ages five to seventeen in poverty as counted in the most recent census data
> 2. the number of children eligible to receive free or reduced priced lunch
> 3. the number of children in families receiving assistance under Aid to Families with Dependent Children
> 4. the number of children eligible to receive medical assistance under the Medicaid program
> 5. a composite of such indicators

Figure 3.1. Title I service eligibility criteria.

tance to the school principal, as it is at the individual school level that total student count must be determined and reported to the central office and ultimately the state. The number of students in the school eligible for "free and reduced lunch" is often used as a baseline for low-income student count. The accuracy of this student head count may mean the difference between a school receiving Title I funds or not being eligible for federal funding.

A district must allocate Title I funds to eligible schools in rank order on the basis of the total number of children from families that meet low-income criteria in each attendance area or school. Allocations to campuses may be reduced by the amount of funds earmarked for a school, by the amount of supplemental state and local funds expended in the school, or for programs that meet the requirements for school-wide programs or targeted assistance schools. This is consistent with regulations for funding for school-wide programs. Provisions must also be made to provide services to students within the district boundaries (see Figure 3.2) but not registered in a district school.[11]

Section 1114—School-wide Program Requirements

School districts can use Title I funds in combination with

other federal, state, and local funds to upgrade the entire educational program of school-wide campuses. In the 1995–96 school year, schools were able to become school-wide programs if 60 percent or more of the children in the attendance area or enrolled in the school were from families that met the district's low-income criteria. In the 1996–97 school year, and all subsequent years, schools may become school-wide programs if 50 percent or more of the children in the attendance area or enrolled in the school are from families that meet the district's low-income criteria. This is a reduction of past percent student enrollment requirements to declare eligibility as a school-wide program.[12]

The implications of this legislation are far reaching and help to answer much of the negative criticism related to instructional approaches in pull-out programs and their impact on student self-esteem and motivation to learn. School-wide programs may provide the vehicle for more innovative programming, collaborative planning and decision-making in program development, implementation and assessment, thematic curriculum development, and fostering school-community links that will provide benefits to all students.[13]

Much has been said in the previous sections about program plans that must be developed and submitted at the local and

---

School districts must reserve funds to provide comparable services to:

1. eligible homeless students who do not attend participating schools, including the provision of educationally related support services to children in shelters

2. children in local facilities for children who are neglected or delinquent

3. children who are neglected or delinquent who attend community day school programs

---

Figure 3.2. Reserve funds for comparable services.

state levels in order to receive federal funds. A local plan, as suggested in Figure 3.3, will help school administrators ensure comprehensive quality services under the Title I guidelines to educationally disadvantaged students.

Goals 2000: Educate America Act

Goals 2000: Educate America Act[14] sets high educational standards for schools throughout the United States. It formalizes into law eight education goals that have been developed at the national level to guide the efforts of communities and states in educational improvement and reform. Title I of Goals 2000: Educate America Act, originally developed under President George Bush, formalized into law six national education goals for school readiness, increased school graduation rates, student academic achievement and citizenship, mathematics and science performance, adult literacy, and safe, disciplined, and drug-free schools. The revised Goals 2000: Educate America Act of 1994, signed into law by President William Clinton,[15] adds two new goals that encourage parent participation and improved professional development for teachers and principals (see Figure 3.4).

It is hoped that these goals will create a new ethic for learning in America, helping children reach challenging educational goals and standards. The object of this act is to help create improved education and training opportunities geared to the needs of states and local communities, to best support children's success in school.

Goals 2000 provides new waiver authority to the U. S. Secretary of Education to cut through federal red tape in education. When a state reform plan is submitted and approved, the state may ask the Secretary to waive requirements of certain federal education programs that the state has determined will impede the implementation of state or local Title I plans. State educational agencies may also submit waiver requests on behalf of local school districts and individual schools. Goals 2000 focuses on the need for a new role of government at all levels and stresses removing unnecessary barriers to educational improvement and supporting those closest to the classroom and community as they work to improve their schools.

- A system to determine eligibility
- Coordination of educational services
- Coordination of efforts with health and social service agencies
- Collaborative planning
- Parental involvement
- Shared responsibility by district administration, school administration, and parents for program monitoring
- Design of assessment procedures and regular program review
- Corrective action when required
- Professional development and description of professional development activities for staff
- Services to private schools if desired and requested
- Services to current and former migrant children on the same basis as other children
- Services to homeless children
- Services to neglected and delinquent youth
- Services to youth in at-risk situations and immigrant children
- Notification to parents and schools of opportunity to operate schoolwide programs
- Description of programs to be conducted in Title I schools
- Coordination of Title I programs with other school programs (i.e., pre-school, vocational, special education, bilingual/ESL, and school-to-work).
- Transition services from pre-school to elementary school

Figure 3.3. Comprehensive Title I local service plan.

SCHOOL READINESS

All children in America will start school ready to learn.

IMPROVED STUDENT ACHIEVEMENT

All students in America will be competent in the core academic subjects.

INCREASED GRADUATION RATE

The high school graduation rate will increase to at least 90 percent.

BEST IN MATH AND SCIENCE

U. S. students will be first in the world in math and science.

ADULT LITERACY AND LIFELONG LEARNING

Every adult American will be literate and possess the skills necessary to compete in the economy of the twenty-first century.

SAFE, DISCIPLINED, AND DRUG-FREE SCHOOLS

Every school in America will be safe, disciplined, and drug-free.

TEACHER EDUCATION AND PROFESSIONAL DEVELOPMENT

All teachers will have the opportunity to acquire the knowledge and skills needed to prepare U. S. students for the next century.

PARENTAL INVOLVEMENT

Every school will promote parental involvement in their children's education.

Figure 3.4. Components of Goals 2000: Educate America Act.

PROGRAM FUNDING

Funding requirements have been an issue of concern under previous Chapter 1/Title I guidelines. Educational agencies have been in agreement that funding should be adequate enough to reflect and meet program goals and that any programs developed by state or local agencies should be cost-effective and equitable, meeting the needs of identified Title I students. Ironically, the same rules that were developed to ensure that extra benefits resulting from designated monies would go to those most in need have undermined many innovations. Consequently, until now, funding structures and regulations have made it difficult for schools to provide the best instruction to Title I students.[16]

A state-wide plan under Part A, Section 1111 of Improving America's Schools Act of 1994 must assure that a state will encourage the use of funds from other federal, state, and local sources for school-wide reform in school-wide programs. Under Title I, funds will be better targeted than in the past to the neediest counties and districts. Those with a poverty rate above the national average will receive a greater share of funds. The changes in the formula are based on the principle that half of all Title I funds should be targeted to the counties in the highest poverty quartile (those with poverty rates of at least 21.5 percent). These counties have 45 percent of the nation's poor children, yet under the current formula receive only 43 percent of Title I funds. The new formula directed an additional $500 million to these high-poverty counties in fiscal year 1995.[17]

Title I, Part A under the reauthorization also provides for program financial assistance through SEAs to LEAs. This assistance has been authorized to meet the special needs of educationally disadvantaged children in school attendance areas with a high concentration of children from low-income families and for children in local institutions for neglected or delinquent children.

Goals 2000 Financial Assistance

The Goals 2000: Educate America Act provides resources to

states and communities to develop and implement comprehensive education reforms aimed at helping students reach challenging academic and occupational skill standards. Congress appropriated $105 million for Goals 2000 in fiscal year 1994, and these first-year funds became available to states on July 1 of that year. The U.S. House of Representatives proposed an increase to $388.4 million, and the U.S. Senate proposed an increase to $428.4 million for future funding.

During the first year of funding, states were requested to submit an application that would describe how a broad-based citizen panel would develop an action plan to improve their schools. Also required as part of the application process was a description by the states of how subgrants would be utilized for local education improvements and improved teacher preservice and professional development programs and activities. Sixty percent of the allotted funds were to be used by the states to award subgrants to local school districts for the development or implementation of these improvements. In succeeding years, at least 90 percent of each state's funds must be used to make subgrants for the implementation of the state, local, and individual school improvement plans and to support teacher education and professional development. Local school districts were required to use at least 75 percent of the funds they received to support individual school improvement initiatives during the first year of the plan. After the first year, districts are required to designate at least 85 percent of the funds to schools.[18]

Title IV of Goals 2000 supports increased parental involvement through funding of parental information and resource centers. The purpose of these centers is to increase parents' knowledge and confidence in child-rearing activities and to strengthen partnerships between parents and professionals in meeting the educational needs of children. Funding for these parent resource centers began in fiscal year 1995.[19]

In the past, federal funding has been based on per pupil allotment for the education of economically disadvantaged children. These children have been identified by local school districts to the state for state reporting requirements and for subsequent allocation of funds back to the local district. Possible changes in funding formulas may result in states receiving combined block grants for both special and compensatory education programs. State education agencies would then distribute funds to the local education agencies.

PROGRAMS

Academic emphasis in Title I programs is placed on the basic skills in reading and mathematics. This includes reading, writing, listening and speaking, as well as performing arithmetical and mathematical operations. Incorporated along with this, programs should also stress the development of thinking skills so that the child will develop the ability to think creatively, make decisions, and solve problems. Knowing how to learn and reason, directing these skills toward the discovery of rules or principles underlying relationships, and then applying that knowledge to solving problems will assist the student in skill development that will be useful not only in the school setting, but in the world beyond school. The fostering of responsibility, self-esteem, sociability, self-management, integrity, and honesty through Title I programs will serve and support the student throughout life.

Numerous suggestions have been made over the years related to improvement and reform of past Title I and Chapter 1 programs. The Commission on Chapter 1 presented a salient critique of Chapter 1 programs along with suggestions for program standards and improvement. The commission's suggestions for successful program development include

1. Clear, high standards for all children regardless of poverty level
2. New systems to assess progress toward standards
3. Ongoing parent information about students' progress and how they can help
4. Heavy investment in teachers, principals, and other adults in the school
5. A match of funding to assure equity
6. Replacing accounting for dollars with accounting for results
7. Integration of health and social service support
8. Rewarding schools that progress and changing those that do not.[20]

Much of the newer legislation reflects these suggestions. Changes that many Title I instructors have desired to implement include cooperative learning groups, heterogeneous grouping, and tutorials in computer-aided instruction.[21] The Improving America's Schools Act of 1994 has taken into account these suggestions for improvement and realigned the emphasis from funding to school and student performance, stressing the importance of professional development at all levels, requiring an integration of student services, parental involvement, and recognition of successful programs.

Migrant Education

Inconsistent attendance and subsequently a lack of instructional continuity is the primary reason migrant children are unsuccessful in school. Under the new legislation, local education agencies must prioritize the use of Title I funds for migrant education into the following two categories: (1) current migratory children, ages 3 to 21 years old, according to need; and (2) formerly migratory children, ages 3 to 21 years old.[22]

Beyond federal regulations regarding the education of migrant children, rules and regulations have been developed at the state levels emphasizing the need for programmatic development serving this particular student population. It is important that any program for migrant children supplement, not supplant, the regular education program. Annual evaluations must show the effectiveness of any program, and parent advisory councils must be established in each district. In addition, each school district should consider establishing a school-community guidance center designed to identify, locate, and assist migrant children with the problems that interfere with their education.[23]

Program Development

Initially, Title I was designed as a pull-out program in which identified students were taken out of their regularly assigned classroom for a designated period of time to receive additional instruction in reading or mathematics by a certified Title I instructor. Educators have felt that this approach is not only ineffective, but also detrimental to a student's confidence and self-image. Standerford conducted an extensive and detailed study on Title I reading programs. It was believed by Standerford and her colleagues that pull-out programs with Title I instruction provided in a room other than the student's regular classroom created an oppressive environment of low expectations, minimum motivation for the student to learn, and a general feeling of hopelessness for the child. In the study, Title I services were provided to students as a supplement to regular instruction within the student's own classroom. The result was higher expectations by teachers and students, better student self-perception, and positive peer acknowledgment fostering motivation to learn.[24]

In addition to the "pull-out" and "send-in" programs, other options for program development are the extended day and add-on programs. These provide the opportunity to extend services to Title I students before or after school or through extended school year and year-round programs. These programs are particularly helpful to those schools serving migrant students.

The proposed expansion of school-wide options for Title I funding and the flexibility of school-level accountability accorded to school-wide programs can be helpful to schools by creating the conditions necessary for transforming schools, particularly those that serve high concentrations of poverty-level students. In schools where the majority of students are economically disadvantaged, it makes little sense to attempt to target Title I programs on individual students. Research has shown that where poverty is concentrated, the poverty level of the school itself is a detriment to the performance of all children in the school. A child from a poor family is more than likely to enter school without adequate preparation. The child may never have heard a bedtime story or may come from a home where no one reads. Survival skills may have taken precedence over social skills. Language skills may be underdeveloped or non-standard, and home and school expectations may be very different.[25] These past experiences place the child at risk of failure upon entry into school. It is the school's responsibility to coordinate and provide the services necessary to afford economically disadvantaged children an equal opportunity for academic success.

Staff training and development is an integral component of any successful program. The new legislation requires the school district to describe the strategy it will use to provide professional training and development for staff in accordance with Part A, Section 1119. This requirement provides the school administrator with the opportunity to train personnel in collaborative planning, site-based management, integrated curriculum techniques, and teaming.[26]

Title I program goals should be achieved through alignment of the regular and specialized curriculum, school guidance programs, student activity programs, and classroom activities. A comprehensive team approach including teachers, social workers, health personnel, parents, school psychologists, and guidance counselors has been found to be most efficient when addressing individual student needs and detecting patterns of troublesome student behavior that may affect student learning.[27]

Parent Involvement

Parent compacts, required under the reauthorized Title I, are agreements between the school and parents that will be developed at the local school level and will identify the mutual responsibility of parents and schools toward helping children succeed in school. Parents and teachers will discuss their agreements and their progress in meeting reciprocal responsibilities at parent-teacher conferences. The use of compacts recognizes the full range of roles that parents can play in their children's education as well as the need for parents and schools to develop partnerships and ongoing dialogue centered around children's achievement. Similar compacts have been used effectively by leading educational innovators to incorporate parents into the learning process.[28] School administrators must work to win the support of Title I parents and learn to respond flexibly and creatively to their children's needs.

Parent involvement is nothing new to Title I programs. In

1976, the Carnegie Corporation awarded the National Coalition of Title I/Chapter 1 Parents a grant to establish the National Parent Center. The center administers programs and serves as a clearinghouse for information concerning parent involvement and education for disadvantaged children. Its mission is to help economically disadvantaged parents to develop the skills and abilities needed to make sound decisions that result in improving the quality of their children's education. Training conferences, technical assistance workshops, scholarships, and publications are offered by the coalition. The purposes of the organization are

1. To provide information to parents that will enable them to help their children to be successful as students as well as adult members of society
2. To promote an exchange of knowledge, experiences and ideas between parents and educators concerning educational programs
3. To inform parents about laws, regulations, and guidelines of the Title I program
4. To develop resources and materials that assist parents and others to understand their roles in the Title I program
5. To serve as a link between parents, the United States Department of Education, state education agencies, and local education agencies
6. To provide parents with information about their rights to be involved in federal education programs
7. To provide technical assistance to parents in their attempts to organize into an effective force in their local communities
8. To monitor federal agency activity that may adversely affect education programs and the role of parents in those programs
9. To act as an advocate for parents in federal agency matters, such as the development of rules and regulations.[29]

THE SCHOOL ADMINISTRATOR'S ROLE

The school administrator's role is to develop and communicate a shared vision for providing effective supplementary services to economically disadvantaged children, enabling them to perform at an academic level with their non-disadvantaged peers. This means establishing direction, aligning people, and motivating others to assist students in reaching the desired performance goals as outlined in school and district Title I plans. Collaboration in plan development will provide opportunities for school personnel, parents, community members, and other agencies to be involved in setting educational goals and assisting students to reach those goals. This collaboration extends to monitoring and evaluating student progress and assessing the overall effectiveness of Title I programs within the school.

As instructional leader, the school administrator should provide assistance with creative curriculum development and implementation to serve the specific needs of disadvantaged children and in the collaborative assessment of instructional programs. Identifying program needs based on student needs and how teachers respond to these needs should guide the school leader's instructional supervision and evaluation. Professional training and growth opportunities for school administration and faculty should include encouraging collaboration among and ensuring the development of appropriate staff development activities in support of Title I programs and instruction (see Figure 3.5).

Five competency areas are important to the school administrator in the support of Title I programs. These include resource allocation, interpersonal skills, communication skills, systems guidance, and technological leadership. As resource allocator, the school principal is involved in budget planning and development including the identification, organization, and distribution of resources, including time, money, material, facilities, and human resources. How federal monies are used in support of Title I programs will be instrumental in supporting the academic development and achievement of economically disadvantaged children.

Interpersonal skills include working with others by participating as a member on teams, teaching new skills to others, serving students, parents, and community in ways that satisfy the educational goals, exercising program leadership, negotiat-

The school administrator's role is to:

- Develop and communicate a shared vision.
- Provide supplementary services for economically disadvantaged children.
- Establish program direction for school, parents, and community.
- Align people and motivate them to serve student needs.
- Collaborate with teachers, parents, and community in plan development.
- Allocate resources to support programs.
- Monitor and evaluate student performance.
- Provide assistance in curriculum development and implementation.
- Assess program effectiveness.
- Identify program needs.
- Provide training and growth opportunities for faculty and staff.

Figure 3.5. The school administrator's role.

ing, and learning to work with people from diverse backgrounds. Communication skills in listening, speaking, and writing will be an asset to school administrators as they interact with and interpret information for a variety of people associated with Title I programs. Communicating a shared vision plays an important role in program development and direction and aids in aligning and motivating people toward the shared goal of student achievement.

Systems leadership requires an understanding of complex relationships, including how social, organizational, and political systems interrelate and influence one another. Required collaboration with constituents beyond the school walls will require systemic knowledge and political skills. Information management includes acquiring and evaluating information, organizing and maintaining information, interpreting and communicating information, and using computers to process information. Technological leadership requires that the school principal understands and works with a variety of technologies through selection, application, and maintenance of equipment. Knowledge of how technological systems work and how to utilize them to operate effectively, monitoring and correcting performance, and how to improve or design systems will result in improved program management and educational support to teachers and students.

The role of the school administrator is complex and varied as it relates to the administration and management of Title I programs. If federal monies are to be obtained and economically disadvantaged students are to be served, it is important for the school leader to become familiar with this newest legislation. It is imperative that school administrators follow the guidelines as they relate to program plan development, collaboration, student identification and assessment, school-wide programs, use of funds, thematic curriculum development, assistive services to students outside the school, and fostering school-community links. Only then will the school administrator's application of knowledge and skills result in disadvantaged children benefiting educationally from this supplement to their regular education program.

REVIEW ACTIVITIES

1. Using Figure 3.1, calculate the numbers of eligible children for each of the five criteria. Which criteria does your district use to determine eligibility for Title I services? Why?
2. Compare your Title I local service plan with the Comprehensive Title I Local Service Plan in Figure 3.3. Which items do you include in your local service plan? Which items do you not include? Discuss the similarities and differences. How would you like to modify your Title I local service plan?

3. Examine the components of Goals 2000: Educate America Act. List characteristics, programs, activities, and statistics of your school district that show how you have met or are meeting these goals. Which goals does your school need to strive toward? How can you strengthen your efforts to attain these goals?
4. Evaluate your school's program development according to the suggestions by the Commission on Chapter 1 for successful program development earlier in the chapter. How successful is your school's program development? How can you strengthen your program development?
5. Identify needs your school has to enhance parent involvement. Review the purposes of the National Coalition of Title I/Chapter 1 Parents National Parent Center.
6. Apply Figure 3.5 to your role as school administrator. Which roles have been successful? Which roles need addressing? How can you maintain your strengths? How can you facilitate the roles that need development?

ENDNOTES

1 Elementary and Secondary Education Act, 20 USC 2701 et seq.

2 Revisions to the Elementary and Secondary Education Act. 1978. P.L. 95-561.

3 Hawkins-Stafford Elementary and Secondary School Improvements Act. 1988. P.L. 100-297.

4 Improving America's Schools Act of 1994: Reauthorizing the Elementary and Secondary Education Act of 1965. P.L. 103-382.

5 Subpart H of 34 CFR Part 200 and Subpart E of 34 CFR Part 201.

6 34 CFR Parts 200 and 201.

7 Improving America's Schools Act of 1994: Reauthorizing the Elementary and Secondary Education Act of 1965. P.L. 103-382. Chapter 1, Part A, Sec. 1111.

8 See Section 1113—Definition of Eligible School Attendance Areas in this Chapter.

9 Improving America's Schools Act of 1994: Reauthorizing the Elementary and Secondary Education Act of 1965. P.L. 103-382. Chapter 1, Part A, Sec. 1112.

10 It is important to note that Section 1113 does not apply to districts with a total enrollment of fewer than 1,000 students.

11 Improving America's Schools Act of 1994: Reauthorizing the Elementary

and Secondary Education Act of 1965. P.L. 103-382. Chapter 1, Part A, Sec. 1113.

12 Improving America's Schools Act of 1994: Reauthorizing the Elementary and Secondary Education Act of 1965. P.L. 103-382. Chapter 1, Part A, Sec. 1114.

13 The information in the previous sections summarizes the essential components of the Improving America's Schools Act of 1994: Reauthorizing the Elementary and Secondary Education Act of 1965. Chapter 1, Part A, Sec. 1111, 1112, 1113, and 1114.

14 Goals 2000: Educate America Act. 1994. 20 USC 5801 et seq.

15 Ibid.

16 United States Department of Education. *Commonly Asked Questions About Improving America's Schools Act of 1993*. (Washington, DC: Author, 1994).

17 Ibid.

18 Goals 2000: Educate America Act. Supporting Communities and States to Improve Student Achievement. United States Department of Education. September 9, 1994.

19 See Section on Parent Involvement in this chapter.

20 Commission on Chapter 1. 1993. "Forum." *Education Week*. (January 13, 1993):46.

21 Texas Education Agency. *Closing the Gap: Acceleration vs. Remediation and the Impact of Retention in Grade on Student Achievement*. The Commissioner's Critical Issue Analysis Series. Number 1. Austin, TX: Texas Education Agency, 1993.

22 See note 14 sup.

23 See note 4 sup.

24 Standerford, S. 1993. "Where Have All the Sparrows Gone: Rethinking Chapter 1 Services." *Reading, Research, and Instruction*, 33:41.

25 Comer, J. P. 1988. "Educating Poor Minority Children." *Scientific American*, 259(5):42–48.

26 McDonnell, L. M. and P. T. Hill. 1993. "Immigrant Education: The Incredible Shrinking Priority." *Education Digest*. Ann Arbor, MI.

27 See note 22 sup.

28 See note 23 sup.

29 National Coalition of Title I/Chapter 1 Parents. *Empowering Parents Everyday!* Washington, DC: National Parent Center. The Center may be contacted at the following address: the National Coalition of Title I/Chapter 1 Parents, National Parent Center, Edmonds School Building, 2nd Floor, 9th & D Streets, NE. Washington, DC 20002.

CHAPTER 4

Reading Programs

THE development of reading skills has always held a high priority in the minds of most educators. Reading, one of the three Rs, should be emphasized at all grade levels according to numerous surveys that have been conducted regarding the public's view toward American education. Grasping an accurate understanding of the place of reading in the total curriculum is fundamental if teachers at all levels are to teach reading skills in the proper amounts at the correct times in the lives of myriad numbers of young people who are students in the schools of this nation.[1] It is a known fact that "when a child reads fluently [s]he is succeeding in extracting meaning from the printed page. In particular, [s]he is deriving meaning as close as possible to those intended by the author."[2] Reading ability correlates closely with students being successful in school. The common characteristics of all reading programs include a philosophy, specific and clearly stated objectives, effective teaching strategies, developmentally appropriate materials, and program evaluation.

As school administrators consider the implementation of a reading program for students in their school and/or school district, what should they consider? What should school administrators know in order to facilitate a reading program that will provide students with the ability not only to read, but also the desire to choose to read and to enjoy reading? As a prelude to compensatory programs and in order to provide appropriate insight into this vital subject, the following topics are discussed in Chapter 4: the historical background of reading instruction, what research tells us about reading, the basic reading theories and models, effective programs that prevent reading failure, the school administrator's role in a reading program, assessing the reading program, reading in the content area, and the impact of early educational experiences.

HISTORICAL BACKGROUND OF READING INSTRUCTION

Reflecting and recognizing the importance of the history of reading instruction and becoming cognizant of the knowledge base is important. "History can provide a fuller view of present practice, stimulate research, and encourage a more realistic perspective of the reading profession."[3] The history of reading instruction encourages "a balance of perspective, provides breadth of approach and interest at a time when too much specialization may be promoting excessive narrowness and limited vision."[4]

A review of the historical background in reading reveals the predominant reason and the importance placed on reading by people in the colonial days. Since religion was the foundation for all human activity in the seventeenth century, children were taught to read so they could read the Bible as reading the scriptures provided the way to salvation. Reading and religion, the "two-R" curriculum, were the dominant courses.

The first recorded type of a book used in colonial schools, the *Hornbook,* originated in medieval Europe. It did not resemble what a book looks like today as the alphabet was covered by a thin transparent sheet made of a cow's horn "tacked to a paddle-shaped piece of wood and often hung by a leather strap around the student's neck. It provided colonial children with their first introduction to the alphabet and reading."[5]

Girls in the colonial era did learn to read, but did not attend secondary school. Boys who had the academic ability and who could afford an education were given the opportunity to attend Latin grammar school. The boys would study and learn Latin and Greek, learn how to conjugate Latin verbs, and learn how to translate the Greek language. The only change in the curriculum for the boys at the Latin grammar school was to read other religious texts and the Bible.

The *New England Primer,* published for American colonists in the late 1600s, was the first real textbook. It gave students a "fear-inspiring dose of Puritan morality from America's first basal reader."[6] The *New England Primer* "was a tiny two and one-half by four and one-half-inch book containing 50 to 100 pages of alphabet, words, and short verses accompanied by woodcut illustrations."[7] Children were taught the alphabet, then vowels, consonants, double letters, italics, capitals, and syllables. The controlled vocabulary was non-existent. The religious orientation of colonial schools was reflected in the *Primer*. An example of a typical verse was

In Adam's Fall
We sinned all.
Thy life to mend,
This Book attend.
The idle fool
Is whipt at School.[8]

In the eighteenth century, new immigrants came to America, the people became optimistic, the westward movement began, and trade and commerce improved. People acquired a commitment to life in the present instead of salvation after death. Hopes and dreams of tomorrow became a part of their new life. "This shift from the spiritual to the secular began to free the curriculum from the tight bonds of religion."[9]

Children learning to read using the *New England Primer* had lessons focused on religion, reading, and morality. In the mid 1800s, words began to be introduced systematically in basal readers. Up until that time "colonial children could meet from twenty to one hundred new words on one page."[10] Also, during this time, writing and arithmetic began to be considered as important as reading.

Noah Webster, of dictionary fame, defined and nourished the new American culture. The *New England Primer* was replaced with Webster's *American Spelling Book.* His influence on reading instruction in America was through his blueback speller as it became the most common elementary textbook. The *American Spelling Book* contained the "alphabet, syllables, consonants, rules for speaking, reading, short stories, and moral advice."[111] Lists of words comprised the largest part of the book.

Of those who had an impact on reading, McGuffey "was known in his own time as an eloquent part-time school advocate, and grape grower more than as the author of his famous readers."[112] McGuffey published a basal series in 1836. The *McGuffey Reader* "emphasized the work ethic, patriotism, heroism, and morality."[113] The first book in the series was called the *Primer* and ended with the *Sixth Reader*. It educated several generations of American children between 1836 and 1920.

McGuffey's readers are significant because they provided reading material for distinct grade levels and the beginning of graded elementary schools. The stories in the McGuffey's readers were written about everyday life and the rewards of good and bad behavior. The basals introduced the word method, silent reading, and reading to get information from content. Literature by American authors, the classics, and fairy tales became the first supplementary reading materials. "Colored pictures, attention to children's interests, and the teacher's manual all appeared by the 1920s. The 'work-pad' was used for 'seat-work' and skills practice in grades one through three."[114]

Since the 1920 era, curriculum materials have encompassed the basal reading stories about Dick, Jane, and Spot that utilized varied methods using large groups, small groups, ability reading groups, multiple basal reading series editions, and trade books. Today there is an abundance of curricular resources (e.g., textbooks, library books, trade books, media, unit plans, and computer software).

A sobering conclusion from a historical review of reading instruction in the United States reveals that "classroom practice and major instructional emphasis are more influenced by the temper of the times and events in society than from the impact of reading research."[115] History has shown us that society does influence reading instruction. For example, some states require a specified time on how much reading should be taught on a daily or weekly basis. A sampling of state requirements for the number of minutes required daily/weekly for reading instruction for elementary and middle school students is as follows:

Connecticut requires weekly reading instructional minutes. Grades 1–3 require 900–1,200 minutes per week; grades 4–5 require 645–900 minutes per week; and grades 6–8 require five periods per week of reading instruction.

Idaho has per week minute requirements for grades 1–6 and hourly times per year for grades 7–8 for language arts instruction. Grades 1–3 require 675 minutes per week, grades 4–6 require 600 minutes per week, and grades 7–8 require 280 clock hours of language arts instruction yearly.

Missouri requires one-half of the 1,800 minutes per week of instructional time for reading, writing, speaking, and spelling. School districts must have a formally adopted time allocation for each subject based on the adopted curriculum and students' instructional needs.

Mississippi compels kindergarten students in low achieving districts to spend less time in pre-reading and reading instruction than do the mid-range and high performing districts. The minutes varied from 100 to 250 instructional minutes per day.

Most districts allocated 120–150 minutes per day of reading instruction in grades 1–3 and 90–150 minutes per day of reading instruction for grades 4–6. Research conducted by the National Association of Educational Progress results showed that 70 percent of students in Mississippi spend 90 minutes or more per day in reading instruction.

Students in grades 7 and 8 have 50- to 60-minute class periods scheduled for reading instruction. Most school districts allocate a 50- to 60-minute class period for one semester at the high school level.

Alabama has each local education agency develop time allocations that reflect a balanced instructional day. There is a recommended list of time requirements by subject area, e.g., language arts for grades 1–3 is 150 minutes daily and for grades 4–6 it is 120 minutes daily.

Hawaii is unique in that it has a single state-wide system, with all schools governed by one state board of education and one superintendent. The school districts, designated geographically, are not fiscally autonomous. However, with school/community-based management, the schools are not restricted in any way in providing programs unique to their communities and students. Certain state-wide policies, regulations, and guidelines apply.

North Carolina has no regulation requiring a specific amount of time for daily instruction in reading, but many local school systems have adopted local requirements. Most elementary schools spend at least 90 minutes on direct language arts instruction with additional time spent in reading through content areas. Most middle schools spend 50 minutes daily, although some have added a double block for reading.

Alaska, Arizona, Arkansas, Delaware, Iowa, Maryland, Nebraska, Oklahoma, Pennsylvania, South Dakota, Virginia, Vermont, and Wyoming are some of the states that have no state regulations requiring a specific amount of time for daily or weekly instruction in reading. Local school districts are empowered to make the decisions based on the needs of students. This allows teachers to use an integrated approach for teaching the elementary school curriculum. For example, each subject area is not restricted to a specified amount of time to be taught. Rather, reading, writing, speaking, and listening become critical components in math, social studies, and science.

WHAT RESEARCH TELLS US ABOUT READING

Research alleges that neither a reading model nor a certain reading approach guarantees that all children will learn how to read. Accordingly, "no one approach to teaching reading yields consistently superior results. A combination is probably best."[16] It is the responsibility of school administrators and teachers to be knowledgeable about what works for students, to diagnose, and to prescribe the proper method for reading instruction.

Children are unique and learn to read just as they have learned to talk and walk. Not all of this happens at the same age. Subsequently, "we won't produce a nation of readers by trying to cram all our young readers into a single mold. The varied nature of student learning should be informing both our classroom practice and our research agenda."[17]

School administrators and teachers must focus on the reasons for reading and on the end result, not the means. Only when we begin to look at and respond to the strengths students possess will the debates and basis of whether students should be taught to read using a skills or a whole language approach to reading instruction be insignificant. The students and how they learn will be significant if "we make the connection between the ways in which children learn language and the ways in which they use language."[18] Reading is a process of organizing knowledge and resources in ways that allow each student the opportunity to predict and understand print.

THE BASIC READING THEORIES AND MODELS

School administrators need to be cognizant of the models and approaches used in teaching reading in order to understand what is happening in the classroom. The model and approach that a teacher chooses to use in reading instruction represents the teacher's implicit theory becoming an explicit theory. Our task as school administrators is to understand the complexity of the literacy behavior of young children, because educators need to "use these understandings to support and enhance children's learning opportunities."[19]

Reading theories can be characterized by three models and four major approaches used in reading instruction. The models of reading differ in terms of their semantic, syntactic, and graphophonemic information. None of the reading models is a complete picture, because they do not encompass the social nature of reading.

The following descriptions of the three models of reading instruction are used only to review inherent characteristics of each model. One reading model cannot be recommended over another because each model has positive instructional purposes that are necessary and beneficial in teaching reading. Teachers are encouraged to use a combination of strategies and techniques in reading instruction. Only then will reading instruction be focused on reading, writing, listening, and speaking—the key elements of language—as an integrated whole, not a jumble of individual skills. Reading instruction will use a comprehensive plan, and it will gain strength by using literature, basals, and whole language. Techniques from all three models will be used to create teaching styles to meet the needs and interests of students.

READING MODELS

Bottom-Up Model

The bottom-up model conjectures that the process of translating meaning begins with print and is initiated by the decoding of print. Phonics instruction is emphasized, which helps students to "acquire independence in word identification."[20] Sounds are associated with graphic symbols, and the process has students learning letters, sounds, and words in isolation before reading sentences, paragraphs, stories, and books. Bottom-up models of reading are described as "data driven" and can be analogous to a person who is learning how to drive a car. For example:

> The beginner finds the mechanics of operating the automobile so demanding that he or she must focus exclusively on driving. However, with practice the skilled driver pays little conscious attention to the mechanics of driving and is able to converse with a passenger or listen to the radio. Likewise, the beginning reader must practice decoding print to speech so rapidly that decoding becomes automatic.[21]

Individual subskills are regarded as hierarchical and are taught in sequence. Some teachers begin with the vowels and their sounds and then the consonants. Others progress through the letters of the alphabet from A to Z. Instruction is based on "sequential, letter-by letter, word-by-word process, as indicated by the isolated phonics and vocabulary instruction and the focus on perfection in oral reading."[22]

To facilitate phonics instruction in the bottom-up model and to enable teachers whose implicit theory places an emphasis on phonics instruction, it is recommended that teachers use a blend of a whole-part-whole sequence. Using this sequence of reading instruction and combining it with excellent literature would be beneficial to students. The whole-part-whole concept can be facilitated by following these three steps.

Reading Models   115

1. *Whole:* Read, comprehend, and enjoy a whole, quality literature selection.
2. *Part:* Provide instruction in a high utility phonic element by drawing from or extending the preceding literature selection.
3. *Whole:* Apply the new phonic skill when reading and enjoying another whole, high quality literature selection.[23]

This method of teaching phonics is a good option for students to learn the letters, sounds, and rules while providing for a natural, meaningful, and intrinsic use of language. The whole-part-whole method combines students' knowledge and reinforces their ability to recognize and pronounce letters and words by using sentences, paragraphs, and stories.

Top-Down Model

The top-down model assumes that the process of translating print begins with the prior knowledge of the reader. It stresses "that information processing during reading is triggered by the reader's prior knowledge and experience in relation to the writer's message."[24] The process is initiated by making predictions or educated guesses about the meaning of the units of print and involves speaking, writing, reading, and listening. The reader decodes graphic sounds to "check out" his or her hypotheses about the meaning of the printed words. The process is conceptually driven. The "Flan and Glock" story provides an example of how reading is conceptually driven.

Flan was a flim.

Glock was a plopper.

It was unusual for a flim and a plopper to be crods, but Flan and Glock were crods. They medged together.

Flan was keaded to moak at a mox. Glock wanted to kead there too. But the lear said he could not kead there.

Glock anged that the lear said he could not kead there because he was a plopper.[25]

By reading the short story above, one could perceive that Flan and Glock are names of two persons and proper nouns. The verbs are medged and keaded. By using "educated guesses," it is understood that Glock was being discriminated against. "Both prior knowledge and graphophonic information were required to make these guesses."[26] The process is a combination of the bottom-up and top-down models. It is difficult to separate the two entirely.

Interactive Model

The interactive model uses prior knowledge and print to combine both the top-down and bottom-up models of reading. "Neither prior knowledge nor graphophonic information is used exclusively . . . [and] the process of reading is initiated by formulating hypotheses about meaning and by decoding letters and words."[27] It assumes that the reader can begin by using either the decoding of graphic symbols, letters, syntactic, and semantic context of a word, or their prior knowledge to make hypotheses about the text. Consequently, "The crucial difference between bottom-up models and the interactive model is that in the latter, information processing occurs from the top-down, as well as from the bottom-up."[28]

The interactive approach provides teachers with a choice and the ability to choose the best way students should be taught. Teachers have the responsibility to diagnose and prescribe the right model for the individual student.

THE FOUR APPROACHES IN READING INSTRUCTION

The four major approaches in reading instruction are prescriptive, basal reading, language experience, and literature based. The two basic criteria that a major approach should meet are that it is (1) observable in actual classroom instruction around the country, and (2) derived from a theoretical base that is top-down, bottom-up, or interactive.[29] These approaches (illustrated in Figure 4.1) can be placed on an instructional continuum with the skills perspective on the extreme left and the whole language perspective at the far right.

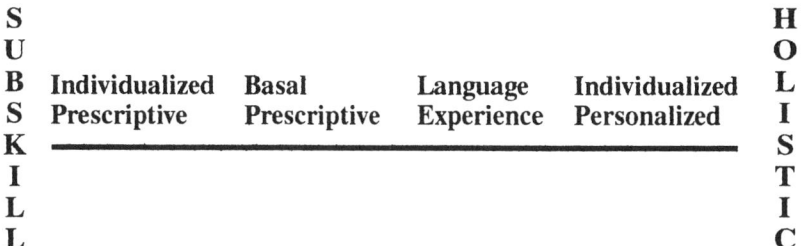

Figure 4.1. Range of four approaches and position on a subskill-holistic instructional continuum. (Adapted from Vacca, J. L., R. T. Vacca, and M. K. Gove. 1987. Reading and Learning to Read. *Glenview, IL: Scott, Foresman and Company, p. 39.*)

Individualized Prescriptive Approach

The individualized prescriptive approach is a skills approach because phonics instruction is emphasized. In listening to reading instruction as it takes place in elementary schools, one is likely to hear the teacher give prescribed commands such as

- "Read the first paragraph on page 22, and tell me what Jane did at the circus."
- "Take time to sound out the words you don't know."
- "The five vocabulary words on the chart need to be memorized for today's lesson."
- "All of you read the following paragraph about the clown out loud."
- "Remember the rule for changing the y to i and adding the ending" or "i before e except after c, or when sounding like /a/ as in neighbor and weigh."

This form of instruction views reading as a part-to-whole process.

The two main methods used to teach phonics are known as the analytic and synthetic phonics methods. The analytic method is preferred, because it places an emphasis on the sound-symbol relationships by using an analysis of words that are familiar to students. An example of the analytic method is as follows:

- Observe a list of known words with a common phonic element, for example, the initial consonant t.

- Begin questioning as to how the words look/sound the same and how they are different.
- Elicit the common phonic element and discuss.
- Have the learners phrase a generalization about the element, for example, all the words start with the sound of the letter t. The sound of the letter t is /t/ as in top.[30]

The synthetic method uses a definite sequence to teach sound-symbol relationships. The sequence is

- Teach the letter names.
- Teach the sound(s) each letter represents.
- Drill on the sound/symbol relationships until rapidly recognized. Discuss rules and form generalizations about relationships that usually apply to words, that is, when vowels are short or long.
- Teach the blending together of separate sounds to make a word. Provide opportunity to apply blending to unknown words.[31]

It is recommended that phonics instruction be used if and when necessary. Teachers should form small groups and provide instruction on skills students need to learn rather than assign page upon page of phonics lessons from a workbook. Always remember that the reason for phonics instruction is to help each student master the ability to read by joining letters, words, sentences, and texts independently. The strongest functional connection between these two skills may run in the reverse direction. It is only the nature of reading that can make the content of a phonics lesson seem sensible; it is only the prospect of reading that can make them seem worthwhile.[32]

Therefore, phonics instruction is a means to an end; it should fulfill some distinctive condition, and it should be associated to students' reading lessons. Since the ultimate goal is to enable students to become independent readers, phonics instruction "must be functional, useful, and contextual to be of value. It also should be planned and systematic."[33]

To help students gain knowledge about letter sounds, it is beneficial to use bulletin boards that are "learning boards" to explain and portray specific reading skills. One favorite that can be used for students of different grade levels is the one on the two sounds made by the letter C,c. This letter can be confusing for students when beginning to read because the two sounds are either the hard /k/ or soft /s/ sound. An example of this confusion and lack of comprehension is related by this personal story. When teaching third grade students, the "C,c learning board" (see Figure 4.2) was on the classroom entry door. One day a fifth-grade student, on her way to music class, stopped and asked, "What does this bulletin board mean?" After the rule was explained by using the cats (each family was a different color to separate visually the different sound classes) she looked at the teacher and said, "Oh! That is what that is all about." How many times had this fifth-grade girl been told the rules for the sounds of the letter C,c? How many times had she been told that it depended on the vowel that followed? How many phonics worksheets had been completed using the vowels a, o, and u with the letter C,c to make the hard /k/ sound in cat, cot, cut, and e, i, y, with the letter C,c to make the soft /s/ sound in cent, city, and cyclone?

Learning bulletin boards are helpful, because students can see and immediately use the information when speaking, reading, writing, and listening. They also provide an exceptional technique to integrate art and reading.

Basal Reading Approach

The use of basal reading material occupies the largest part of the instructional continuum and can be described as a comprehensive reading program. The directed reading lesson or directed reading activity is a familiar method for organizing instruction with basal reading materials. "Even with the rise in popularity of whole language and literature-based reading programs, teachers in more than 90 percent of U.S. classrooms use basal reading programs."[34]

Basal readers do furnish a structure, and most students do learn to read with them. However, basal readers fail to provide adequate practice in reading. "Basal activities and materials can be the basis for a good developmental reading program, but they

Figure 4.2. The sound of the letter (learning board). McEathron, M. 1952. Your child can read. Buffalo, NY: Kenworthy Educational Service, Inc., p. 18. (Adapted and reproduced by permission.)

should be seen only as a starting point and should be heavily supplemented with other activities and materials."[35]

The major components of basal reading programs are

- the readiness program
- pre-primer and primer levels
- word identification strand
- comprehension strand
- literature

- language arts
- management

School administrators and teachers must analyze the available materials used in reading instruction and differentiate between the "pros and cons" when using this approach in reading instruction.

> Basals are neither a method nor an approach to teaching reading. They are simply a carefully crafted set of materials. The core of the reading program is the teacher. It is the teacher who should decide how and when to use basals and whether to choose alternative materials.[36]

Those who have a rigid reliance on the old paradigm of basals and ignore the teacher as core of the reading program mortify an effective reading program. The basal reader should be considered as one resource and not the only resource.

Language Experience Approach

The Language Experience Approach (LEA) is characteristic of the interactive and top-down models and is very personal. In the LEA, "the student—either individually or as a part of a small group—dictates a story about an actual, personal experience."[37] It integrates the processes of thinking, speaking, listening, writing, and reading. A child's story is typed or written by the teacher or another person, read aloud, and can be made into a book. This approach gives students, with the ability, an opportunity to use their prior knowledge and personal experiences. Stories use words that are familiar and utilized in the everyday language of students. A description of the LEA approach is as follows:

> What I can think about, I can talk about,
> What I can say, I can write (or someone can write for me),
> What I can write, I can read (and others can read too),
> I can read what I have written, and I can also read what other people have written for me to read.[38]

Literature-Based Approach

The literature-based approach is located at the far right of the continuum. It can be described as the approach that utilizes characteristics from the interactive and/or top-down model of reading instruction. "Literature-based reading programs are used by teachers who want to provide for individual student differences in reading abilities and at the same time focus on meaning, interest, and enjoyment."[39]

How can a teacher get ready and plan for using this approach? The most important components are to designate a time each day for reading and to have an abundance of books available that students will enjoy and choose to read. These books can be of varied reading levels, topics, types, and interest. Interest is the key motivator in getting students to read. The number of books must be adequate for the number of students in the classroom.

The following questions and answers will assist in use of the literature-based approach in reading instruction.

(1) How do I set up a classroom library? Stock the library with all types of books—trade books, library books, Caldecott Medal books, Newbery Medal books, new books, little books, picture books, poetry books, paperbacks, fat books, thin books, fairy tale stories, cowboy stories, mysteries, silly stories, historical fiction, nonfiction, autobiographies, biographies, books on dinosaurs, birds, animals, famous people, and outer space. Also, choose books that represent ethnic and minority groups, mainstream Americans, and traditional and nontraditional families. Acquire science, music, social studies books—and any books that interest students.

(2) Where can I find these books? Buy, borrow, collect, find, and order them from book clubs. Use resources—school, city, university, and state libraries. Check out the rummage and garage sales in your area. Ask school administrators, colleagues, parents, grandmothers, grandfathers, students, uncles, aunts, and friends for books. Explore and look in the boxes in the attic, the basement, and the garage. Shop at book stores.

(3) Where should this reading area be located? Choose a corner or a special place in the classroom for reading. Organize the reading area, and make it comfortable by having carpeting, rugs, pillows, or bean bags on the floor for students to sit or stretch out on. Any furniture can be used, even an old bathtub—just create an environment that enhances students' reading.

(4) What does the teacher do when the children are reading? The change from product-to-process oriented instruction changes the teacher's role. The teacher is the facilitator, assisting the students when help is requested, making competent instructional decisions, helping students select books at proper reading levels, and modeling reading.

In more and more of today's classrooms, the teacher often assumes a role of facilitator of learning, rather than dispenser of information. The teacher conferences with a student on a regular basis in a special place, away from other students, and no distractions are allowed! These conferences are about 5 to 10 minutes and are done on a one-on-one basis. The teacher uses a class list to make certain all students have a scheduled time. The teacher and the student have selected a procedure for recording the individual student's reading selections, e.g., title, author, main idea, favorite character, and type of literature. The teacher could even have students retell a portion of the story that has been read. Retelling is excellent for measuring comprehension.

(5) What do students do when the teacher is having a conference? Students will be cognizant of the rules established for the reading area and select a book to read. When choosing books to read, students should

1. Choose a middle page of the book.
2. Read the page silently.
3. When the student encounters a word that is unknown or confusing, put down a thumb. When a second word is unknown, put down a finger. If all fingers are used for the one page, the book is too difficult, and the student should choose another book.

Students may choose a story, poem, or a play, and read it with someone from their peer group. "The Small Grouper"[40] can be of assistance if the teacher desires to pair students using a sociometric technique. The teacher may have the students read portions of these books, stories, and so on orally before reading to the teacher. Most important, students will spend this time reading, either silently or orally. Also, students may be doing journal writing, writing letters, writing poetry, writing books, publishing stories—the list is endless. The teacher and the students will have ways to share these activities using Author's Chair, class books, individual books, plays, and newspapers.

(6) How will the teacher assess student learning? Assessment will be observational and ongoing. The teacher uses "kidwatching," informal reading inventories, anecdotal records, checklists, observation, and portfolios of stories written and read orally by students. The strengths and needs of each child will be recorded in a notebook, or on a card, or any method used by the individual teacher.

(7) How will group or individual assignments be made? Assignments will be based on the needs of the student. The assignments can be individual or small group work. The teacher will become cognizant of the needs of individual students by reviewing the records of individual conferences to determine which students have the same reading problems, such as vowels, suffixes, prefixes, compound words, etc. These students can be brought together as a group and taught the skill. Grouping is a quick way to teach the same skill to several students at the same time, e.g., a few students need instruction on vowel sounds.

There are hundreds of other cooperative or independent activities, such as creative writing, research, crafts, science experiments, and social studies projects that can be included with this approach. The objective is reading, reading, and more reading for the literature-based approach. Research strongly supports a literature-based program, because literature gives students an excellent opportunity to learn about themselves and their world. Literature-based reading instruction creates a community of readers.[41]

To capture and to explore what works in reading instruction, school administrators and teachers must be aware of how and what turns students on to want to read. It is important to find out what students perceive and how students can be motivated. Motivation and developing self-esteem are key ingredients to what will get students reading, which promotes literacy.

PREVENTIVE PROGRAMS USED IN READING INSTRUCTION

The detrimental effects of reading failure are widely acknowledged. Research shows "that children who encounter problems in the beginning stages of learning to read fall further and further behind their peers—the poor do get poorer."[42] Therefore, school administrators should consider redirecting many of the dollars spent annually on marginally, if at all, effective compensatory and special education programs toward preventing initial reading failure.

Programs for students who are at risk of reading failure are Reading Recovery, Early Intervention in Reading (EIR), the Boulder Project, Success For All, the Winston-Salem Project, and Students Achieving Independent Learning (SAIL). These six preventive reading programs are similar, because they are developed on the axiom that students who are low-achievers can experience success in reading if they are provided supplemental quality instruction in first grade.

READING RECOVERY

An example of a reading program that has been developed by educator and psychologist Marie Clay of New Zealand and used in that country since 1970 is the Reading Recovery Program. Clay defines Reading Recovery as "a strategic process that takes place in the reader's mind; that reading and writing are interconnected, reciprocal processes; that it is most productive to intervene early, before children become trapped in a cycle of reading failure."[43]

The state of Ohio has experienced success with the program since 1984.

Reading Recovery is getting more recognition today because it seeks to help students who are at risk due to the consequences caused by failure in reading. Past experience has shown that for some children, whatever the reason, regular classroom instruction

> is not sufficient for them to become readers and writers. They need extra help to make that critical breakthrough that suggests that they understand the underlying processes. Traditional remedial programs do help but do not make it possible for at-risk readers to "catch up"; these programs do not usually create independent readers who can keep on learning.[44]

Reading failure is costly in dollars and to the individual student.

> Viewed from the short-term perspective of annual costs, Reading Recovery is less expensive than first grade retention, but more expensive than typical Chapter 1 services or special education services. However, [as illustrated in Figures 4.3 and 4.4], the short-term investment in Reading Recovery has significant long-term payoffs.[45]

Reading Recovery offers an effective way for schools to use financial resources for the good of students. It is a cost-benefit program.

Students who cannot read suffer from low self-esteem and have academic difficulties. Reading Recovery is a one-time intervention that occurs when students are enrolled in first grade. Its aim is to assist those children who are in the lowest 20 percent in reading and writing achievement. Its purpose is to help children "without regard to intelligence, ethnic group, language achievement, school history, physical handicaps, or learning abilities."[46] The goal of the program is to provide assistance and one-on-one, individualized instruction for students so they have the opportunity to develop into independent readers. The duration of Reading Recovery instruction is 12 to 16 weeks. Students will be in a pull-out program, but Reading Recovery is not intended to be a substitute for the school district's selected reading and writing instruction; it is a supplementary program.

The Reading Recovery teacher must receive special training through inservice education, because Reading Recovery is not a teacher-proof, commercially prepared package. The training continues for a year, and teachers learn how to design intervention strategies to meet individual learning needs. Students will receive instruction on a one-on-one basis, and each lesson will be for one-half hour daily. The teacher directs "the reading of familiar 'little' books, takes a 'running record' of independent reading, works with the student on reading strategies as needed, supports the child in writing a message or a story, and reads a new 'little' book with the child."[47] Each teacher works individually with four children per day and undertakes other educational duties during the rest of the day.

Intervention	Annual Cost	Average Years In Program	Total Program Time	Total Cost per Student
Retention(first Grade)[1]	$5,208 (all costs)	1 Year	1,080 hrs.	$5,208 (all costs)
Chapter 1[2]	$943	5 years	525 hrs.	$4,715*
Special Education[3] ("learning disabled")	$1,651	6 Years	1,512 hrs.	$9,906
Reading Recovery[4]	$2,063	1/2 year	40 hrs.	$2,063

*Cost in 1990-91 dollars; inflation and salary increases are not included.

[1] Cost for one child retained in first grade who received *all school services* (food, transportation, etc.) for one year, assumed to be the annual per pupil expenditure nationwide for current operations of $5,028, in 1990-91, as reported in *Estimates of School Statistics: 1990-91*, National Education Association (1991). The time for this intervention was estimated assuming a 6-hour school day x a 180-day school year.

[2] Annual *teacher salary cost* of instruction for one student in Chapter 1 pull-out program. Calculated by dividing the national average of teacher salaries for 1990-91 (33,015) reported in NEA *Estimates of School Statistics: 1990-91*, by the average number of Chapter 1 students taught by each Chapter 1 teacher per year. The average number of student taught per teacher was calculated from data in the U.S. Department of Education report *The Current Operation of the Chapter 1 Program* (1987), and assuming a 6-hour teacher day with 7 classes of 5 students each, equaling a teacher load of 35 students. The study also was the source of data used to calculate the time for this intervention: an average Chapter 1 pull-out resource session of 35 minutes per day x 180 days per year x 5 years, which is the average length of time students receive Chapter 1 services in elementary school.

[3] Annual *teacher salary cost* of instruction for one student classified as "learning disabled" taught in pull-out resource room program for one year. Calculated by dividing the national average of teacher salaries for 1990-91 ($33,015) by the average total number of students classified "learning disabled" taught by each teacher in a resource room pull-out program (a teaching load of 20 students per day), as reported in the U.S. Department of Education study *Patterns in Special Education Service Delivery and Cost* (Moore et al., 1988). The time for this intervention was also calculated from data in the study, which reports the typical student classified as "learning disabled" spends 7 hours per week in resource pull-out programs. Given a 36-week school year, this is 252 hours per year, or 1,512 hours over the course of 6 years of elementary school.
NOTE: These costs only include teacher salaries. Costs do *not* include items such as the *annual costs of assessment* of students, which was reported in the study *Patterns of Special Education Services and Delivery and Cost* to be $1,273 per Special Education student in 1985-86. Estimates also do not include time and salary costs for Special Education students beyond sixth grade.

[4] Annual *teacher salary cost* of Reading Recovery instruction for one student calculated by taking half the national average of salaries for teachers for 1990-91 ($33,015 divided by 2 = $16,508) and dividing this number by the average number of student (8) taught by one Reading Recovery teacher teaching Reading Recovery half of each day for one year. The time for this intervention was calculated using a tutoring session of 30 minutes each day, for a 16-week period.

Figure 4.3. *Reading recovery savings: comparison of teacher time and salary costs per pupil, with grade retention, Chapter 1, and Special Education in the elementary grades (in 1990–1991 dollars). (Source: Dyer, P. C. 1992. "Reading Recovery: A Cost Effectiveness and Educational-Outcomes Analysis," ERS Spectrum, 10:1. Reproduced by permission.)*

• Expected benefits from one Reading Recovery teacher working one year:	
Avoid 2 grade one retention, @ $5,208 each	$10,416
Avoid need to serve two students in Chapter 1 programs (each child served for five years), @ $5,208 each	$9,430
Avoid misclassification of one Special Education student in "learning disabled" resource program (child served for six years during elementary school)	$9,906
Total cost savings	$29,752
• Less cost of one Reading Recovery teacher (half year's full-time salary)	(16,508)
• Net savings per Reading Recovery teacher	$13,244

Figure 4.4. *Potential long-term reading recovery cost-benefit for one reading recovery teacher working with eight students during one year (in 1990–1991). (Source: Dyer, P. C. 1992. "Reading Recovery: A Cost Effectiveness and Educational-Outcomes Analysis,"* ERS Spectrum, *10:1. Reproduced by permission.)*

The primary principle of the Reading Recovery program correlates with what most school administrators and teachers believe about children and their ability to learn to read. The effects of implementing a Reading Recovery program in a school can be assessed as having immediate effects as well as long-range effects on students. These effects are as follows.

Immediate Effects of Reading Recovery

- reduces retention in first grade
- reduces referrals to special programs
- builds self-esteem in students
- develops independent readers, writers, and problem solvers
- achieves higher test scores
- turns good teachers into better teachers
- provides a vehicle for parental involvement

Long-Range Effects of Reading Recovery

- reduces the dropout rate
- produces a more literate community

The Reading Recovery program reduces reading failure and

is designed to assist those students who are at risk before they become labeled and categorized as remedial. Reading Recovery can also be an asset to the model, strategy, or method used by the teacher in individual classrooms for reading instruction. Some fundamental theoretical assumptions of Reading Recovery that correlate with other reading models are as follows:

- Reading is a strategic, in-the-head process.
- Reading and writing are reciprocal processes.
- Children learn to read by reading.
- School literacy instruction influences children's conceptions of reading.
- It is productive to intervene early.
- Knowledgeable and sensitive teachers are the key.[48]

Reading Recovery saves money and reduces a school district's dependence on the current practices of retaining, labeling, tracking, and categorizing students. These are not even educational practices. They are educational stumbling blocks for some students.

If a company offered a better product that would cost less and take less time to develop, business and industry would not hesitate 1 minute to have that product become a reality. American students, teachers, parents, and taxpayers deserve no less. With the research evidence that Reading Recovery is not only educationally effective, but also cost-effective, this early intervention deserves careful consideration by all those responsible for the education of children.[49]

EARLY INTERVENTION IN READING (EIR)

The Early Intervention in Reading approach is an alternative to the Reading Recovery tutorial program. EIR is a helpful, in-class program developed by Barb Taylor, a professor at the University of Minnesota. It is supported by sound instructional practices and based on research. The EIR program "makes use of quality literature, develops students' phonemic segmentation and blending ability, and teaches students to use phonic, syntactic, and context clues as they read."[50] The EIR program is cost-effective and uses small group instruction within the classroom. First-grade students who are low achievers in reading are given supplemental quality instruction. It is not a pull-out program like Reading Recovery. First-grade teachers receive training in using special intervention procedures within their regular classrooms. The purpose of EIR is similar to Reading Recovery as it also believes "that supplemental quality instruction provided early in first grade for low-achieving readers will help students get off to a better start and will prevent them from experiencing unnecessary failure."[51]

Classroom teachers are required to receive initial training in the Intervention in Reading procedures. This training could be during an all-day workshop during the summer before a school district implements the program. It would also be necessary to have several follow-up meetings, after the school term has begun, to answer questions and concerns teachers have about the program.

EIR Program Materials

- thirty-six picture books that greatly appeal to first-grade children
- summaries of these picture books on a chart and in booklet form
- fourteen additional short, easy-to-read picture books
- all materials ranging from forty to 200 words in length and are divided into four levels on the basis of length
- summaries on the charts and in the booklets identical in format and spread out over three to six pages[52]

EIR Program Procedures

- Day 1 is spent working with the teacher 15 to 20 minutes per day.
- Children will spend 3 days working on a story summary. The teacher reads the original picture book on the first day.
- Days 2 and 3 are spent working with the teacher. Children re-read the story summary from the chart with little assistance from the teacher.

- Children spend additional time working with the trained teacher aide or a project assistant for 5 minutes or in pairs for 5 to 10 minutes.
- Children are to read their story summaries with a minimum accuracy of 93 percent by the end of day 3.
- Children at the conclusion of the program make a transition to independent reading.

The Early Intervention in Reading program has proven to be successful in helping students who are

> at risk of falling behind in reading in first grade. The program is used by classroom teachers as an in-class supplement to the regular first-grade reading program, has helped many low-achieving first-grade students experience considerable success in reading.[53]

Some of the stories used in the Early Intervention in Reading program are listed in Figure 4.5.

It is important that school administrators remember the teachings of John Dewey that school is not a preparation for life, but it is life. Time spent reading is an important determinant in success in reading.

THE BOULDER PROJECT

The Boulder Project, an exclusively first-grade intervention program, involves Title I teachers and students from two schools. Teachers in the Boulder Project may or may not recognize (their choice) ongoing classroom reading instruction; regardless, it does not address the complex issue of how to improve poor classroom reading instruction.

The characteristics of the Boulder Project are as follows:

- It is a pull-out program that is exclusively supplementary to the regular reading program.
- It assumes no responsibility for the students' regular classroom reading instruction.
- Small groups are created for reading instruction.
- A Title I teacher works with three children for 30-minutes each day while a teacher's aide instructs

Some of the stories used in the Early Intervention in Reading program

Books from Group A:
Children listen to full story and read 40-60 word summaries (October-November)
Ask Mr. Bear. Marjorie Flack
You'll Soon Grow into Them, Titch. Pat Hutchins
Herman the Helper. Robert Kraus
Just for You. Mercer Mayer
Who Took the Farmer's Hat? Joan Nodset
Imogene's Antlers. David Small

Books from Group B:
Children listen to full story and read 60-90 word summaries (November-January)
Charlie Needs a Cloak. Tomie dePaloa
Three Kittens. Mirra Ginsburg
Good Night, Owl. Pat Hutchins
Geraldine's Blanket. Holly Keller
Round Robin. Jack Kent
Owliver. Robert Kraus

Books from Group C:
Children listen to full story and read 90-150 word summaries, and also read 50-150 word books (January-March)
A Dark, Dark Tale. Ruth Brown (book read by students)
Hattie and the Fox. Mem Fox
The Three Billy Goats Gruff. Paul Galdone
The Chick and the Duckling. Mirra Ginsburg (book read by students)
The Doorbell Rang. Pat Hutchins

Books from Group D
Children read these 100-120 word books (March-April)
Herman the Helper. Robert Kraus
Just for You. Mercer Mayer
The Bear's Toothache. David McPhail
There's a Nightmare in My Closet. Mercer Mayer
Noisy Nora. Rosemary Wells

Note: Books were grouped A-D according to summary or book length. Basic procedure: After hearing a book read aloud, the children saw the teacher read the story summary aloud from a large classroom chart; on subsequent days the teacher and students worked further at reading the summary.

Figure 4.5. Stories in Early Intervention Reading Program.

another group (the teacher and aide exchange groups at mid-year).
- The Title I teacher plans and coordinates students' instructional programs.
- The focus of the program is on (1) repeated reading of predictable trade books, (2) teaching word identification through the use of analogy or word patterns, (3) writing words from word pattern instruction, e.g., in, pin, tin, and (4) writing about topics of choice in notebooks.[54]

The positive result reported for the Boulder Project is that some at-risk students made progress with very small-group instruction.

SUCCESS FOR ALL PROGRAM

Success for All is considered as a total school reading program for kindergarten through third grade. The program focuses on both regular classroom instruction and supplementary support. The Success for All program depicts the following features.

- Students in grades 1–3 are heterogeneously grouped in classrooms of approximately twenty-five students, except for a 90-minute daily reading period when students are regrouped by reading level across the three grades in groups of fifteen to twenty students (this allows whole group, direct instruction and eliminates xeroxed copies and workbooks).
- Title I teachers, school-wide special education teachers, and Success for All tutors provide classroom reading instruction in order to reduce reading group size.
- Individual tutoring sessions of 20 minutes supplement group instruction for those students who are falling behind.
- Tutoring sessions emphasize the same strategies and skills as classroom reading activities.
- Whenever possible, the classroom teacher is also the child's tutor.
- The program provides preschool and full-day kindergarten experiences for all students and

implements a clearly defined approach to teaching reading.
- Kindergarten and first-grade textbooks specifically written to include vocabulary that exercises phonic skills are used.

The Success for All reading program has been implemented mostly in schools with a low socio-economic population in Baltimore, Maryland, and Philadelphia, Pennsylvania. Also, most children attend a half-day preschool and a full-day kindergarten.[55]

THE WINSTON-SALEM PROJECT

The Winston-Salem Project, used in first-grade classrooms in two schools in Winston-Salem, North Carolina, serves students from middle-class backgrounds in one school and low socio-economic backgrounds in the other school. Distinctive characteristics of this reading program comprise the following:

- Classroom instruction is reorganized into four 30-minute blocks in which students are taught reading in heterogeneous groups.
- The Basal block consists primarily of selective use of instructional suggestions from a recently published basal reading program that includes an anthology of children's literature and accompanying paperback books.
- The Writing block consists of five 10-minute mini lessons and student independent writing activities.
- The Working with Words block consists of word wall activities in which students manipulate groups of letters to form as many words as possible.
- During the Self-Selected Reading block, students read self-selected books, including informational books related to science and social studies topics.
- Students spend a considerable amount of time in reading related activities—a total of 3 hours and 15 minutes.
- At-risk students are given an additional 45 minutes of small group [five to six students] instruction in reading. Title I and special education teachers teach reading during these 45 minutes.

- Writing portfolios are kept for students, and teacher observations are considered important.[56]

Because some children needed help in reading beyond the first grade, the Winston-Salem Project was extended into second grade.

STUDENTS ACHIEVING INDEPENDENT LEARNING (SAIL)

The Students Achieving Independent Learning reading program is designed to help all students, particularly low achievers. Students in the SAIL program "learn to use a repertoire of learning strategies, initially with extensive modeling/coaching support, but with teacher assistance diminishing over time until students are competent, independent readers/thinkers/learners."[57] Characteristics of the SAIL reading program entail the following:

- The program promotes frequent and extensive student reading and encourages reading throughout the day.
- Children's literature is the primary source of instructional reading material. Selected basal stories or articles that children enjoy are also used.
- Instructional purposes are based on the needs of children.
- Students are encouraged to set their purposes for reading.
- To increase student motivation, SAIL teachers help students develop personal goals for improving their reading ability.
- Students are taught to use strategies to monitor understanding and solve problems as they read.
- The teacher ensures that students understand that getting the "gist" is a primary goal for reading. The "gist" prompt is "What's the story about?"
- During reading, students monitor their understanding of what they are reading by making predictions, visualizing, summarizing, and/or thinking aloud.
- The SAIL teacher frequently models the use of

strategies, e.g., I'm going to show you how good readers read.
- Students are taught how to activate and use background knowledge while (rather than before) reading.
- Vocabulary is dealt with as it occurs in the text.
- Student responses are accepted nonjudgmentally.[58]

The SAIL reading program helps students become successful readers by showing them steps that they can take throughout the reading process to increase their understanding. Title I test scores have shown "that SAIL instructed students clearly outperform their non-SAIL counterparts in both reading comprehension and math problem solving."[59] Accordingly, the students in the SAIL program view themselves as competent, successful readers.

IMPLEMENTING A READING PROGRAM

What type of a reading program will help meet the literacy needs of students today and equip them for future years? Why is it that more students have not been given the opportunity to practice reading? It is a well known fact that to become good and proficient at any skill one needs to practice. It is time to endorse and implement reading programs that allow children to read. Utilizing children's books can help achieve greater levels of success in learning reading skills and also reading for enjoyment. Five recommended principles that can make a difference in reading ability for students are

1. Children learn to read by reading.
2. Reading should be easy—but not too easy.
3. Instruction should be functional and contextual.
4. Make connections. Build a bridge between children's experiences and what they are about to read.
5. Build self-esteem.[60]

These five principles can be a part of the self-fulfilling prophecy. School administrators know the positive results of expressing to students that they have confidence in them. Therefore, apply these principles, this prophecy, and believe in your students. Also, school administrators should help teachers gain the knowledge and expertise to diagnose, prescribe, and make learning to read important and relevant.

Reading instruction must become focused on reading as a language and a thinking process. In order to promote reading instruction that will be language-conscious and alleviate the differences between language learning in school and the language students use at home or in their life space, the following will be helpful:

- Instead of learning words to read, read to learn words.
- Instead of learning phonics to read, read to learn phonics.
- Instead of beginning readers reading to their teacher, the teacher should read to them.
- Instead of teachers or materials asking questions, children should ask them.
- Instead of thinking of children as deriving meaning from print, think of children bringing meaning to print. Meaning is not in the ink found on a page of print, but in the minds of students.[61]

Learning to read must be perceived as language learning. School administrators and teachers should work collaboratively so that students will be given the opportunity to "link their linguistic competence and cognitive abilities."[62] Reading is a meaningful and enjoyable process. Use what each student has in his or her cognitive map to facilitate learning how to read.

Informal Reading Inventories

An informal reading inventory (IRI) provides information about the independent, instructional, frustration, and listening capacity for each student. Teachers who have completed a course in remedial reading instruction should have exposure to varied reading inventories. It is recommended that the IRI be given by the school's reading specialist or a teacher who has had specific training in the administration and interpretation of an IRI.

Informal reading inventories that can be purchased commercially are

- Analytic Reading (1–8), Merrill Publishing Company
- Basic Reading (1–8), Kendall/Hunt Publishing Company
- Classroom Reading (1–8), Brown Publishers
- Qualitative Reading (1–8), Scott, Foresman/Little, Brown
- Burns/Roe Informal Reading (1–12), Houghton Mifflin
- Ekwall Reading (1–12), Allyn and Bacon

Reading Interest Inventories

Another reading inventory that provides teachers with reading material that can help in "turning students on to reading" is the interest inventory. These inventories are comprised of teachers' questions, or they can be purchased. Listed below are thirty sample questions (see Exhibit 4.1) that can be used to create an interest inventory for students in your classroom and/or school.

An interest inventory gives teachers information about students' interests and attitudes toward reading. It provides teachers with needed insights for accruing books that students will be eager to read. Always remember, each child is a unique individual and possesses different likes and dislikes. The ultimate goal in reading instruction should be to motivate each student to read, comprehend, and enjoy various print media.

Students' strengths and weaknesses can be assessed by asking some general questions about a school district's literacy program, which is dependent on the adopted reading philosophy, goals, and objectives. Relevant questions are as follows:

- Where are students in their literacy development?
- At what level are they reading?
- Are they reading up to their ability?
- How well do they comprehend what they read?
- How adequate are students' reading vocabularies?
- What word attack skills do they use effectively?
- Do they know how to study?
- What comprehension and word attack strategies do students use?
- What are their attitudes toward reading?

> **EXHIBIT 4.1**
>
> **Reading Inventory Questionnaire (Elementary)**
>
> 1. Who are you?
> 2. How old are you?
> 3. When is your birthday?
> 4. How would you describe yourself?
> 5. Do you live in a city or in the country?
> 6. What sports do you enjoy?
> 7. Who is your hero? Why?
> 8. What is the name of your favorite book?
> 9. Why did the author write the book?
> 10. Who is your favorite character from a book that you read?
> 11. What do you like to read?
> 12. Would you like to have time during class to read on your own?
> 13. Do you read at home?
> 14. Do you like to have someone read to you?
> 15. Do you like to read out loud?
> 16. Do you have a library card?
> 17. What is your favorite subject?
> 18. What animals do you like?
> 19. If you would go to the movies, what would you choose to see?
> 20. What section of the newspaper do you like the most?
> 21. What magazines do you read?
> 22. I wish I had more time in school to _____.
> 23. What is something special that you can do that you would enjoy teaching or showing the class?
> 24. How many people are in your family?
> 25. If you could visit any country, what country would you choose? Why?
> 26. What is your hobby?
> 27. What is your favorite thing to do after school?
> 28. What do you want to be when you grow up?
> 29. I enjoy _____.
> 30. Reading is _____.

- What kind of books do they like to read?
- Do they read on their own?
- Do they enjoy reading?
- How well do they write?
- What kinds of writing tasks have they attempted?
- Are students' reading and writing improving?
- Which students seem to have special needs in reading and writing?[63]

The information from the aforementioned questions provides school administrators and teachers with insights on what type of reading instruction is needed for students in that school or school district.

The school administrator must choose teachers who have certain qualities, because any reading program is only as good as the teacher who is teaching reading in the classroom. The qualities that are considered important for an effective teacher are

- warmth: The teacher should have a caring attitude for all students and a concern for their social, emotional, and intellectual needs.
- enthusiasm: Arousing interest in the teaching and learning processes is essential for being an effective teacher.
- cognitive organization: The teacher must know how to organize learning material for students (e.g., the teacher needs to diagnose and prescribe the correct reading materials and use the proper instructional approach for the students).
- indirectness: The teacher uses varied instructional methods that will best connect students with the subject (students of all ages remember 90 percent of what they say as they do a task).[64]

The above qualities are analogous to what effective teachers do. For example, the "mediocre teacher tells. The good teacher explains. The superior teacher demonstrates. The great teacher inspires."[65]

The school administrator should also consider the qualities of McGregor's X and Y theories and Ouchi's Z theory in selecting teachers for reading instruction. Flexibility is one of the greatest assets of teachers. They must have the knowledge and expertise to modify reading instruction to fit the needs of the students. McGregor's X and Y and Ouchi's Z theories, illustrated in Figure 4.6, can be utilized as a beginning point in deciding the type of teacher who should be facilitating reading instruction for students in our schools.

Effective teachers understand the nature of reading, serve as role models, and enjoy reading. They truly believe that reading is a part of language and important in communication, more than completing skill exercises or a complex skill. Reading "instruction demands much more than merely drilling children, asking them for correct answers, and following the suggestions

Theory X	Theory Y	Theory Z
1. Students dislike work and will avoid it.	1. Learning is as natural as play.	1. Students and teachers work as a team.
2. Students must be forced to work.	2. Students are self-motivated and will strive to accomplish obectives.	2. Teachers clarify objectives to gain students' support for learning.
3. Students want to be directed and will avoid responsibility.	3. Students will learn to accept and seek responsibility.	3. Teachers and students view learning as a journey.

Consider your approach to the teaching and learning processes and determine whether you are an X, Y, or Z type teacher.

Figure 4.6. Theories X, Y, and Z teacher characteristics. (Source: Boschee, F. 1989. Grouping = Growth. *Dubuque, IA: Kendall/Hunt Publishing Company, p. 21. Reproduced by permission.*)

offered in the teacher's manual."[66] Effective reading teachers do not look for a panacea; they monitor students' comprehension, not by placing an emphasis on correct answers and rote memory, but by utilizing open-ended questions that use "why" and "how" to facilitate and place an emphasis on comprehension, analysis, synthesis, and evaluation that causes students to think.

Effective reading teachers also value the importance of having students who "like to read and that . . . read willingly in order to acquire information and enrich their lives."[67]

IMPROVING READING SKILLS IN SECONDARY SCHOOLS

Where does content area reading fit into a secondary school curriculum? Where does content area reading fit when teachers have academic degrees in secondary education? Objections by secondary school teachers to reading in the content area are usually verbalized with statements such as

- "My curriculum is hands-on. We don't do any reading."
- "I deal mainly with numbers."
- "It's a fad. What'll we do next year?"
- "It's not my job! I'm not the reading teacher."[68]

Reading in the content area should be a natural component of every curriculum. Reading is not a subject but rather a body of skills that should be taught and reinforced by every content teacher who uses printed matter. Too, "reading instruction is not, and should not, be construed as being the sole responsibility of the elementary teacher."[69] Unfortunately, formal reading instruction ends at the sixth grade level in far too many schools. Instead, reading skills development should be viewed as a lifetime process and extends from birth to death.

> One of the myths about teaching reading skills [at the secondary school level] is that these competencies cannot or should not be promoted in a subject matter class. When printed matter is used, the teacher is obligated to teach the vocabulary, comprehension, and study skills related to that subject area. The vocabulary of science, for example, is unique to that area and the placement of reading skill competency as the sole responsibility of a special reading teacher for teaching subject matter reading skills is both unfair and unrealistic. Reading skills must be taught in a meaningful context and not in an educational vacuum.[70]

Skills Necessary for Effective Reading Instruction

To be an effective teacher of reading in the content area, secondary school teachers should encompass a body of skills that will enable them to help students with their reading proficiencies. To be able to read and comprehend content material, the students should develop reading competencies with teacher guidance. The reading competencies listed in Exhibit 4.2 in the form of behavioral objectives should build the core of such a body of skills.

The list of skills presented in Exhibit 4.2 will have a different level of significance for the various content areas in the secondary schools. However, nearly all of them will apply to the social studies and literature areas, and many will be important to all other areas that use print media as the major thrust of instruc-

EXHIBIT 4.2

Essential Reading Skills (Secondary)

Students should be able to:

1. Analyze words through the use of phonics, structural analysis, and text clues.
2. Employ the use of different kinds of abridged and unabridged dictionaries for finding the meaning of words, their origin, and correct pronunciation.
3. Make use of certain visual clues in print materials for understanding concepts, formulas, experiments, and new vocabulary.
4. Understand and develop the vocabulary which is unique to a given content area.
5. Evaluate and compare the truthfulness and authenticity of an explanation of a topic which is presented in a number of different sources.
6. Review material which has been read in order to form accurate conclusions and main ideas about the topics explored.
7. Make outlines of required reading materials in preparation for a test.
8. Perceive the order of events and capture the main idea of the topic.
9. Select carefully those resource books which are most likely to contain desired information.
10. Develop the ability to use the library resources wisely when seeking information about a given topic which has been assigned.
11. Detect propaganda techniques which may be included in newspapers and popular journals.
12. Utilize classroom and media references correctly when seeking information in the World Almanac, encyclopedias, and other sources.
13. Develop an interest in reading widely in many different sources after a subject has been introduced.
14. Arrive at appropriate conclusions and generalizations after reading several paragraphs from a chapter of material.
15. Analyze cause and effect relationships when a number of topics are considered.

tion. Regardless, the goal of all content teachers should be to help each student gain maximum proficiency in as many of the skills as possible.

Building Motivation to Read in the Content Area

How can secondary school students be motivated to read? Can they be motivated? A number of techniques that have been

> **EXHIBIT 4.2 (continued)**
>
> **Essential Reading Skills (Secondary)**
>
> Students should be able to:
>
> 16. Know how to adjust reading rate in light of the nature and type of reading material being read.
> 17. Understand the meaning and importance of references and footnotes as an aid to increasing comprehension of both literal and interpretive questions.
> 18. Read orally with clarity and purpose with an absence of omissions, substitutions, and hesitations.
> 19. Develop the ability to summarize and organize a body of data which has been collected from a number of sources.
> 20. Construct and utilize class notes properly during and after class sessions.
> 21. Understand the function and importance of such textbook sections as the preface, glossary, table of contents, and index of a given book or series of books.
> 22. Read and follow directions which relate to such topics as experiments and projects.
> 23. Utilize the SQ3R (survey, question, read, recite, review) reading-study formula in areas where it would seem to apply.
> 24. Comprehend the meaning and function of such items as formulas and scientific laws.
> 25. Understand the importance of punctuation marks and the meanings they convey in a body of material.
> 26. Withhold judgment about an idea or topic until all information has been perused about the subject.
> 27. Locate written statements which support a certain point of view on a topic that is controversial in nature.
> 28. Draw appropriate conclusions from scanning pictures, illustrations, and other graphic aids which accompany a particular chapter or section of material.
> 29. Apply and adapt what has been read to real life situations.
> 30. Derive meaning from words, phrases, sentences, paragraphs, and chapters in that order.[7]

highly successful for building motivation are available. A brief description of several strategies are provided below. Each instructor should select and utilize those that seem most applicable to the content area he or she is teaching.

1. To uncover each student's likes and dislikes with regard to various types of print media, an interest inventory is one of the most effective ways. For example, the teacher may ask students to respond to questions similar to the following:

- What are the names of three of your favorite television programs?
- If you had several hours to spend in a large library, what types of books would you select to read?
- Of all the books that you have read, which one has been your favorite?
- When you look at a daily newspaper, which section do you generally read first?
- Place a check mark beside each of the following types of books that you enjoy reading:

  ___ mysteries ___ stories about heroes
  ___ sports stories ___ biographies
  ___ science fiction ___ novels
  ___ history ___ reference books

2. Developing a cheerful and inviting classroom environment is conducive for building reading interests of students. A table could be placed in one corner of the room where various resource books from a given content area are displayed. The books should be rotated with newer volumes in evidence on a regular basis. Students should be invited to review one or more books during the course of the semester or school year.

3. Business and other community leaders may be invited to speak to the students regarding new books or articles that they have read or published. This type of activity creates the impression that "important" people read books and enjoy the experience.

4. Several companies produce tapes and computer software that serve to introduce books that have been written on various subjects. Some of the programs give a short introduction to the material, pose questions to arouse interest, and invite learners to read the total volume.

5. The use of bibliotherapy to motivate reluctant readers to read and enjoy is useful. The bibliotherapy technique focuses on students who have experienced a difficult problem or challenge. Books that deal with the problem or challenge—death, divorce, drugs or alcohol, poor self-concept—will be useful for those readers.

There are several sources available for finding information

about books to be used for bibliotherapy purposes. One of the most useful volumes is *Bookfinder* published by American Guidance Services, Inc., Circle Pines, MN 55014.

6. There are a large number of magazine and book clubs available for students of various ages. Many of these sources contain selections that are very interesting material for all students, especially those who are unmotivated and not inspired to read. (Contact the school librarian for up-to-date sources).

7. Many local and state educational agencies sponsor reading clubs for secondary students. Content teachers should become informed about the clubs and urge students to participate actively in such organizations.[72]

Teachers need to be good role models and provide an academic setting that will allow success to be possible for the reader. The strategies provided for teachers in the content area should be of significant help in building levels of motivation for reading by students.

THE IMPACT OF EARLY EDUCATIONAL EXPERIENCES

What if all children would be given the opportunity to attend full-day preschools and kindergartens that would provide them with beginning reading instruction and related educational experiences? Would we still need "backload" remedial reading programs? According to prevailing research, the answer is an overwhelming NO. Two national studies have recently confirmed that specific kinds of educational experiences provided for children by both parents and teachers, from preschool through high school, can make a significant difference in their reading ability as young adults.

The Kindergarten Reading Follow-up (KRF) study examined long-term effects on children of being taught to read in kindergarten; and the Reading Development Follow-up (RDF) study sought to identify specific kinds of experiences that foster high levels of reading achievement in high school seniors. The results of these two studies provide some straightforward guidelines for cultivating literacy development. The implications are clear:

students who are provided with more of these specific kinds of experiences across their development will have higher reading achievement levels than those who have less.

Early Educational Experiences

Early language and educational experiences for children are particularly critical to adult literacy levels. Although early childhood experiences have long been known to be important in terms of general intelligence development, the RDF study confirmed that the specific kinds of early educational experiences students have are highly predictive of later reading abilities as well. That is, those high school seniors who are provided with more reading, language, and other kinds of both direct and indirect educational experiences during their preschool years have higher overall levels of reading competency than those provided with less.

Such preschool activities as learning nursery rhymes and stories, watching Sesame Street, playing word and number games, being read to, attending nursery/preschool, and participating in special lessons, such as swimming, dance, or music, are all positively related to students' reading ability in high school. Finally, later "high stakes" schooling experiences, such as placement in remedial/developmental classes and/or a particular type of high school academic track, could be linked to the student's level of involvement in early educational experiences.

Early Reading Instruction

Children who learn to read early, either indirectly through home and family experience, or directly through formal beginning reading programs implemented in preschools and kindergartens, are typically good readers in the primary grades.[73] Until recently, however, it was unclear as to whether this advantage was maintained through high school.

The findings of the KRF study clearly indicate that those students who began their formal reading instruction in kindergarten have higher reading achievement scores, both at the end of their kindergarten year and as seniors in high school, than those students who did not.[74,75] Also, compared to other high school seniors in the same school districts, those who received the kindergarten reading instruction had better grades, attendance, and attitudes toward reading, as well as less need for remediation. More importantly, these same results held up across ethnic, gender, and social class groups. Perhaps the most astounding finding was that those students in the study who were provided with formal reading instruction in kindergarten were, as a group, from "lower" social class backgrounds than those students who were not; yet, they scored higher on all indicators of educational achievement as high school seniors than their higher socioeconomic status peers who attended elementary schools in the same school districts.

Elementary Schooling Experience

In regard to elementary schooling experience in general, the RDF Study[76,77] found that those students who participated in activities and classes with an academic emphasis, and avoided remedial classes and/or repeating grades, had higher achievement levels than those who did not. The more classes and situations in which students participated that had an academic and/or accelerated emphasis (including skipping a grade or double promotion), as opposed to a non-academic and/or remedial or developmental emphasis, the higher their reading achievement was in their senior year of high school. More specifically, those students who spent more time writing stories or papers, doing math problems, reading books, working on science projects, and/or working on spelling and language lessons had good school attendance records and high levels of reading achievement.

Secondary School Experiences

At the secondary level, those students who spent more time in organized extracurricular activities, had higher reading achievement scores as seniors than those who spent more time in unorganized extracurricular activities, such as watching television, talking on the phone, or hanging out at the mall. Also, the students who were programmed through an academic track, as opposed to a vocational track, and/or those who took more than 1 year of high school math, science, and foreign language courses had better reading skills at the end of their senior year of high school than those who did not. Finally, those students who spent less time working in part-time jobs, paid or unpaid, had better reading skills than students who worked more.

Parental Involvement and Support

Specific experiences provided by parents, at every schooling level (i.e., pre-through high school), were clearly related to adult literacy levels. Results indicated that if parents expect their children to become literate adults, then they must provide guidelines for their behavior and encourage participation in reading and reading-related activities, at least through high school. For example, having rules concerning the student's bedtime, household chores, and/or homework, along with giving rewards for school work, providing books and magazines, and taking the student to the library, museum, and concerts, were all shown to contribute to the level of a student's high school reading achievement. Moreover, parental expectations in regard to students' educational attainment are extremely important. The students who did well in school and/or indicated that they wanted to continue their education beyond high school had parents or guardians who expected them to do so and provided them with the necessary support and encouragement.

The findings of both the Reading Development Follow-up Study and the Kindergarten Reading Follow-up Study emphasize the responsibility of parents, educators, and policy makers in regard to literacy development. Today, however, the vast majority of preschool children are not provided with the kinds of early educational experiences that generate success in literacy development; yet, amazingly, educational leaders and local, state, and national policy makers seem puzzled as to why so many students graduate from high school as functional illiterates.

If our nation's schools are going to have an impact on future literacy rates, "front loading" is essential. This means that all children must be given the opportunity to attend full-day preschools and kindergartens that provide them with beginning reading instruction and related educational experiences now known to be critical to literacy development. Subsequently, school districts and policy makers must be ready to present new and compelling evidence for *not* providing early childhood teachers with valid programs that would enable them to teach the appropriate language and beginning reading skills to students in their preschool and kindergarten classes.

THE SCHOOL ADMINISTRATOR'S ROLE

The roof is leaking! Quick, get the buckets! In this metaphor, a reading program was a once-beautiful home that deteriorated over time. The owners, realizing this, try to repair the obvious damage, but somehow they overlook the leaky roof. So they redo the plaster, repair the windows, replace the doors—giving attention to everything but the roof. The house continues to deteriorate, and nobody seems to notice the roof. But until the roof is repaired, the house will never be beautiful or fully functional.[78]

Where is the leaky roof in our reading programs? Is it the spectacular changes in children who now attend school? Is it the continuous use of traditional solutions? Or, is it both? School administrators must be cognizant of these elements in selecting a reading program.

Understanding the Spectacular Changes in Children

Education demographer Harold Hodgkinson believes that the spectacular changes in children who now attend school constitute the leaky roof in our reading programs. Fully, one-third of the nation's children are at risk of failure before they enter kindergarten. The assertion is supported by the statistics issued by the United States House of Representatives Select Committee on Children, Youth, and Families, which show that

- One-fourth of all preschool children in the U.S. live in poverty.
- Seven out of ten women with children are active members of the work force.
- The work force has quadrupled in the past 20 years, pushing the number of single-parent families toward 25 percent; 16.2 million children are being raised in single-parent families, and that number is expected to increase 30 percent by the year 2000.
- Fifteen million children are being raised by single mothers whose annual income averages about $11,400 in 1988 dollars, while the average couple makes $34,000. The number of babies born addicted to cocaine reached 350,000 a year by 1989; those who survive birth are poorly coordinated and have strikingly short attention spans.[79]

For better or worse, the family image has changed significantly. The traditional household of one mother, one father, and two children has decreased from 60 percent in the 1950s to 4 percent today. Also, communities across America are experiencing more violent and higher crime rates, more poverty among the populace, a neglect of disadvantaged youth by public institutions, and the dissipation of good teachers. In general, at-risk youth are not confined to the ghetto, the poor, or newly arrived immigrants. Rather, they are symptomatic of disturbing conditions in all American communities.

At-risk children "require a very high level of psychological and academic development . . . to be successful both in school and later in adult life."[80] Subsequently, school administrators will have to learn new strategies and behaviors on how to organize effective reading programs. The ability to work smarter, not harder, will become the measure of achievement. In reality, it is a social and educational intervention that is analogous to Albert Einstein's statement that "Perfection of means and confusion of ends seem to characterize our age."[81]

Recognizing a Proven Solution

A local strategy for school administrators is to underwrite and support an intervention reading program to supplement the school district's current reading program. Imagine what a school could be like if all children could experience prosperity in reading. Could the school dropout rate decline? Could society be more literate? Positive reading results could influence most or all of America's education goals.

The school administrator is the educational leader. The school administrator, teachers, and school community will need to decide what reading program, model, or approach will be the best for students. The question "How should reading be taught?" cannot be answered without knowing the needs, interests, and abilities of students. Teachers must use "reflective decision" making skills and the knowledge that they have learned to choose the model, strategy, and/or approach best for students as this will be determined by a student's abilities and capabilities.

Assessing the Reading Program

The changes in society and the research findings about reading instruction and how students master this complex activity of learning how to read has brought focus on various components and conditions that are instrumental in a good reading program. Schools can no longer be satisfied with teaching students how to identify and how to pronounce words. Reading experts state that

> before students can truly be said to be readers, they must have the ability to read the words they see, understand the ideas those words convey, integrate information from a variety of sources, and use all the information to understand complex ideas.[82]

According to recent research, a good reading program should include the following components and characteristics:

- phonics instruction
- the opportunity for children to do "meaningful" reading
- an emphasis on comprehension, not just word attack skills
- opportunities for listening, speaking, reading, and writing
- inclusion and applicability in all curricular subjects[83]

School administrators need to evaluate the reading instruction that is practiced in the classrooms and ensure that these components and characteristics are included in the reading program.

In conclusion, the fifteen goals for reading listed below will serve as a guide in choosing reading instruction:

- Incorporate both whole-language and skill-based instruction into the reading curriculum.
- Extend and deepen formal reading instruction in content areas and in middle and secondary schools.
- Enrich materials and motivate students to read for pleasure and as a habit.
- Vary and extend teaching capabilities.
- Establish or extend school district reading priorities, goals, and standards.
- Reach problem students.
- Teach higher level skills.
- Offer more effective inservice training.
- Encourage greater comprehension.
- Individualize instruction to a greater degree.
- Make greater, more effective use of computers.
- Seek new materials, more time, and higher scores for reading instruction.
- Involve parents more deeply.
- Establish stronger leadership structures in the reading program.
- Increase the use of children's literature in reading instruction.[84]

The decision on how to teach reading will be dependent on the school district's philosophy; school administrators' and teachers' philosophies; interpretation of research; the students' prior experience with print, prior knowledge; and level of instruction. Educators should always be aware that reading is a part of the language process and that the school administrator has the responsibility to provide the environment for students to master the task of reading.

Every American child deserves a school that takes to heart its most challenging and important mission—to teach all students to read. The child who attends such a school is much more likely to become a productive and contributing adult—and a happier one, too.[85]

School administrators have the moral obligation to do whatever is necessary to guarantee that all students receive reading instruction that will provide them success in learning how to read, learning how to comprehend, and learning to read for enjoyment. The reading success of individual students and productivity of educational systems is preeminent to the school administrator. Research has provided the basis for promising techniques and approaches that can be used in different school districts to provide all students with the ability to become literate during their first years of school and to put students on the road to success in life.

REVIEW ACTIVITIES

1. Create a chart that highlights the characteristics of the three models—bottom-up, top-down, and interactive—used in reading instruction.
2. Apply the four approaches in reading instruction—prescriptive, basal reading, language experience, and literature based—to the three models of reading instruction.
3. Create a general inventory of classroom "libraries" in your school. Which areas need reading materials? Which areas have particularly well stocked, appealing, and used "libraries"? How can your school increase student access to reading and reading activity?
4. Create a chart of preventive programs used in reading instruction. Include a brief description, benefits, and applications of each program.
5. Compare the reading program in your school to the components and characteristics of a good reading program on page 149. Identify the strengths and weaknesses of your school's reading program. As an administrator, what steps can you take to improve the reading program of your school?
6. Use brainstorming to compile a list of ways your school can increase parental involvement and support of reading and

reading-related activities to enhance student competency in reading.

ENDNOTES

1 Cushenbery, D. C. 1985. *Improving Reading Skills in the Content Area.* Springfield, IL: Charles C. Thomas, Publisher.

2 Somerfield, M., M. Torbe, and C. Ward. 1985. *A Framework for Reading: Creating a Policy in the Elementary School, A Language for Life: The Bullock Report* (6.39). Portsmouth, NH: Heinemann, p. 64.

3 Cranney, A. G. and J. S. Miller. 1987. "History of Reading: Status and Sources of a Growing Field." *Journal of Reading,* 30(5):390.

4 Ibid., p. 390.

5 Sadker, M. P. and D. M. Sadker. 1994. *Teachers, Schools, and Society.* Third edition. New York: McGraw-Hill, Inc., p. 115.

6 Sadker, M. P. and D. M. Sadker. 1994. *Teachers, Schools, and Society.* Third edition. New York: McGraw-Hill, Inc., p. 172.

7 Ibid., p. 115.

8 Ibid., p. 115.

9 Ibid., p. 172.

10 Vacca, J. L., R. T. Vacca, and M. K. Gove. 1991. *Reading and Learning to Read.* Second edition. New York: Harper Collins Publishers, p. 269.

11 Sadker, M. P. and D. M. Sadker. 1994. *Teachers, Schools, and Society.* Third edition. New York: McGraw-Hill, Inc., p. 115.

12 Cranney, A. G. and J. S. Miller. 1987. "History of Reading: Status and Sources of a Growing Field." *Journal of Reading,* 30(5):390.

13 Sadker, M. P. and D. M. Sadker. 1994. *Teachers, Schools, and Society.* Third edition. New York: McGraw-Hill, Inc., p. 115.

14 Vacca, J. L., R. T. Vacca, and M. K. Gove. 1991. *Reading and Learning to Read.* Second edition. New York: Harper Collins Publishers, p. 269.

15 Cranney, A. G. and J. S. Miller. 1987. "History of Reading: Status and Sources of a Growing Field." *Journal of Reading,* 30(5):390.

16 Gunning, T. G. 1992. *Creating Reading Instruction for All Children.* Boston: Allyn and Bacon, p. 391.

17 Harris, P. 1989. "New Findings in the Great Debate." *Phi Delta Kappan,* 71:259.

18 Taylor, D. 1989. "Toward a Unified Theory of Literacy Learning and Instructional Practices." *Phi Delta Kappan,* 71:192.

19 Ibid., p. 193.

20 Trachtenburg, P. 1990. "Using Children's Literature to Enhance Phonics Instruction." *The Reading Teacher,* 43:648.

21 Vacca, J. L., R. T. Vacca, and M. K. Gove. 1991. *Reading and Learning to Read.* Second Edition. New York: Harper Collins Publishers, p. 20.

22 Jones, L. L. 1982. "An Interactive View of Reading: Implications for the Classroom." *The Reading Teacher,* 35:773.
23 Trachtenburg, P. 1990. "Using Children's Literature to Enhance Phonics Instruction," *The Reading Teacher,* 43:648.
24 Vacca, J. L., R. T. Vacca, and M. K. Gove, 1991. *Reading and Learning to Read.* Second edition. New York: Harper Collins Publishers, p. 20.
25 Ibid., p. 21.
26 Ibid., p. 21.
27 Ibid., p. 21.
28 Jones, L. L. 1982. "An Interactive View of Reading: Implications for the Classroom." *The Reading Teacher,* 35:774.
29 Vacca, J. L., R. T. Vacca, and M. K. Gove. 1991. *Reading and Learning to Read.* Second edition. New York: Harper Collins Publishers, p. 37.
30 Ibid., p. 262.
31 Ibid., p. 262.
32 Adams, M. J. 1990. *Beginning to Read: Thinking and Learning about Print.* Cambridge: MIT Press, p. 272.
33 Gunning, T. G. 1992. *Creating Reading Instruction for All Children.* Boston: Allyn and Bacon, p. 79.
34 Samuels, S. J. and A. E. Farstrup, eds. 1992. *What Research Has to Say About Reading Instruction.* Newark, DE: International Reading Association, p. 146.
35 Au, K. and J. M. Mason. 1989. "Elementary Reading Programs," in *The Administration and Supervision of Reading Programs.* B. Wepner, J. T. Feeley, and D. S. Stricland, eds. New York: Teachers College Press, p. 64.
36 Gunning, T. G. 1992. *Creating Reading Instruction for All Children.* Boston: Allyn and Bacon, p. 365.
37 Samuels, S. J. and A. E. Farstrup, eds. 1992. *What Research Has to Say About Reading Instruction.* Newark, DE: International Reading Association, p. 296.
38 Baghban, M. 1981. "Practicality and Literacy," a paper presented at the *26th Annual Meeting of the International Reading Association,* New Orleans, LA, April 17–May 1, 1981, ERIC Reproduction Service No. ED 206 411, p. 13.
39 Vacca, J. L., R. T. Vacca, and M. K. Gove. 1989. *Reading and Learning to Read.* Second edition. New York: Harper Collins Publishers, p. 42.
40 The program features of "The Small Grouper" include the following:
- partitions students into small groups (four, five, or six students in a group)
- saves hours of manual effort
- provides clear, concise reports
- identifies isolates, neglectees, and group leaders
- places each student with one of his/her choices

To order "The Small Grouper," send $195.00 to Floyd Boschee, 117 Willow Street, Vermillion, SD 57069. Please indicate disk size, IBM-compatible (with 640K RAM, hard disk, and mouse recommended) or Macintosh.

41 Boschee, F., B. M. Whitehead, and M. A. Boschee. 1993. *Effective Reading Programs: The Administrator's Role.* Lancaster, PA: Technomic Publishing Company, Inc., pp. 49–52.
42 Pikulski, J. J. 1994. "Preventing Reading Failure: A Review of Five Effective Programs," *The Reading Teacher,* 48(1):38.
43 Dyer, P. C. 1992. "Reading Recovery: A Cost-Effectiveness and Educational-Outcomes Analysis," *ERS Spectrum,* 10(1):10.
44 Pinnell, G. S. 1989. "Reading Recovery: Helping At-Risk Children Learn to Read," *The Elementary School Journal,* 90(2):180.
45 Dyer, P. C. 1992. "Reading Recovery: A Cost-Effectiveness and Educational-Outcomes Analysis," *ERS Spectrum,* 10(1):15.
46 Ibid., p. 10.
47 Ibid., p. 11.
48 Pinnell, G. S. 1989. "Reading Recovery: Helping At-Risk Children Learn to Read," *The Elementary School Journal,* 90(2):169–170.
49 Dyer, P. C. 1992. "Reading Recovery: A Cost-Effectiveness and Educational-Outcomes Analysis," *ERS Spectrum,* 10(1):18.
50 Taylor, B. M., R. A. Short, J. J. Frye, and B. A. Shearer. 1992. "Classroom Teachers Prevent Reading Failure Among Low-Achieving First Grade Students," *The Reading Teacher,* 45:593.
51 Ibid., p. 593.
52 Ibid., p. 593.
53 Ibid., pp. 596–597.
54 Pikulski, J. J. 1994. "Preventing Reading Failure: A Review of Five Effective Programs," *The Reading Teacher,* 48(1):33–38.
55 Ibid., pp. 32–38.
56 Ibid., pp. 32–33.
57 Bergman, J. L. 1992. "SAIL—A Way to Success and Independence for Low-Achieving Readers," *The Reading Teacher,* 45:598.
58 Ibid., pp. 598–601.
59 Ibid., p. 602.
60 Gunning, T. G. 1992. *Creating Reading Instruction for All Children.* Boston: Allyn and Bacon, pp. 14–17.
61 Tovey, D. R., L. G. Johnson, and M. Szporer. 1986. "Remedying 'The 180° Syndrome' in Reading," *Childhood Education,* 63(1):12–14.
62 Ibid., p. 15.
63 Gunning, T. G. 1992. *Creating Reading Instruction for All Children.* Boston: Allyn and Bacon, p. 460.
64 Boschee, F. 1989. *Grouping = Growth.* Dubuque, Iowa: Kendall/Hunt Publishing Company, p. 22.
65 Alcorn, M. D., J. S. Kinder, and J. R. Schunert. 1964. *Better Teaching in Secondary Schools.* Revised edition. Chicago: Holt, Rinehart and Winston, Inc., p. 6.
66 Hayes, B. L. 1991. *Effective Strategies for Teaching Reading.* Boston, MA: Allyn and Bacon, p. 11.

67 Ibid., p. 9.
68 McAloon, N. M. 1994. "Content Area Reading—It's Not My Job!" *Journal of Reading,* 37:332.
69 Roe, B. D., B. D. Stoodt, and P. C. Burns. 1983. *Secondary Reading Instruction: The Content Area.* Boston: Houghton-Mifflin Company, p. 5.
70 Cushenbery, D. C. 1985. *Improving Reading Skills in the Content Area.* Springfield, IL: Charles C. Thomas Publisher, p. 5.
71 Ibid., pp. 14–16.
72 Ibid., pp. 101–102.
73 Mason, J. 1984. "Early Reading from a Developmental Perspective," in *Handbook of Reading Research.* D. Pearson, ed. New York: Longman, pp. 505–543.
74 Hanson, R, and D. F. Siegel. 1988. "The Effect on High School Seniors of Learning to Read in Kindergarten." Technical Report No. 1., Garden City, CA: Hanson Research Systems.
75 Hanson, R., and D. F. Siegel. 1991. "The Long-Term Effects of Seniors Learning to Read in Kindergarten: A Twelve-Year Follow-Up Study." [ED 323 494]
76 Siegel, D. F. 1987. Identification and Validation of Process Factors Related to the Achievement of High School Seniors: A Follow-Up Study. Unpublished doctoral dissertation, University of Tulsa.
77 Siegel, D. F. 1990. "The Literacy Press: A Process Model for Reading Development." *Journal of Educational Research,* 83:336–347.
78 Hodgkinson, H. 1991, September. "School Reform vs. Reality," *Phi Delta Kappan,* 73:9–16.
79 Anderson, T. R. and J. Jeffrey. 1992. "Restructuring Schools with the Forgotten Solution: Community Education," in *Educational Restructuring and the Community Education Process,* Larry E. Decker and Valerie A. Rommney, eds. Alexandria, VA: National Community Education Association, p. 26.
80 Comer, J. P. 1987. "New Haven's School—Community Connection," *Educational Leadership,* 44(6):13.
81 Amundson, K. 1988. *Challenges for School Leaders.* Arlington, VA: American Association of School Administrators, p. 51.
82 Kline, L., B. Brodinsky, and K. Amundson. 1990. *Teaching Reading.* American Association of School Administrators, Critical Issues Report, p. 1.
83 Ibid., pp. 2–3.
84 Ibid., p. 8.
85 Ibid., p. 1.

CHAPTER 5
Bilingual Education

Once upon a time, a Mother mouse was training her little one in the art of self-preservation. "If you hear a meow," she said, "sit tight and don't venture out of the hole." And the little mouse heard a meow and stayed still as instructed. A few moments later the little mouse heard "Bow wow," and with Mother mouse's okay, ventured out and was quickly seized and eaten by a big black cat who, with a satisfied smile remarked, "That's one of the advantages of being bilingual." (Author Unknown)

DESCRIPTION AND OVERVIEW

SCHOOL classrooms across America are quickly filling with large and growing numbers of children who are of limited English proficiency (LEP). These language-minority children speak virtually all world languages including many languages indigenous to the United States. In addition, the cultural heritage of these children differs widely from their English proficient peers. United States immigration policies are responsible in part for the presence of these limited English speaking children in American schools.[1] These policies have been supported, in part, by federal legislation related to equal educational opportunities for all children and youth. The federal government, as demonstrated by Title VI of the Civil Rights Act of 1964 and section 204(f) of the Equal Education Opportunities Act of 1974,[2] has expressed a special and continuing obligation to ensure that states and local school districts take appropriate action to provide equal educational opportunities to all children and youth of limited English proficiency. This federal obligation includes assisting states and local school districts in developing the capacity to provide programs of instruction that offer limited English proficient (LEP) children and youth an equal educational opportunity.

Limited English speaking children face many challenges in receiving an education that will enable them to obtain the education and income that will provide the means to participate fully as contributing members in American society. These challenges include

- segregated education programs
- disproportionate and improper placement in special education and other special programs due to the use of inappropriate evaluation procedures
- the limited English proficiency of their own parents, which hinders the parents' ability to fully participate in the education of their children
- a shortage of teachers and other staff who are professionally trained and qualified to serve such children and youth[3]

International communication has become a daily occurrence in government, business, commerce, and family life. As the world becomes increasingly interdependent, multilingual skills constitute an important national resource that deserves protection and development. Quality bilingual education programs can enable children and youth to learn English and meet high academic standards, including proficiency in more than one language. The use of a child's or youth's native language and culture in classroom instruction can

- promote self-esteem and contribute to academic achievement and learning English by limited English proficient children and youth
- benefit English proficient children and youth who also participate in such programs
- develop our nation's national language resources, thus promoting our nation's competitiveness in the global economy[4]

The bilingual education policy of the United States has most recently been revised and outlined by Congress in Title VII, Part A of Improving America's Schools Act of 1994: Reauthorizing the Elementary and Secondary Education Act of 1965.[5] This federal policy has been developed to ensure equal educational opportunity for all children and youth and to promote educational excellence among children with limited English proficiency. To support these goals, Congress has made available federal assistance grants not only to state and local educational agencies, but also to institutions of higher education and community-based organizations to build their capacity to establish, implement, and sustain programs of instruction for children and youth of limited English proficiency.

The purpose of this act is to educate limited English proficient children and youth to meet the same rigorous standards for academic performance expected of all children and youth (see Figure 5.1). This includes meeting challenging state content standards and challenging state student performance standards in academic areas by

- developing systematic improvement and reform of educational programs serving limited English proficient students through the development and implementation of exemplary bilingual education programs and special alternative programs

---

- Program improvement and reform
- English and native language skills
- Bilingual and multilingual skills
- Multicultural understanding
- Native American assistance
- Research and technical assistance
- Instructional training and development

Figure 5.1. Bilingual education program purposes.

- developing bilingual skills and multicultural understanding
- developing the English of such children and youth and, to the extent possible, the native language skills of such children and youth
- providing similar assistance to Native Americans with certain modifications relative to the unique status of Native American languages under Federal law
- developing data collection and dissemination, research, materials development, and technical assistance that is focused on school improvement for limited English proficient students
- developing programs that strengthen and improve the professional training of educational personnel who work with limited English proficient students[6]

HISTORICAL BACKGROUND

Bilingual education has been heralded by many as one of the most significant and widespread movements in American education in the twentieth century. Bilingual education was first implemented in the public schools in the late 1960s. These programs were a direct result of legislative mandates for bilingual programs in schools where linguistic differences existed in the student population. This legislation recognized that students whose first languages were other than English, and whose cultural backgrounds were different than the majority student population, could not be served with the same academic approaches that were used to serve English proficient students. Funding was provided at both the federal and state levels to support these programs. The implementation of bilingual education programs at the school level resulted in modifications to the daily school routine and imposed new responsibilities on the school administrator and teaching staff.

Federal initiatives and subsequent court cases in the 1960s and 1970s prompted the nation's school systems to identify and develop methods of instruction for LEP students in an effort to provide these students equal educational opportunity under the law. Schools at this time lacked basic information and competence in the ability to implement bilingual education programs. In order to develop these programs, a new type of school administrator with specialized training in bilingual education was often required to manage the services needed to address the needs of the targeted student population.

Title VII, Part A of Improving America's Schools Act of 1994: Reauthorizing the Elementary and Secondary Education Act of 1965 is the most recent revision of federal guidelines related to bilingual education programs and extends program development and grant opportunities under this act until the year 2000. Title VII, Part A broadens the scope of past programs to include funding grants for bilingual education in early childhood, elementary, and secondary school programs. The program scope has been broadened to foster language enhancement, language acquisition, parent and community involvement, cultural enrichment, the use of technology, support for innovative program development, service to private school students, as well as the inclusion of English proficient students in bilingual education programs to enhance multilingualism among the nation's students.

RESEARCH AND LEGAL BASE

The history of bilingual education legislation reflects the history of conflict in American education. Progress attained in the legislative changes produced during the 1960s demonstrates that in most instances bilingual education legislation emerged as an attempt to respond to social unrest related to the education of linguistic minorities in America's schools. It was found that large numbers of LEP students were not progressing academically at the same rate as their age appropriate peers. Academic and social problems that existed in school districts with large LEP populations underserved by a traditional, English-only educational system prompted litigation that contributed to legal resolutions and some mitigation of social tensions.

Conflict and controversy continued to be associated with bilingual education policy and practices in American school systems even after the passage of several federal legislative and landmark cases. The Bilingual Education Act of 1968[7] gave bilingual education national prominence and served as a catalyst in correcting some of the misconceptions associated with its concept. The optional programs under this act called for instruction for LEP students in a program that was well-organized and encompassed parts of all of the regular school curriculum. These programs were also required to include study of the history and culture associated with the mother tongue of LEP students and to develop and maintain the students' self-esteem and pride in both cultures.

As a result of this act, numerous projects were funded in various states across the nation. However, due to slow program implementation, stronger legislation was eventually required. The passage of the Bilingual Education Act of 1974, amending the previous acts of 1964 and 1968,[8] made bilingual education no longer optional, but mandatory in all schools receiving federal funds. Programs proliferated during the period that followed the passage of this legislation. The Bilingual Education Act of 1974 broadened the scope of mandatory instructional programs by defining transitional native language instruction through bilingual education as

> instruction given in, and study of English to the extent necessary to allow a child to progress effectively through the educational system, native language of the children of limited English speaking ability, and such instructions given with appreciation for the cultural heritage of such children, and with respect to elementary school instruction, such instruction shall, to the extent necessary, be in all courses or subjects of study which will allow a child to progress effectively through the educational system.[9]

This act was also amended, and one of the most important aspects of the Bilingual Education Act of 1978 was the clarification of bilingual education program goals. The amendments emphasized that the goal of bilingual education was to help develop the English language skills of students who were deficient in these skills, while simultaneously providing instruction in the native language so that students would be afforded the opportunity to progress effectively and successfully through the educational system. Local projects were required to set goals for children involved in bilingual programs and to provide necessary follow-up services for children who were exited from the program. More stringent requirements for parental involvement in the bilingual education programs were also included.[10]

Legal challenges began to emerge throughout the United States. The first of these court cases was *Cisneros v. Corpus Christi*.[11] This case was a reinterpretation of the 1954 landmark desegregation case *Brown v. Board of Education of Topeka*.[12] The Cisneros case held that Hispanics, as in the case of Blacks, are an identifiable ethnic minority for purposes of desegregation and for designing a remedy that could include bilingual education. This case was supported by *United States v. Texas* in which the court stated "we see no reason to believe that ethnic segregation is any less detrimental than racial segregation."[13] The rationale of *Brown v. Board of Education of Topeka* was also applied to the bilingual education of American Indian students in *Natonabah v. Board of Education of Gallup-McKinley County School District* in New Mexico and *Geraud v. Schrader* in Wyoming.[14]

The Tenth District Court of Appeals in *Keyes v. Denver* ruled that maintaining a segregated school even for the purpose of bilingual instruction violates the Constitution of the United States. The court stated that bilingual education is not a substitute for desegregation, and although bilingual instruction may be required to prevent the isolation of minority students in predominantly English speaking schools, such instruction must be subordinate to a plan of desegregation.[15]

The movement toward implementation of bilingual education programs in schools was further reinforced by the landmark United States Supreme Court decision in *Lau v. Nichols*.[16] In this case, Chinese-American students attending public schools in San Francisco, along with their parents, filed suit claiming that their right to equal protection under the Fourteenth Amendment to the Constitution and their rights under Title VI of the Civil Rights Act of 1964 were being denied by the public schools. The issue at hand was whether non-English speaking students were denied an equal educational opportunity when taught in a language they cannot understand. Title VI of the Civil Rights Act of 1964 states that "no person in the United States shall, on the ground of race, color, or national origin, be excluded from participation in, be denied the benefit of, or be subjected to discrimination under any program or activity receiving Federal financial assistance."[17] In their decision, the court unanimously agreed that

> It is not equality of treatment merely by providing students with the same facilities, textbooks, teachers, and curriculum; for students who do not understand English are effectively foreclosed from any meaningful education. . . . There is nothing less equal than the equal treatment of unequals."[18]

The Supreme Court based its decision in *Lau* on Title VI of the Civil Rights Act of 1964 and ruled in favor of the students and their parents. *Lau* became the law of the land regarding the education of non-English speaking students and provided the impetus for implementation of bilingual education programs in schools throughout the United States. One of the most significant results of the *Lau* decision was an intensive evaluation of school districts by the Department of Health, Education, and Welfare (HEW) and the Office of Civil Rights (OCR) to determine the extent of violations identified by the court's decision in *Lau*. These investigations gave rise to the *Lau Remedies,* commonly referred to as the *Lau Guidelines* issued jointly by HEW and OCR in 1975.[19] Although never enacted by Congress or officially adopted as federal policy, the *Lau Guidelines* eventually became publicly recognized, even by many courts, as the minimal standards for designing or evaluating an educationally effective program to overcome discriminatory practices against limited English speaking students.

Following *Lau*, Congress passed the Bilingual Education Act of 1974. This law specifies that programs "of bilingual education shall be developed in consultation with parents of children of limited English speaking ability, teachers, and where applicable, secondary school students."[20] The Bilingual Education Act of 1988[21] reaffirmed these principles, detailing federal regulations and appropriating funds for program development and implementation through 1993. *Lau* also became the catalyst for numerous court cases that followed, which tested and challenged the new laws.

The findings in *Rio v. Read* in 1974[22] helped define the responsibility of a school district, stating that unless the school district's program was academically effective for students, it would be in violation of the *Lau* decision. The courts found that an ineffective program would be the same as if no program was offered. That same year in *Serna v. Portales Municipal Schools*,[23] the court found that any student who does not understand English and is not provided with bilingual instruction is precluded from any meaningful education.

Morgan v. Kerrigan[24] found Boston, Massachusetts, to be out of compliance with *Lau* in service to its Hispanic, limited English speaking student population. While Hispanic students requiring bilingual instruction numbered over 32,600 in Boston city schools, Boston's plan required bilingual programs only for other less numerous linguistic minority groups. These other linguistic groups included Chinese, Italians, French-Haitian, Greeks, and Portuguese.

In *Aspira of New York, Inc. v. Board of City of New York*,[25] the court ruled that all Hispanic students should be given a test to determine their proficiency in English language usage. Those students who fell below the established cut-off score of the twentieth percentile were to be given bilingual instruction. The instruction was to continue until the limited English proficient students successfully achieved a score on the test higher than the twentieth percentile. In 1979, the bilingual educational needs of handicapped students were addressed in *Jose P. v. Ambach*.[26] In this case, the court stated that failure to provide bilingual education to disabled students may violate the Rehabilitation Act of 1973.[27]

Although most legal activity has focused on limited English proficient students, the special needs of students who speak various English dialects were also addressed by a Michigan federal court. In this case, the court ruled that school districts must offer assistance in learning to use standard English to students who speak "black English." The students and parents in this case alleged that their rights under the Equal Education Opportunities Act of 1974 had been violated by the school district. This statute states

> No state shall deny equal educational opportunity to an individual on account of his or her race, color, sex, or national origin, by ... (f) the failure by an educational agency to take appropriate action to overcome language barriers that impede equal participation by its students in its instructional program.[28]

The court held that the students' rights under Section 1703(f) of Title 20 of the Equal Educational Opportunities Act had been violated because the education agency failed to take appropriate action to overcome the students' language deficiencies. The court did not require the creation of a bilingual education program or teaching in black English. The school board was, however, ordered to develop a plan in which teachers would become aware of the language used in students' homes and in the community so that they might identify children who used the dialect and in turn use that knowledge to instruct the students more effectively in standard English.[29]

Title VI Language Discrimination Guidelines were established and published in 1980.[30] These regulations contain the basic components of the *Lau v. Nichols* guidelines, which include identification, assessment, program assignment, and exit criteria. Specific requirements differ in each of these areas. These regulations specify that no minimum number of students within the general student population are required before bilingual education programs must be implemented. The guidelines do, however, provide that alternative organizational methods for instruction may be used by a school administrator when student populations from a particular language background become too small to combine conveniently into a single class with a single teacher.

Mexican-American children and their parents brought suit against the Raymondville, Texas, Independent School District (ISD) in *Castaneda v. Pickard* in 1981,[31] alleging that district policies and practices deprived them of their rights under the Fourteenth Amendment to the Constitution, Title VI of the Civil

Rights Act of 1964, and the Equal Educational Opportunities Act of 1974.[32] The school district offered bilingual education programs in kindergarten through third grade only. Parents and students claimed that the district discriminated against them by failing to implement adequate bilingual education programs to overcome the linguistic barriers that impede their equal participation in the educational programs of the district. The lower court found that Raymondville ISD did not violate any constitutional or statutory rights. An appeal was made to the higher court that found that Title VI was not violated since the district program was not intended or designed to discriminate against Mexican-Americans. The higher court did find, however, that the school district was in violation of Section 1703(f) of the Equal Educational Opportunities Act[33] by not providing teachers who were competent to teach in a bilingual education program. The court ordered the district to remedy this problem as well as conduct an evaluation and replacement, as needed, of testing materials used to assess the academic performance of the limited English proficient students.

The following three-part test to be used by school administrators when evaluating the effectiveness and equality of their bilingual education programs is the primary legal guideline resulting from the Castaneda case:

- Is the program educationally sound?
- Are the practices and programs of the school reasonably calculated to implement effectively the educational theory adopted by the school?
- Are the practices accomplishing the desired objectives?[34]

School administrators should be aware that many states, including Massachusetts, Texas, California, Illinois, and Connecticut, passed legislation related to bilingual education that predates federal legislation. The federal law applies to all public schools; however, state laws may go further than the federal law and provide more extensive educational requirements for non-English speaking students. It is, therefore, imperative that school administrators familiarize themselves with state and local policies to remain in compliance with the law.[35] Figure 5.2

1954	*Brown v. Board of Education of Topeka*
1964	Title VI of the Civil Rights Act of 1964
1968	Bilingual Education Act of 1968 (Title V of the Elementary and Secondary Education Act of 1965)
1970	*Cisneros v. Corpus Christi*
1972	*United States v. Texas*
1973	Keyes v. Denver Natonabah v. Board of Education of Gallup-McKinley County School District
1974	*Lau v. Nichols* *Rios v. Read* *Serna v. Portales Municipal Schools* Equal Educational Opportunity Act Bilingual Education Act of 1974
1975	*Morgan v. Kerrigan*
1976	*Aspira of New York, Inc. v. Board of City of New York*
1978	Bilingual Education Act of 1978
1979	*Jose P. v. Ambach* Martin Luther King, Jr. Elementary Schools v. Ann Arbor
1980	Title VI Language Discrimination Guidelines
1981	*Castaneda v. Pickard*
1988	Bilingual Education Act of 1988
1995	Bilingual Education Act of 1994 (Title VII, Part A of *Improving America's Schools Act of 1994: Reauthorizing the Elementary and Secondary Education Act of 1965*)

Figure 5.2. Chronology of bilingual education legislation.

provides a chronological summary of bilingual education legislation.

PROGRAM FUNDING

The first legislation making bilingual education mandatory was Title VII of the Elementary and Secondary Education Act, also known as the Bilingual Educational Act of 1968. This was followed by the Bilingual Education Act of 1978 and subsequently by several reauthorizations and amendments.[36] These acts created a discretionary grant program providing federal financial assistance, primarily to local school districts, to develop and implement "new and imaginative ... school programs." These grants were to meet the special needs of children between the ages of 3 and 18 years who had limited English speaking ability and came from low-income families.[37] The Bilingual Education Act of 1978 and its amendments did not require school districts to provide bilingual programs. Rather, the law provided financial assistance to districts that desired to implement such programs.[38] Subsequent amendments to the law extended the fiscal authorization to school districts, expanded the purpose and scope of the act through increased authorizations for new and existing programs, and broadened the act to serve those students who could not "read, write, or understand English at the level appropriate for their age and grade."[39]

The most recent reauthorization of this funding statute is Title VII, Part A of Improving America's Schools Act of 1994: Reauthorizing the Elementary and Secondary Education Act of 1965, hereafter referred to as the Bilingual Education Act of 1994. An appropriation of $215 million for fiscal year 1995 and additional assistance as may be necessary for each of the 4 succeeding fiscal years has been made for the purpose of carrying out the general intent of the act.[40] This financial assistance has been appropriated under Sections 7112 through 7115 to assist local educational agencies, institutions of higher education, and community-based organizations develop and enhance their capacity to (1) provide high quality instruction through bilingual education or special alternative instructional programs for children and youth of limited English proficiency; (2) develop proficiency in English and, to the extent possible, their native language; and (3) meet the same challenging state content standards expected for all children and youth as required by Section 1111(b) of Improving America's Schools Act of 1994: Reauthorizing the Elementary and Secondary Education Act.[41] Funding opportunities are listed in Figure 5.4 on page 177.

Program Development and Implementation Grants

Grants are available to local educational agencies to develop and implement new comprehensive, coherent, and successful bilingual education or special alternative instructional programs for LEP students. These include programs for early childhood education, kindergarten through twelfth grade education, gifted and talented education, and vocational and applied technology education (see Figure 5.3). Each grant will be awarded to a local education agency for a period of 3 years and must be used to improve the education of LEP students and their families by

1. Developing and implementing comprehensive preschool, elementary, or secondary bilingual education or special alternative instructional programs that are coordinated with other relevant programs and services to meet the full range of educational needs of limited English proficient students
2. Providing inservice training to classroom teachers, administrators, and other school or community-based organizational personnel to improve the instruction and assessment of language-minority and limited English proficient students[42]

Further, grants under Section 7112 may be used to improve the education of limited English proficient students and their families by

1. Implementing family education programs and parent out-

- Comprehensive K-12 curriculum development
- In-service training for teachers, administrators, and support personnel
- Family education programs
- Student tutorials
- Academic counseling
- Career counseling
- Enrichment activities
- Early Childhood Programs
- Gifted and Talented Programs
- Vocational and Applied Technology
- Alternative Instructional Programs

Figure 5.3. Program development and improvement grants.

reach and training activities designed to assist parents to become active participants in the education of their children
2. Improving the instructional program for limited English proficient students by identifying, acquiring, and upgrading curriculum, instructional materials, educational software, and assessment procedures and, if appropriate, applying educational technology
3. Compensating personnel, including teacher aides who have been specifically trained or are being trained, to provide services to children and youth of limited English proficiency
4. Providing tutorials and academic or career counseling for children and youth of limited English proficiency
5. Providing such other activities, related to the proposed of this part, as the Secretary may approve[43]

Supplemental Programs

Grants are available to agencies desiring to develop and implement early childhood education or family education programs, or to conduct an instructional program that supplements the educational services provided by a local education agency. This funding is available to (1) one or more local education agencies; (2) one or more local education agencies in collaboration with an institution of higher education, community-based organization, or local or state education agency; or (3) a community-based organization or institution of higher education that has an application approved by the local education agency. Appropriation of funds by these agencies must emphasize and support the need for early childhood, elementary, and secondary education programs.[44]

Enhancement Projects

Program enhancement projects will be supported by grants for the purpose of innovative, locally designed, focused projects to expand or enhance existing bilingual education programs. These grants will be for a period of 2 years and are to be used to provide inservice training to classroom teachers, administrators, and other school or community-based organizational personnel to improve instruction and assessment of language-minority and limited English proficient students. Grants under this section may be used for

1. Implementing family education programs and parent outreach and training activities designed to assist parents to become active participants in the education of their children
2. Improving the instructional program for limited English proficient students by identifying, acquiring, and upgrading curriculum, instructional materials, educational software, and assessment procedures and, if appropriate, applying educational technology
3. Compensating personnel, including teacher aides who have been specifically trained or are being trained, to provide services to children and youth of limited-English proficiency

4. Providing tutorials and academic career counseling for children and youth of limited English proficiency
5. Providing intensified instruction[45]

School-wide and System-wide Projects

Comprehensive school-wide grants are available under Section 7114 and system-wide improvement grants under Section 7115 to implement school-wide and system-wide bilingual education programs or special alternative instruction programs. The purpose of these grants is to reform, restructure, and upgrade all relevant programs and operations serving children and youth of limited English proficiency within an individual school or district that has significant concentrations of such children and youth within their student populations. The grant monies may also be utilized in either program for the same educational purposes as outlined in Section 7112 for program development, implementation, and enhancement projects. Grants can be terminated at any time by the Secretary of Education if it is determined that students in the school-wide or system-wide programs are not being taught to and are not making progress toward achieving challenging state content standards and challenging state student performance standards, or if dual-language programs are not promoting student dual-language abilities.[46]

Paraprofessionals and Instructional Aides

A variety of other funding sources may be used by schools and school districts to supplement the cost of paraprofessionals linguistically fluent in the students' native language as tutors and instructional aides. These include bilingual allotments available through state compensatory funds and other supplementary funds, including other Title programs under Improving America's Schools Act of 1994: Reauthorizing the Elementary and Secondary Education Act of 1965. Caution should be exercised by school administrators to ensure that required bilingual education programs are provided with state funds and that federal funds are used only to supplement and not to supplant state foundation program efforts.[47]

Native American, Alaska Native, Native Hawaiian, Native Pacific Islander, Residents of Territories, and Commonwealth of Puerto Rico

Native American and Native American languages, as defined in Section 103 of the Native American Languages Act, including native residents of outlying areas, have a unique status under federal law. This status requires special policies within the broad purposes of the Bilingual Education Act of 1994 to serve the educational needs of language-minority students in the United States.[48] Program grants are available for Native American and Alaska Native children enrolled in school, residents of the Territories and Freely Associated Nations, Native Pacific Island children, and children in the Commonwealth of Puerto Rico under Sections 7104, 7105, 7122, and 7136 of the Bilingual Education Act of 1994.

Programs designated under Section 7104 may be developed for individuals served by elementary, secondary, and post-secondary schools operated predominately for Native American or Alaska Native children and youth, an Indian tribe, a tribally sanctioned educational authority, a Native Hawaiian or Native American Pacific Islander native language education organization, or an elementary or secondary school that is operated or funded by the Bureau of Indian Affairs. For the purpose of funding, an agency serving these student populations will be considered as a local educational agency.[49] Programs developed under Section 7105 must address the needs of residents of the Territories and Freely Associated Nations in the outlying areas. The term *local educational agency,* under this section, includes public institutions or agencies whose mission is the preservation and maintenance of native languages.[50]

Programs for Native Americans and Puerto Ricans are authorized under Section 7122 of the act. These include programs that serve Native American children, Native Pacific Island children, and children in the Commonwealth of Puerto Rico. Designated bilingual education programs may include programs of instruction, teacher training, and curriculum development, evaluation, and testing designated for Native American children and youth learning and studying Native American languages. Programs are also authorized for children and youth of limited Spanish proficiency. The expected outcome of the bilingual education programs serving these children must be increased English proficiency.[51] Section 7136 outlines the provision of grants for the

> development, publication, and dissemination of high-quality instructional materials in Native American and Native Hawaiian languages and the language of Native Pacific Islanders and natives of the outlying areas for which instructional materials are not readily available.[52]

Priority will be given to applications under this section of the act to the development of instructional materials in languages indigenous to the United States and outlying areas that are consistent with voluntary national academic content standards and challenging state academic content standards (Figure 5.4).

- Program Development and Implementation Grants
- Supplemental Program Grants
- Enhancement Project Grants
- Comprehensive School-Wide Grants
- System-Wide Project Grants
- Paraprofessional and Instructional Aide Grants
- Native Language Grants

Figure 5.4. Funding opportunities.

INSTRUCTIONAL PROGRAMS

Children entering schools throughout the United States using languages other than English should presently be provided with programs in either Bilingual Education or English as a Second Language (ESL). Bilingual Education and ESL are closely interrelated, and English language proficiency is a common objective of both programs. Bilingual education offers instruction to groups of children with the same home language background. The children are grouped together, and the home language is used in class. The program includes an English language teaching component. An ESL program provides instruction to children of diverse language backgrounds attending school together in the same class. Typically, the home languages of the children are not used in class.

Confusion often exists among parents as well as professionals regarding the differences between the two programs. In addition, school administrators often make the mistake of incorrectly, or out of necessity, assigning bilingual and ESL certified teachers to a program or class that does not match their instructional expertise. In an attempt to clarify terminology and come to an agreed upon definition used in bilingual education programs, research activities have been authorized through the Office of Educational Research and Improvement in collaboration with the Office of Bilingual Education and Minority Language Affairs under this act that support

> establishing (through the National Center for Educational Statistics in consultation with experts in bilingual education, second language acquisition, and English-as-a-second-language) a common definition of "limited English proficient student."[53]

It is obvious from the language of the Bilingual Education Act of 1994 that the emphasis of local education agencies is to be on bilingual education programs serving children and youth from early childhood through secondary school. The rationale as described in the act is to emphasize multilingualism and dual-language abilities directed toward the United States remaining competitive in world economic markets. Multilingual communication occurs daily in families, government, businesses, and commerce, and a purpose of this act is to develop and protect bilingualism as a valuable national resource.

The implementation of bilingual education programs requires the formulation of rules and regulations at the federal, state, and local levels describing the type of bilingual education programs that are required and permitted to be implemented under the Bilingual Education Act of 1994.

Program assessment needs and requirements are outlined as part of the act. A successful bilingual education program rests on the academic achievement of LEP students. This does not mean that the student will only be functional in two languages. It means that all LEP students in a school have been afforded the opportunity to meet challenging state and federal academic content standards set for America's school children and youth. A successful bilingual education program will not only offer academic and cultural training, but will provide the same enrichment activities, tutorials, academic, and career counseling from early childhood through secondary programs in a student's native language as provided to students in English.

BILINGUAL EDUCATION

Bilingual education consists of primary native language instruction in areas such as mathematics, science, and social studies. This is provided to assist the student in developing cognitive/academic concepts. ESL instruction is provided to assist the student in the development of oral and written English language skills and to reduce language barriers to understanding subject matter taught in English. Native language literacy skills, whether in English or another language, are necessary for successful second language development. Exemplary bilingual education programs provide students with instruction in both their native language and in English. These programs are aimed at developing and maintaining student self-esteem and pride in both cultures without disruption to their cognitive/academic development. The programs recognize that the stronger the students' cognitive and academic proficiency in their first language, the stronger their proficiency in a second language. A bilingual education program encompasses both the mainstream curriculum and the history and culture associated with the native language.[54]

ENGLISH AS A SECOND LANGUAGE

English as a second language (ESL) consists of monolingual English instruction using specialized ESL methods to teach oral and written English. The classes are often taught in simplified English with many visual aides in the subject areas using ESL techniques. In English subject classes, vocabulary and grammatical structure are taught, not in isolation, but in meaningful contexts relevant to the students' learning experiences and to their lives as members of linguistically and culturally diverse communities. Exemplary ESL programs incorporate cultural aspects of the students' backgrounds into meaningful language learning experiences and apply ESL techniques to content areas taught through English. An ESL program may also provide native language support to the student.[55]

INSTRUCTIONAL APPROACHES

The ideal approach for meeting the needs of students of limited English proficiency is to provide an educational atmosphere and programs in the affective, linguistic, and cognitive domains. Essential to all programs are a positive classroom climate and activities for the development of a positive self-concept that are integrated into all instructional activities throughout the day. Instruction should be provided for developing comprehension, speaking, reading, and written composition in the home language and in English. Mathematics, science, health, and social studies should also be provided in both the home language and in English. All of these classes and individual courses should be taught by a certified bilingual education teacher. Students may receive instruction for other required subjects along with enrichment and elective subjects such as music, art, theater arts, and physical education in regular classes with all students.[56]

The preferred bilingual education classroom is self-contained and staffed with a teacher certified in early childhood, kindergarten, elementary, or secondary education as appropriate, and also trained in bilingual education instruction. An ESL classroom should be self-contained with a teacher certified in early childhood, kindergarten, elementary, or secondary education as appropriate, and a bilingual or ESL endorsement. The use of parents or paraprofessionals who are native speakers in the home language of the students for tutoring students is a desirable option that can be instituted by the school administrator.[57]

According to Teachers of English to Speakers of Other Languages (TESOL), there are three major types of bilingual education programs offered in schools throughout the United States: transitional, maintenance, and two-way. Following are the three program options and recommendations as outlined by TESOL.[58]

Transitional Bilingual Program

A transitional bilingual program provides instruction and cognitive development using a student's dominant language only until the student has acquired sufficient proficiency in English to function effectively in a monolingual English setting. The goal of this type of program is to develop proficiency in English, using two languages to accomplish the task. This academic model often fails to recognize how long it takes to develop both cognitive and academic literacy in a second language. A 1- to 2-year period of instruction is generally long enough for young learners to acquire basic social language skills in English. This is not, however, long enough to develop the cognitive and academic language proficiency needed for school success. Proficiency in this area may take from 5 to 9 years. Transitional bilingual programs usually do not take into account the research finding that most long-term bilingual instruction is more efficient and more cost-effective than most short-term instruction.

Maintenance Bilingual Program

A maintenance bilingual program uses content-subject instruction in both the home language and English to achieve the goal of strong literacy in two languages. Recognizing that becoming truly bilingual and bicultural takes many years, a maintenance program views the development of bilingual proficiency as an asset that more than justifies the investment of time. The ultimate goal of this type of program is to enrich the student's linguistic repertoire by adding a second language as an alternate means of learning and communicating.

Two-Way Bilingual Program

A two-way bilingual program is an integrated model that enables learners from linguistically and culturally diverse communities, as well as learners who come from homes where only English is used, to learn each other's languages and cultures. As in the maintenance program, enrichment and dual language proficiency is a goal.

RECOMMENDED PROGRAMS

None of the three instructional programs described above are remedial in nature. TESOL strongly recommends the use of maintenance and two-way programs because they are designed to

- recognize that a strong first language (oral and written) leads to a strong second language
- assure sufficient time to acquire the strong classroom language and academic concepts needed for successful academic-language learning, going beyond the acquisition of social language skills
- have a strong, carefully integrated ESL component; promote bilingualism and biculturalism as assets, while showing respect and appreciation for students' language rights[59]

This recommendation for the use of maintenance and two-way bilingual instructional programs coincides with the recommendations, funding incentives, and desired outcomes of the newly authorized Bilingual Education Act of 1994.

INTENSIFIED INSTRUCTION AND PROGRAM INNOVATION

Intensified instructional programs may be developed and implemented through specialized programs to assist limited English proficient students under Section 7117 of the Bilingual Education Act of 1994. Suggestions for these special programs include an extended or expanded school calendar that includes before- and after-school programs, year-round school, and specialized programs during the summer months. Supplementary instruction or activities, including educationally enriching extracurricular activities during times when school is not routinely in session, may also fit well into an expanded calendar. Other ideas that might be implemented by a school include expanding the use of professional and volunteer aides who are proficient in the native language of the students, parent and community involvement, and applying educational technology to instruction. All will assist the school administrator in accomplishing improved student achievement outcomes.[60]

Educational technology incorporated into bilingual education programs has the potential for improving the education of language-minority and LEP students and their families. Parent and community participation in bilingual education programs contributes to program effectiveness. Funding has been provided to develop and implement highly focused, innovative, locally designed projects to expand or enhance existing bilingual education or special alternative instructional programs for LEP students. These grants are available to provide inservice training for classroom teachers, school administrators, and other school or community-based organization personnel to improve the instruction and assessment of language-minority and LEP students. These grant monies may also support

1. The implementation of family education programs and parent outreach and training activities designed to assist parents to become active participants in the education of their children
2. Improving the instructional program for LEP students by identifying, acquiring, and upgrading curriculum, instructional materials, educational software, and assessment procedures and, if appropriate, applying educational technology
3. Compensating personnel, including teacher aides who have been specifically trained or are being trained to provide services to children and youth of limited English proficiency
4. Intensified instruction and other related activities[61]

Instructional program enhancement and innovation are listed in Figure 5.5.

- Educational technology applications
- Parent and community involvement
- Alternative instructional programs
- Family education programs
- Parent outreach and training activities
- Upgrading K-12 curriculum and instruction
- Personnel training
- Intensified instructional programs
- Tutorials for children and youth
- Community-based collaborative programs
- Academic and career counseling

Figure 5.5. *Instructional program enhancement and innovation.*

BICULTURAL PROGRAMS

Throughout the history of bilingual education in the United States, an emphasis has been placed on incorporating cultural knowledge into programs and generally reinforcing the native culture of the limited English proficient student. The Bilingual Education Act of 1994 once again supports the integration of cultural knowledge into academic programs and enhancement projects in an attempt to promote self-esteem and academic achievement on the part of the LEP student. Family culture is highly personal and important to all children and youth. When educators ask a child to choose between the culture of their family and the culture of the school, we are setting the child up for academic failure.[62] Care must be taken by the school administrator to ensure that cultural diversity is supported and opportunities for celebration and sharing are provided to children and youth to reinforce self-esteem and, ultimately, academic achievement. The incorporation of family and community members in the development and implementation of regular, intensified, enriched, and expanded school programs will have a positive effect on both student attendance and achievement.

The Bilingual Education Act of 1994 calls for not only the development of bilingual skills, but also study of the history and culture of a student's mother tongue, multicultural understanding, cultural enrichment, appreciation of cultural heritage, and pride in both native and American cultures. As part of this act, the school administrator has the opportunity to enhance both bilingual language skills and multicultural awareness among the entire school population through instructional leadership in curricular development and monitoring instructional content to ensure bicultural understanding.

PARENT INVOLVEMENT AND SUPPORT

Parents of children in bilingual education and ESL programs, including those who come from language backgrounds other than English, have much to contribute to the school community. These parents have the same rights as any other parents regarding the education of their children. These rights include communication with school teachers, administrators, and staff; receiving communications from the school in their stronger language, which may not be English; volunteering and assisting at school; participating in their children's learning activities at home; and participating in governance and advocacy activities. These activities might include parent-teacher organizations, school management teams, and school board meetings. It is the obligation of the school administration to provide interpreters for these parents and guardians as necessary.[63]

The limited English proficiency of parents of LEP students hinders their ability to participate in school programs and discuss the academic standing of their children. Research shows that greater parental participation in a child's education results in academic success for the student. Parent participation in school programs has been supported in this act through the allocation of grant monies to foster and support family training programs, family outreach centers, and community-based programs that may be developed in cooperation with the school. Funding is available for collaborative activities with institutions of higher education, community-based organizations, local or state educational agencies, private schools, nonprofit organizations, or businesses to carry out programs supporting bilingual education.[64]

ADMINISTRATOR'S ROLE

Bilingual education programs offer many opportunities for the school administrator to lead the development of instructional programs that will serve and enhance the academic performance and needs of all students in the school. Too often, historically, the specialized needs of limited English proficient children have been overlooked, neglected, or given only the attention that was required. This may have been the result of social pressures directed toward the use of English-only curriculum, instruction, and language usage in school classrooms. The newly authorized Bilingual Education Act of 1994 addresses and stresses the importance of student populations becoming bilingual and multilingual in an effort to meet the ever-changing needs of society, a society that has undergone numerous transformations as a result of United States immigration policies and the nation's need to compete effectively in world economic markets. Here is an opportunity for the school administrator to view bilingual education through a different lens, not as just another compensatory program that must be implemented, but rather as an asset to the intellectual development of both limited English and English proficient students.

Among the numerous tasks of the school administrator is the alignment of educational goals supported through coordination of the curriculum, correlation of services, and allocation of resources. The Bilingual Education Act of 1994 serves as a clear guideline for these administrative tasks in the creative development of programs and services for limited English proficient students.

School administrators support student achievement goals through alignment of the curriculum, staff selection and development, classroom instructional activities, guidance programs, and enrichment activities. Coordination of the curriculum to serve both limited English and English proficient students to become bilingual may involve the development of new courses, collaborative planning on unit and lesson plans, team teaching, parental and community involvement, and shared responsibility for student achievement in dual-language enhancement and dual-language acquisition. Assessment of learner needs, both present and future, will allow the school administrator to plan strategically toward the dual-language development of all students. The goal should be to provide high quality instruction to all students through reinforcement and development of Early Childhood, K–12, Gifted and Talented, and Tech Prep/Vocational programs supporting dual-language acquisition and cognitive/academic development.[65]

The allocation of resources must be adequate, cost-effective, and equitable to support programs that reflect school goals. Resources available through grant monies provide a monetary source for school administrators to support traditional and innovative instructional and enrichment programs. The purchase of instructional materials, educational software, and applied technology equipment will enhance and provide creative alternatives to traditional instructional programs. Personnel selection and training to support educational goals is an administrative function that cannot be overlooked. Building budgets must reflect staff development needs for teachers, administrators, instructional aides, and parent and community volunteers. Adequate compensation for paraprofessionals and classroom aides to support instruction is made possible through grants provided in the Bilingual Education Act of 1994. Monetary support is also available for family education. Parent outreach programs and training can be developed and provided by the school so that parents can develop the skills to become active participants in their children's education.

Correlation of services is supported in the Bilingual Education Act of 1994 to enhance opportunity for program support. Creativity is once again the key for the school administrator. Enrichment programs offered through an extended or expanded school calendar can provide opportunities for collaboration with parents and community members or organizations to support cultural knowledge or provide academic tutorial programs. Grants provide monetary resources for creative collaboration between the school and institutes of high education or community-based programs. Within the school, correlation of service can be effected through cooperation of various components of school staff in program development and the integration of academic and career counseling with academic instruction and enrichment programs. Combining after-school tutorials with parent-education programs can encourage parents not only to acquire English language skills, but also to become involved in their child's education, thus supporting school programs directed toward English language proficiency and academic success.

In preparing students for the world beyond school, the school administrator must look beyond the walls of the school to local and national needs. These needs have driven school improvement and reform efforts in the past and will continue to influence instructional and programmatic decisions directed toward improved educational programs for the twenty-first century.

REVIEW ACTIVITIES

1. Explain why school administrators must familiarize them-

selves with state and local policies rather than just federal laws to remain in legal compliance.
2. Assess the needs for bilingual program development and supplemental programs in your school. Create a list of grants that are available to help you address these needs.
3. Compile a list of funding sources available to you for enhancement projects. How may these grants be used?
4. Discuss the purposes of school-wide and system-wide project grants.
5. Explain why school administrators must ensure that required bilingual education programs are provided with state funds and federal funds are used only to supplement state foundation program efforts.
6. Make a chart to compare the differences between Bilingual Education and English as a Second Language (ESL).
7. Using the Bilingual Education Act of 1994 as a guideline, align educational goals supported through coordination of the curriculum, correlation of services, and allocation of resources for your school to creatively develop programs and services for limited English proficient students.

ENDNOTES

1 Stewart, D. 1994. "Immigration Laws Are Education Laws Too." *Phi Delta Kappan,* 75(9):556–558.

2 Civil Rights Act of 1964, Title VI. 42 U.S.C.A. Secs. 2000D-D-1; Equal Education Opportunities Act of 1977, Sec. 204(f). 20 U.S.C. Sec. 1703.

3 Improving America's Schools Act of 1994: Reauthorizing the Elementary and Secondary Education Act of 1965. PL 103-382. Title VII, Part A. Sec. 7102(5).

4 Improving America's Schools Act of 1994: Reauthorizing the Elementary and Secondary Education Act of 1965. P.L. 103-382. Title VII, Part A. Sec. 7102(a)(14).

5 Improving America's Schools Act of 1994: Reauthorizing the Elementary and Secondary Education Act of 1965. P.L. 103-382. Title VII, Part A.

6 Improving America's Schools Act of 1994: Reauthorizing the Elementary and Secondary Education Act of 1965. P.L. 103-382. Title VII, Part A. Sec. 7102(16)(c).

7 Bilingual Education Act of 1968. Title VII of the Elementary and Sec-

ondary Education Act of 1965 and amended in 1967. Elementary and Secondary Education Act, 20 U.S.C. 2701 et seq.

8 Bilingual Education Act of 1974. 20 U.S.C. Sec. 880b et seq. (1976).

9 20 USCA et seq. (Supp 1975) Sec. 58061.

10 Bilingual Education Act of 1978. P.L. 95-561 (1978); 20 U.S.C. Secs. 3282-3341(1988).

11 Cisneros v. Corpus Christi Independent School District, 467 F.2d 142 (5 Cir 1972), cert. den. 413 U.S. 922, 93 S. Ct. 3052, 37 L.Ed.2d 1044 (1973). The rationale of Brown has also been applied to Mexican-American students in Arvizu v. Waco Independent School District, 495 F.2d 499 (5 Cir. 1974) and Morales v. Shannon, 516 F.2d 411 (5 Cir. 1975). This was further supported by the Office of Civil Rights Memorandum of 1970. Office for Civil Rights. Identification of Discrimination of Denial of Services on the Basis of National Origin. 35 Fed. Reg. 11,595 (1970).

12 Brown v. the Board of Education of Topeka, 347 U.S. 483, 74 S.Ct. 686 (1954).

13 United States v. Texas, 342 F. Supp. 24 (E.D. Tex. 1971), aff'd, 466 F.2d 518 (5th Cir. 1972).

14 Natonabah v. Board of Education of Gallup-McKinley County School District, 355 F.Supp. 716 (D.N.M.1973); Geraud v. Schrader, 531 P.2d 872 (Wyo. 1975).

15 Keyes v. School District No. 1, Denver, 413 U.S. 189, 93 S.Ct. 2686 (1973).

16 Lau v. Nichols, 483 F.2d 791, 797 (9th Cir. 1973), rev'd, 414 U.S. 563 (1974).

17 Title VI of the Civil Rights Act of 1964. 42 U.S.C. Sec. 2000(d)et seq. (1970).

18 See note 15 sup.

19 Lau Remedies. Office of Civil Rights, Task-Force Findings Specifying Remedies Available for Eliminating Past Educational Practices Rules Unlawful under Lau v. Nichols, Sec IX, pt. 5 (1975) H. Teitelbaum and R. Hiller. 1979. A Handbook of the Enforcement of Lau v. Nichols, B 97–98. Washington, DC: Office of Civil Rights.

20 See note 8 sup.

21 Bilingual Education Act of 1988, Pub.L. No. 100-297, 102 Stat. 274 (1988).

22 Rios v. Read, 480 F. Supp. 14 (E.D.N.Y. 1978).

23 Serna v. Portales Municipal Schools, 499 F.2d 1147 (10th Cir. 1974).

24 Morgan v. Kerrigan, 401 F.Supp. 4341 (E.D.Tex. 1981).

25 Aspira of New York, Inc. v. Board of Education of City of New York. 423 F.Supp. 647 (S.D.N.Y. 1976).

26 Jose P. v. Ambach. 3 E.H.L.R. 551:245 (E.D.N.Y. 1979).

27 Vocational Rehabilitation Act of 1973. 42 U.S.C. 12131 et seq.

28 Equal Educational Opportunities Act of 1974, Section 204; 20 U.S.C. Sec. 1703(f) (1976); Title VI Language Discrimination Guidelines, 45 Fed. Reg. 152.52056 (1980).

29 Martin Luther King Junior Elementary Schools Children v. Ann Arbor School District Board, 473 F. Supp. 1371 (E.D. Mich. 1979).

Endnotes 191

30 Title VI Language Discrimination Guidelines, 45 Fed. Reg. 152.52056 (1980).
31 Castaneda v. Pickard. United States Court of Appeals for the Fifth Circuit, 648 F.2d 989 (1981).
32 See notes 16 and 29 sup.
33 See note 29 sup.
34 See note 31 sup.
35 A variety of sources were used for this section including Alexander, K. and M. D. Alexander. 1992. *American Public School Law*. Third edition. St. Paul, MN: West Publishing Company.; Fischer, L., D. Schimmel, and C. Kelly. 1991. *Teachers and the Law*. Third edition. New York: Longman; Imber, M. and T. Van Geel. 1993. *Education Law*. New York: McGraw-Hill, Inc.; Kemerer, F. R. and J. B. Hairston. 1990. *The Educators Guide to Texas School Law*. Second edition with 1991 Supplement. Austin: University of Texas Press; Legislative Service Bureau. 1994. *The School Code of 1976: State of Michigan*. (Updated through Public Act No. 328 of 1994). Lansing: Legal Editing and Law Publications. McCarthy, M. M. and N. H. Cambron-McCabe. 1992. *Public School Law: Teachers' and Students' Rights*. Third edition. Boston: Allyn and Bacon; Reutter, E. E., Jr. and R. R. Hamilton. 1976. *The Law of Public Education*. Second edition. Mineola, NY: The Foundation Press, Inc.; Schoop, R. J. and D. R. Dunklee. 1992. *School Law for the Principal: A Handbook for Practitioners*. Boston: Allyn and Bacon; Yudof, M. G., D. L. Kirp, and B. Levin. 1992. *Educational Policy and the Law*. Third edition. St. Paul, MN: West Publishing Company.
36 20 U.S.C. Secs. 32-3341 (1988) amended by the Bilingual Education Act of 1988, P.L. 100-297, 102 Stat.274 (1988).
37 Bilingual Education Act of 1978. P. L. 95-561 (1978).
38 Shoop, R. J. and D. R. Dunklee. 1992. *School Law for the Principal: A Handbook for Practitioners*. Boston: Allyn and Bacon.
39 P. L. 93-380 (1974); P. L. 95-230 (1978); and P. L. 95-561 (1978).
40 Improving America's Schools Act of 1994: Reauthorizing the Elementary and Secondary Education Act of 1965. P.L. 103-382. Title VII, Part A. Sec. 7103.
41 Improving America's Schools Act of 1994: Reauthorizing the Elementary and Secondary Education Act of 1965. P.L. 103-382. Sec. 1111(b).
42 Improving America's Schools Act of 1994: Reauthorizing the Elementary and Secondary Education Act of 1965. P.L. 103-382. Title VII, Part A. Sec. 7112(b)(2)(A).
43 Improving America's Schools Act of 1994: Reauthorizing the Elementary and Secondary Education Act of 1965. P.L. 103-382. Title VII, Part A. Sec. 7112(b)(2)(B).
44 Improving America's Schools Act of 1994: Reauthorizing the Elementary and Secondary Education Act of 1965. P.L. 103-382. Title VII, Part A. Sec. 7112(c)(d).
45 Improving America's Schools Act of 1994: Reauthorizing the Elementary and Secondary Education Act of 1965. P.L. 103-382. Title VII, Part A. Sec. 7113(b)(2)(B).

46 Improving America's Schools Act of 1994: Reauthorizing the Elementary and Secondary Education Act of 1965. P.L. 103-382. Title VII, Part A. Sec. 7114(b)(3) and Sec. 7715(b)(4).

47 See note 5 sup.

48 Improving America's Schools Act of 1994: Reauthorizing the Elementary and Secondary Education Act of 1965. P.L. 103-382. Title VII, Part A. Sec. 7102.

49 Improving America's Schools Act of 1994: Reauthorizing the Elementary and Secondary Education Act of 1965. P.L. 103-382. Title VII, Part A. Sec. 7104.

50 See note 48 sup.

51 Improving America's Schools Act of 1994: Reauthorizing the Elementary and Secondary Education Act of 1965. P.L. 103-382. Title VII, Part A. Sec. 7122.

52 Improving America's Schools Act of 1994: Reauthorizing the Elementary and Secondary Education Act of 1965. P.L. 103-382. Title VII, Part A. Sec. 7136.

53 Improving America's Schools Act of 1994: Reauthorizing the Elementary and Secondary Education Act of 1965. P.L. 103-382. Title VII, Part A. Sec. 7113(a)(3).

54 Teachers of English to Speakers of Other Languages, Inc. 1992. *TESOL Statement on the Role of Bilingual Education in the Education of Children in the United States.* Alexandria, VA: Author. The organization can be contacted at Teachers of English to Speakers of Other Languages, Inc., 1600 Cameron Street, Suite 300, Alexandria, VA 22314-2751 USA.

55 Ibid.

56 Texas Education Agency. 1994. *Texas Administrative Code and Statutory Citation: Adaptations for Special Populations.* Title 19, Part II, Chapter 89, Subchapter A. March 1994 Update. Austin, Texas: Author.

57 Ibid.

58 See note 53 sup.

59 See note 53 sup.

60 Improving America's Schools Act of 1994: Reauthorizing the Elementary and Secondary Education Act of 1965. P.L. 103-382. Title VII, Part A. Sec. 7117.

61 Improving America's Schools Act of 1994: Reauthorizing the Elementary and Secondary Education Act of 1965. P.L. 103-382. Title VII, Part A. Secs. 7112, 7113, 7114, 7115.

62 Beyer-Houda, B. 1995. "Preparing School Administrators for Multicultural Settings." *Catalyst for Change,* 24(2):20–22.

63 Improving America's Schools Act of 1994: Reauthorizing the Elementary and Secondary Education Act of 1965. P.L. 103-382. Title VII, Part A. Sec. 7112.

64 Improving America's Schools Act of 1994: Reauthorizing the Elementary and Secondary Education Act of 1965. P.L. 103-382. Title VII, Part A. Sec. 7116(g)(C).

65 Improving America's Schools Act of 1994: Reauthorizing the Elementary and Secondary Education Act of 1965. P.L. 103-382. Title VII, Part A. Sec. 7112(a).

CHAPTER 6

Vocational, Tech-Prep, and Career Education Programs

AS school administrators consider implementation of vocational, tech-prep, and career education programs for their schools and/or their districts, they are likely to ask the following questions about each program and how it might best be implemented.

WHAT ARE VOCATIONAL EDUCATION, TECH-PREP EDUCATION, AND CAREER EDUCATION PROGRAMS?

Vocational Education

The primary purpose of a vocational education program has always been to help give the nation's work force the marketable skills needed to promote economic growth and to live productive lives through activities supported since 1917 through several federal programs. The purpose stated in the latest version of vocational funding, a change in the Carl D. Perkins Act (proposed as the Carl D. Perkins Career Preparation Education Reform Act of 1995), is to help states to expand and improve their programs of vocational education and to provide equal opportunity in vocational education for populations that have historically been underserved.[1]

The wide range of activities that are supported under the current Perkins Act includes professional development for teachers, development of curricula, field testing and dissemination of curricula, and support for state efforts to develop performance standards and measures for their programs. States may also use grant funds to promote partnerships among business, education, industry, and labor to improve career preparation for young people.

Tech-Prep Education

Tech-prep education, a key strategy for building a school-to-work system, had its roots in the late 1970s and early 1980s through the efforts of vocational/technical educators attempting to reform and improve the curricula for their fields. Tech-prep formulates a different kind of technical education curriculum first planned for the non-college-bound student but later evolved to include all students. It consists of a planned sequence of study for a technical field over 4 years beginning in the junior year of high school. The sequence extends through the last 2 years of high school and on through 2 years of post-secondary occupational education or some type of apprenticeship arrangement of at least 2 years following secondary instruction, and culminates in certification or in an associate degree. As of May 1994, approximately 800 consortia composed of high schools and 2-year post-secondary institutions across all fifty states and the District of Columbia were involved in tech-prep program agreements.[2]

Tech-prep programs require a formal, program-specific articulation agreement between the institutions involved at the secondary and post-secondary levels. (An articulation agreement is a formal linking where secondary and post-secondary institutions commit to the joint development and implementation of tech-prep curriculum and instruction.) Tech-prep is then made available to all secondary students, including those preparing for college, those who have selected vocational/technical training, and those students in the general track. Tech-prep is designed to prepare students for direct entry into the work place as technically skilled employees or for further education beyond the associate degree leading to baccalaureate and advanced degrees.

Career Education

Although many of the activities of career education, such as career guidance and career development, have been taking place in some form in schools since the turn of the century, the concept of career education in the schools is credited to U.S. Commissioner of Education Sidney P. Marland, early in his tenure (1970–1973), who coined the phrase in a speech to the National Association of Secondary School Principals in January of 1971. He talked about career education being a blending of vocational education, general education, and college-preparatory education rather than being a substitute for any of them.[3] Several different working definitions came out of early state programs after Commissioner Marland's speech, and in November 1974, the U.S. Office of Education issued its official definition of career education as being "the totality of experiences through which one learns about and prepares to engage in work as a part of her or his way of life."[4] Career education in schools today seeks to promote self-awareness, to provide job and role information, and to teach decision-making and goal-attaining skills. Career education is most often found in the form of career planning or preparation, career development, or career guidance/counseling. Vocational testing; discussions about the meaning and value of work; career planning/preparation classes; evaluation of skills, talents, and interests; visits to college and university classes; shadowing experiences of adults at work; volunteer work experiences; paid internships with professionals; exposure to typical and atypical career models; and mentorships all exemplify the various aspects of career education. One responsibility of the school administrator with regard to career education is to inform teachers in every course at every level that they should emphasize, where appropriate, the career implications of the content they are teaching. This helps give more meaning and relevance to the academic subject matter, provides a positive motivation, as well as shows the importance of the content as preparation for a later career.

WHAT IS THE BACKGROUND AND LEGAL BASE FOR EACH PROGRAM?

Vocational Education

After several years of discussion, federal support for vocational education began in 1917 with the Smith-Hughes Act, which was passed in response to the perception that the classical high school curriculum was not meeting the changing needs of industry, because the factory system was replacing the apprenticeship system and large numbers of immigrants needed to be quickly absorbed into an expanding labor force. With states and local school districts being required to match federal funds, this law funded the development of vocational programs in high schools as a separate track with governance of the programs also being separate at the state level. It was also aimed at supporting teacher training and teacher salaries in vocational education, but was primarily focused on preparing students for employment in agriculture, trades and industries, and home economics. In the years from 1917 to 1963, a variety of federal laws, such as the 1918 Vocational Rehabilitation Act, the 1920 Smith-Bankhead Act, the 1929 George-Reed Act, the 1934 George-Ellzey Act, the 1937 George-Deen Act, the 1937 National Apprenticeship Act (Fitzgerald Act), the 1943 Vocational Rehabilitation Act (Public Law 78-16), the 1946 George-Barden Act (Public Law 80-402), the 1958 National Defense Education Act (Public Law 85-864), the 1961 Area Redevelopment Act (Public Law 87-27), and the 1962 Manpower Development and Training Act (Public Law 87-415), encouraged a variety of state and local activities resulting in expansion nationally of the availability of vocational education.

Changing conditions, especially the growth of community colleges, the civil rights movement, and the welfare of the poor and other special populations brought about revisions and consolidation of the laws dealing with vocational education with passage of the 1963 Vocational Education Act (Public Law 88-210). The Elementary and Secondary Education Act of 1965 (Public Law 89-10), amendments to the Vocational Education Act in 1968 (Public Law 90-576) and 1976 (Public Law 94-482), and the passage of the Carl D. Perkins Vocational Education Act in 1984 (Public Law 98-524) further extended the emphasis on civil rights, created set-aside monies for disadvantaged and disabled individuals, and introduced sex equity issues into vocational education. On the governance side, these laws and amendments also increased emphasis on planning and accountability, and phased out support for program maintenance, while at the same time called for program improvement.

Vocational education was further expanded by the 1988 Omnibus Trade and Competitiveness Act (Public Law 100-418), which authorized new vocational training programs; the 1990 Carl D. Perkins Amendments (Public Law 101-392); the 1991 Rehabilitation Act Amendments (Public Law 102-52), which reauthorized vocational rehabilitation services; and the 1992 Job Training and Reform Amendments (Public Law 102-367), which amended the 1984 Carl Perkins Act.

The current Carl D. Perkins Act (under consideration by congress for FY '96), called the Carl D. Perkins Career Preparation Education Reform Act of 1995, focuses on improving the occupational education of those people hit hardest by declining wages in low-skill jobs. This includes people who are economically or educationally disadvantaged, disabled, limited English proficient, or those in other special populations.

Tech-Prep Education

The tech-prep education program is considered the cornerstone of the Carl D. Perkins Vocational and Technology Act Amendments of 1990.[5] This legislation represented the first major federal initiative promoting some type of comprehensive sustained links between secondary and 2-year post-secondary institutions. The purpose of the law was to provide planning, demonstration, and incentive grants for the development of 2 + 2 articulated curriculum in technical education leading to a 2-year associate degree, a certificate, or an apprenticeship program.

A tech-prep program combines an academic focused education with a technical education. The foundation of the program is based on skills in higher-level math, science, communications, technology, and uses applied technologies as appropriate.

The principles and practices of tech-prep education programs in the schools will help foster a school-to-work transition system that is innovative in educational reform in the United States.

Tech-Prep programs:

- provide a career path that is intended to prepare students for highly-skilled technical occupations, which is accomplished by formally linking secondary and

post-secondary institutions and integrating into an educational program academic and occupational learning
- offer opportunity for students to directly enter into the work place as a qualified technician or to continue with further education leading to advanced degrees beyond the associate degree level
- are available to all students at the secondary level
- form consortia that are local in nature and bring about partnerships involving secondary and post-secondary education, business, industry, labor unions, and community-based organizations
- address change in a systematic and structural manner

This arrangement helps to break down traditional barriers between levels of education, academic and vocational/technical education, and between education and employers by requiring communication, coordination, cooperation, and collaboration in order to be effective.

Career Education

Early conceptualization and promotion of career education took place under the auspices of the U.S. Office of Education in its Bureau of Adult Vocational and Technical Education (BAVTE), which under the 1972 Educational Amendments (Public Law 92-318) became the Bureau of Occupational and Adult Education (BOAE). The purpose of the BOAE was to design, establish, and conduct occupational education, which was a forerunner to career education. Also under the Educational Amendments of 1972 was the establishment of the National Institute of Education (NIE), which had as one of its directives the mission to improve career education.

The Educational Amendments of 1974 (Public Law 93-380) appropriated funds specifically earmarked for career education and officially established an Office of Career Education with a director who reported to the Commissioner of Education. This law also established a National Advisory Council on Career Education whose function was to make legislative recommendations to the Congress. In 1978, the Career Education Incentive Act (Public Law 95-207) further authorized the formal establishment of a career education program for the elementary and secondary schools.

The 1993 Goals 2000: Educate America Act (Public Law 103-227), which provided resources to states and communities to ensure that all students reach their full potential, and established a National Skills Standards Board to facilitate the development of rigorous occupational standards, and the 1993 School-to-Work Opportunities Act (Public Law 103-239), which established a national framework where states and communities can develop systems to prepare young people for first jobs and continuing education, compose two of the latest legislative actions aimed at furthering career opportunities for students.

HOW IS EACH PROGRAM FUNDED?

Vocational Education

The history of funding for vocational education has gone from about $52 million under the Smith-Hughes and George-Barden acts, to $60 million in 1964, to $225 million in 1967, to $355 million in 1969, to $565 million in 1973. The current Perkins Act would authorize approximately $1.141 billion for state grants and an additional $37 million for national leadership activities in fiscal year 1996. A 10-year reauthorization is also being requested to allow time for the systemic reform needed for full implementation of a school-to-work system in every state.

Tech-Prep Education

The history of financial backing for the tech-prep or 2 + 2 approach to secondary/post-secondary articulation has been funding in the amounts of $63.4 million for FY '91, $90 million for FY '92, $104.6 million for FY '93, $104.1 million for FY '94, and $108 million for FY '95. Fiscal year '96 funding is in a restructured Perkins Act that would consolidate twelve existing programs into two major programs as talked about above in the vocational education section. The first program would be a $1.1 billion State Grants program (which would include the tech-prep program) designed to be more flexible and supportive of state and local reforms begun under the School-to-Work Opportunities Act, and the second program, a $37 million National Programs authority that would support research, development, evaluation, demonstrations, and other initiatives in such areas as high-quality professional development for vocational educators, innovative uses of technology, curriculum development, and program performance standards.[6]

Career Education

Until 1971, the federal funds invested in the concepts of career education originated in vocational education appropriations. This was most noticeable in the Vocational Education Acts of 1963 and 1968 where the assignment of vocational education started to change from an emphasis on meeting the skill needs of the labor market to a greater concern for personnel employability. This change broadened the definition of vocational education and at the same time focused funding in contexts contributing to career education.[7] Federal funding by program for career education came with the official announcement of career education as a policy direction by the U.S. Office of Education and the selection of six sites in the summer of 1971 as the large-scale demonstration models of career education in public school systems. Since 1971, funding for career education has been through the same type of mechanisms found in vocational education and the tech-prep program. In 1994, using the Congressional appropriation under the Carl Perkins Act and the Job Training Partnership Act, all states received development grants in the form of awards of $200,000 to $750,000. States were to use this money to develop plans to implement school-to-work systems, with implementation grants starting to be awarded in the middle of the year. The plan being for all states to have implementation grants in the next 4 years. The next round of funding for these plans is incorporated into the consolidated Carl Perkins Act under consideration by Congress for 1996 and beyond.

New Funding Guidelines

Funds for all three of these programs in FY '96 and beyond would continue to be distributed to states, under the consolidated plan, by a formula based on population and the relative per capita income among the states, but would be simplified. States would distribute funds available for secondary education services and activities to local education agencies (LEAs) or consortia of LEAs. They would distribute funds available for post-secondary services and activities to eligible institutions or consortia of institutions including institutions of higher education, LEAs providing education at the post-secondary level, area vocational education schools providing education at the post-secondary level, or Bureau of Indian Affairs (BIA)-controlled or tribal-operated post-secondary institutions.

States, from their allotments, could retain up to 20 percent in fiscal years 1996 and 1997 and up to 15 percent in fiscal years 1998 through 2005 for state-level activities. States could use up to 5 percent of the amount retained for administration; the remainder would be used for state leadership activities that further the development, implementation, and improvement of state-wide school-to-work opportunities systems and are integrated with broader education reform activities underway in the state and activities the state carries out in other programs.

At least 80 percent of the state allotment would be distributed to local agencies in fiscal years 1996 and 1997, and 85 percent in 1998 through 2005, which formulates an increase from the current level of 75 percent. States will continue to set the allocation of funds between secondary and post-secondary levels, but could directly fund consortia of secondary and post-secondary institutions, such as tech-prep consortia.

WHAT DO SOME EXISTING AND INNOVATIVE PROGRAMS LOOK LIKE?

Vocational Education

No comprehensive approach exists that can provide a framework for serving all students in a school with vocational education programs. However, the following three models all contain elements that prove essential to the success of meeting the needs of all students.

Estrella Mountain High School in Laveen, Arizona, serves predominantly Pima and Maricopa Native Americans and hosts a successful flower production business run by teen parents and their agriculture teacher. The project was started as a way to get girls back into school and also get them the skills that would qualify them for jobs or go on to college. The project involves community partners and the Arizona State Department of Education.[8]

A program started in Tennessee by the singer and actress Dolly Parton in conjunction with the Sevier County Schools is called the Buddy Contract Program and was designed to prevent students from dropping out of school. This program starts with career planning information and assigns all seventh grade students a "buddy" or partner classmate who shares the goal of staying in school. The contract states that if they stay in school, upon graduation they will receive a financial reward of $1,000 and will be eligible for additional scholarship assistance for further schooling. Over the next 6 years, the school, community, and the Dollywood foundation work with these students in intervention programs, math and reading programs, internships, parental involvement, and the use of applied technology.[9]

A project called Voc-Fest aimed at increasing the nontraditional enrollment in vocational programs is in Flagstaff, Arizona. This program consists of about 400 eighth grade students having a hands-on opportunity to explore career options at the high school campus where they will be going next year. After taking an interest inventory, discussing their results, and as a part of choosing their high school courses, students go on campus to explore traditional and nontraditional classes with high school students acting as guides and role models. Follow-up activities to the exploration day include writing assignments and decision-making activities that include parents and the business community.[10]

Tech-Prep Education

Several tech-prep programs around the country are briefly

outlined below with the type of program they have instituted and their linkages between secondary and post-secondary institutions.

Students in a chemical technology program take courses at their local high school and at the Community College of Rhode Island. They follow an articulated curriculum that includes algebra and trigonometry and technology courses as well as modern technical physics. Those students in electronic engineering technology take a course in technical math but take the regular college physics course.[11]

Of two programs in California, the first, a home economics program, comprises the basis for linking Rowland High School, Mt. San Antonio Community College, and California State University at Long Beach. The second program is a fashion merchandising program called the East Gabriel Valley Regional Occupational Program, which links 17 high schools with Los Angeles Trade and Technical College and with California State University Los Angeles. In both programs, a portfolio achievement process, separate from other student records, was developed to track students through each program.[12]

An engineering technology program forms the basis in Oregon for involving five area high schools, Portland Community College, and the Oregon Institute of Technology.[13]

Career Education

Several career education programs that have been developed for use in the schools around the country are described below.

Academy of Finance

The Academy of Finance is an intensive 2-year, academic and work experience program designed to prepare high school students in grades 11–12 for entry-level careers in financial services. This constitutes a highly structured academic/work experience program offering a viable option for students lacking concrete career plans or interests. It provides an avenue for career preparation in financial services, an opportunity for women and minorities to gain access, and a substantive approach for involving businesses in preparing youth for entry-level jobs. This program supports the existing curriculum and consists of seven courses that are finance or finance related plus a college-level finance course, a 7-week paid summer internship at a financial services institution between the student's junior and senior years, participation in finance-related activities, an annual conference, speakers, and tours. Participation in this program prepares students for productive employment by stressing communication skills, analytic thinking, and workplace basics, such as appropriate dress, punctuality, and cooperation.

This program recommends a 6-month start-up period for planning and teacher training. A start-up guide, curriculum materials, technical assistance, training, and support are provided as part of this program. If a school district becomes part of this program, it is required to support some continuous teacher training in the form of annual staff development conferences and additional professional development activities developed with the local advisory board.

Start-up and ongoing costs and support are shared by the local school district, an institution of higher education, and local business sponsors. The first year shared non-personnel costs are estimated to be around $26,000, which includes a $4,000 adoption fee (for curriculum support materials, newsletters, directory training, and technical assistance in perpetuity) and covers teacher training, materials, special events, and three director's conferences. In addition, the partnership of school/business negotiates the sharing of costs for the full-time program director's and administrative support salaries. The school district budgets for teacher salaries; business sponsors budget for paid internships and on-site teacher training; and institutions of higher education contribute tuition costs for a college class. Beyond the training, curriculum, and support materials, a technical assistance team visits new sites during the start-up phase.[14]

Career Education Responsiveness to Every Student (CERES)

The Career Education Responsiveness to Every Student Program (CERES) is a comprehensive program developed in California to enhance instructional time and better prepare students for employment trends of the future. The purpose of the program is to provide students with the basic academic and employability skills necessary for competent, productive performance both during the time they are in school and after they leave the school setting. The program is tailored to the developmental ages of students at different grade levels with three common objectives: (1) students will identify and practice responsible work habits, (2) students will acquire knowledge of diverse occupations, which includes preparation, training, and job duties, and (3) students will apply basic skills to career decisions and actions involving job seeking and job retention.

The program's activities are transportable and can be implemented without disrupting existing programs. The program can be adopted by individual teachers and/or schools. One day of training is required to get the program started, and one day of follow-up inservice is recommended thereafter. CERES materials are self-contained, easy to use, and do not require extensive supplementary resources. Awareness material for the program is available at no cost. Staff are available for out-of-state awareness sessions, training, and follow-up activities.[15]

Careerways 2000

The Careerways 2000 program was developed to help students be more aware of what they need to be successful in both their academic work and the work-a-day world of tomorrow. The program was designed to focus students' attention on those skills, attitudes, and abilities that will afford them the widest variety of educational opportunities and career options in the future.

The curriculum package consists of six 30-minute videotapes and a Careerways 2000 Teacher's Guide, which is divided into seven instructional units, each containing a number of student activities. Each activity contains a lesson plan, necessary teacher background materials, and student worksheets. The seven units focus on (1) key aspects of decision-making, (2) the arts, (3) business and finance, (4) industry, (5) the media, (6) service, and (7) science and technology. The program can be implemented as a self-contained career education course of study or as individual units in a specific subject content area. Careerways 2000 addresses the National Goals for Education and is most appropriate for those audiences seeking an emphasis on decision-making and communication skills, gender equity, at risk, and the infusion of vocational education and academics.

The cost of the Careerways 2000 program is approximately $450 dollars per set of six videotapes and the Teachers Guide. Additional copies of the guide and the individual videotapes may be purchased separately for about $75 each. Awareness materials are available at no cost, and program staff are available to attend awareness conferences or to conduct program training. The costs of trainers and travel can be negotiated.[16]

Center for Educational Development (CED)/Career Guidance Project

The CED is an interdistrict project model developed in the Tucson School District that coordinates and delivers a variety of career education services to other schools in Pima county. This infusion model is designed to develop knowledge and skills in self-awareness and career exploration. CED has several main components: (1) direct services to students; (2) services to school staffs who want help in planning or implementing career education activities; (3) selection and maintenance of up-to-date career education media and materials; (4) coordination of community resources, such as volunteer aides, speakers, and work exposure/work experience sites; (5) conduct parent discussion groups; and (6) other services, such as development of a career education implementation unit and services to special education teachers.

The infusion model approach is to demonstrate the relationship between academic subjects and particular occupations or the world of work as a whole. Infusion redirects the focus and intent of school subjects without changing content. For example, addition may be taught by totaling prices on equipment invoice checks in a simulated auto parts store instead of by adding numbers on blank paper. Activities at the high school level are aimed at giving students career exploration and uses of academic skills in various careers.[17]

Project Discovery

Project Discovery is a career exploration and assessment system developed in Kentucky to provide students with hands-on work experiences. Forty-two programs comprise the entire Project Discovery system. Students, following detailed instructions, use many of the same tools, equipment, and materials as a trained worker in a particular field. Students are able to sample a variety of work activities to identify likes and dislikes or self-perceived abilities and gain an understanding of the basic work requirements and competencies of the occupational/vocational area. Work performance benchmarks are provided in the materials that help compare a student's specific knowledge, skills, and abilities to the actual ones required in the occupation. A guidance and counseling component is also available to aid in the exploration and assessment interpretation.

The program is designed to be used as self-contained units. Instructor's notes, student instructions, work performance benchmarks, supplies, materials, and tools and equipment are included. Nineteen of the forty-two modules are designed with "special editions" for special-needs populations, including disabled readers.[18]

WHAT RESOURCES AND SUPPORT ARE NECESSARY FOR IMPLEMENTATION AND MAINTENANCE OF EACH PROGRAM?

The current Carl D. Perkins Act under consideration aims to transform vocational education, tech-prep education, and career education into a component of true career preparation by building into every phase of planning and implementing Perkins-funded activities the belief that all students, including special populations, can achieve to high standards. Compared to earlier vocational education laws, this newest version broadens the base of students who will benefit. Instead of just students in a vocational education track or vocational classes, the services are to be designed to benefit all students in a school. It focuses on providing challenging education that will prepare all students for a range of career opportunities, rather than preparing some students for specific low-skill jobs, some for challenging careers, and yet others for higher education but not work.

Federal support under the proposed Carl D. Perkins Career Preparation Education Reform Act will take the structure of a performance partnership, a more flexible alternative to both the current array of categorical programs and the block grant approach, which simply combines funds into grants without accountability for results. The focus of the program will be moved away from process and will concentrate more on outcomes, which will empower communities to make their own decisions about administrative structuring while at the same time providing incentives based on performance. Federal, state, and local entities will jointly design the program, will work together to eliminate barriers to success, and will be responsible for measuring program results.

Local agencies are to use these funds to provide services and conduct activities that would further the development, implementation, and improvement of school-to-work opportunities. Local recipients would be required to focus assistance under Title I of Perkins on schools or campuses that serve the highest numbers or percentages of students who are members of special populations. In addition, services and activities of sufficient size, scope, and quality to be effective will be provided.

HOW DO YOU ASSESS EACH PROGRAM AFTER IMPLEMENTATION?

It is not sufficient to look only at resources, treatments, and outcomes that are found in traditional assessment models when trying to fully understand how and where these programs work and have an impact. In exchange for increased flexibility, the new performance partnership plans will require evaluation of program accomplishments based on objective, measurable performance goals and indicators. Building on the systems of standards and measures developed under the 1990 Perkins Act, states will be required under the new Perkins Act to establish, by July 1997, performance goals and indicators defining the level of performance to be achieved by students served under the act, and then use these factors to evaluate the quality and effectiveness of the services provided by their local agencies and institutions.

Programs supported under the new law must also give priority to the integration of academic and vocational instruction, classroom-based and work place-based learning opportunities, secondary and post-secondary education, and meaningful career guidance and other related activities. Performance indicators will need to focus on such areas as achievement in challenging state academic standards and industry-based skill standards, receipt of a high school diploma, skills certificate or post-secondary certificate or degree, and job placement, retention, and earnings in the career major.

WHAT IS THE SCHOOL ADMINISTRATOR'S ROLE IN THE PROGRAM?

If a school district is going to successfully implement a new program or change an existing program of vocational education, tech-prep education, or career education, it must first be identified as a high priority by the board and superintendent, and then adequate resources of personnel and funding must be allocated. The person most responsible for the planning, leadership, facilitation, and implementation of the program, however, is usually the building principal. Planning for a program generally involves the orderly sequencing of personnel, resources, and activities in a time framework. While this will require numerous detailed steps, the actual ordering of these steps will depend upon the unique conditions found in each community, as well as the skill and experience of the developers.

Involvement of many individuals in the form of discussion groups or committees is crucial to the success of any change taking place in an organization. The role of the administrator in this setting comprises one of leadership and facilitation. A general action or strategic plan outlining the role of the administrator in four phases is presented here as one method or approach that could be taken toward program implementation.

Phase I

1. Assess the needs and study the readiness for change in your current educational system.
2. Inventory and assemble all of your available resources.

Phase II

3. Seek cooperation of the necessary organizations, institutions, and individuals at all levels.
4. Organize the interested teachers, other individuals, and groups into a network of support for planning and ongoing activities.
5. Have a clear understanding among all participants of the program concepts and begin to establish the educational objectives.
6. Begin planning the program and activities most appropriate for your community's needs.

Phase III

7. After the program has been planned, the individual activities defined, and an evaluation process determined, full-scale implementation of the program takes place.
8. Put the evaluative process in operation for purposes of determining how the implementation is working.

Phase IV

9. Create a feedback loop to utilize evaluation findings for improvement and making necessary changes in the program.
10. Maintain and sustain the program through an ongoing process of review and revitalization as necessary for change.[19]

SUMMARY

The answers to the questions posed above emerge from observations of the programs in action, from prior and current practices, from research, and from theory. Current application of the information toward implementation of these programs in your own schools and districts will require administrators to study over a period of time the needs of the students in their schools and the needs of the surrounding community before initiating or changing programs. Paying close attention to the results of program review and assessment after implementation will also constitute a necessary task if administrators are to adequately serve the community with the best programs possible.

REVIEW ACTIVITIES

1. Examine the existing programs that your own school district or school has in place, and compare them to the example programs described in Chapter 6. What are some of the apparent similarities and differences between the programs as compared to the programs in your district or school?

    How would you go about convincing your school board or superintendent to consider changing or adopting a new program?

    Who are the key players in each area that need to be identified when you attempt to implement a new program or adopt a major change in an old one?

2. You have just been selected by your school board to conduct a needs assessment of the community and surrounding area regarding a tech-prep program. What specific stakeholder individuals and groups from your school district would you select to be represented during the planning stages for this assessment? Provide a brief rationale for each selection you make.

    Develop a timeline of proposed meetings you would hold in relation to completing a needs assessment; include the individuals and groups to be involved in each meeting.

    What resources will you need from the school district and from the community to successfully complete this task?

3. Carefully review the discussion about the new federal funding guidelines that will be taking place with passage of the consolidated laws for the years 1996–2005.

How might these changes benefit the local school district in the implementation and ongoing maintenance of funded programs?

What steps will need to be taken at the local level, the district level, and the state level to implement an ongoing assessment program?

4. Think of a program that you have been involved with that has been implemented or has been changed in a major way. What were the reasons behind the implementation or the changes? Was the implementation or change successful? Why or why not? Review the four-phase plan for implementation discussed earlier, and apply it to the process you encountered. Which steps were present and which ones were missing and to what degree?

ENDNOTES

1 U.S. Congress. House. Committee on Economic and Educational Opportunities. 6 Apr. 1995. Carl D. Perkins Career Preparation Education Reform Act of 1995. Hearing. 104th Cong., 1st session.

2 U.S. Department of Education. Office of Educational Research and Improvement. 1994. *Tech Prep and School-to-Work Fact Sheet.* Washington, DC: OERI.

3 Marland, S. P. 23 Jan. 1971. "Career Education Now." Speech delivered at the convention of the National Association of Secondary School Principals, Houston, TX.

4 U.S. Department of Health Education and Welfare. 1975. *Policy Paper of the U.S. Office of Education (DHEW Publication No. [OE] 75-00504).* Washington, DC: GPO, p. 4.

5 Hull, D. and D. Parnell. 1991. *Tech Prep Associate Degree: A Win/Win Experience.* Waco, TX: Center for Occupational Research and Development.

6 U.S. Department of Education. February 1995. *Department of Education Fiscal Year 1996 Budget Summary and Background Information.* Washington, DC: GPO.

7 Hoyt, K. B., R. N. Evans, E. F. Mackin, and G. L. Mangum. 1972. *Career Education: What Is It and How to Do It.* Salt Lake City, UT: Olympus Publishing Co.

8 For further information about this project, contact Estrella Mountain High School, P.O. Box 809, Route 2, Laveen, AZ 85339.

9 For more information about this program, contact Director, Dollywood Foundation, 1020 Dollywood Lane, Pigeon Forge, TN 37863-4101.

10 For further information about Voc-Fest, contact Special Grants Coordinator, Northern Arizona University, P.O. Box 6025, Flagstaff, AZ 86011-6025.

11 Mamaras, J. and P. Neri. 1992. *2 + 2 Program Guide: Tech-Prep Associate Degree Program.* Warwick, RI: Community College of Rhode Island.

12 Stanley, P., B. Morse, and C. Kellett. 1992. "Tech Prep 'Plus': In California, Win+Win+Win=Bachelor's Degree," *Vocational Education Journal,* 67(4): 32–33.

13 Hata, D. 1990. *Model 2 + 2 + 2 Tech Prep Program in Engineering Technology.* Portland, OR: Portland Community College.

14 For more information on the Academy of Finance Program, contact National Academy Foundation, 235 Park Avenue South, New York, NY 10003.

15 For further information on the CERES Program, contact Program Director, CERES, 3425 Pioneer Road, Hughson, CA 95326.

16 For further information on the Careerways 2000 Program, contact Careerways 2000 Disseminator, Los Angeles Unified School District, 1320 West Third Street, Room 406, Los Angeles, CA 90017.

17 For further information on the Center for Educational Development model, contact Director, Center for Educational Development (CED), 620 North 7th Avenue, Tucson, AZ 85705.

18 For further information about Project Discovery, contact Education Associates, Inc., 8 Crab Orchard Road, P.O. Box Y, Frankfort, KY 40602.

19 The four-phase model is adapted from *Career Education: A Handbook for Implementation,* available from the U.S. Office of Education, Washington, DC: U.S. GPO, (1972), 69.

CHAPTER 7
Multicultural Education

TO gain perspective on what multicultural education programs are, we must look at what programs were historically and where they are evolving. To begin, we must first define what we mean by *multiculturalism*. As we strive to define multiculturalism, we need to clarify the root word *culture*. It "connotes a complex integrated system of beliefs and behaviors that may be both rational and nonrational. Culture is a totality of values, beliefs, and behaviors common to a large group of people."[1] Therefore, multicultural education can be portrayed as a multifaceted, change-oriented approach that emphasizes equity and intergroup harmony. It is a belief and a process whose major goal is to transform the educational structure in our schools so that "male and female students, exceptional students, and students who are members of diverse racial, ethnic, and cultural groups will have an equal chance to achieve academically"[2] and to become productive citizens.

For too long, American schools have presented a shallow, Eurocentric viewpoint. Only the achievements of European-Americans (mostly male) have been trumpeted, while those of other groups have been overlooked. In a pluralistic democracy, such a limited view is unacceptable because all students in the United States should learn about their own culture, the cultures of others, gender, exceptionalities, as well as ethnic, racial, and social-class virtues. Multicultural education, in moderation, has the potential to unite a deeply divided society and create an authentic unity. Conversely, if carried to extremes, multicultural education can nurture a subgroup orientation. We have a choice—we can be overcome by whatever the future brings, or we can help shape it.

HISTORICAL BACKGROUND

The civil rights movement of the 1960s generated several related movements to make education more equitable for various groups. In addition to movements such as desegregation, bilingual education, special needs education, and the use of mainstreaming to make public schools more accessible to more students, some form of multicultural education was launched with the intent to change the content and processes in schools.[3]

Portraits of Multicultural Education

Like many of the movements in the 1960s and early 1970s, multicultural education has gone through various phases of development since inception. To underscore this development, the four phases of multicultural education are described in sequential form (see Exhibits 7.1–7.4).[4] Multicultural education has taken on very different meanings as it evolved. In Phase 1, the multicultural curriculum was focused on racism. During Phase 2, ethnic studies became more global and less politically oriented. In Phase 3, the multicultural curriculum shifted away from one variable (focus on minority groups) to involvement of the total school. Currently, the multicultural curriculum, known as Phase 4, deals with the educational problems of all cultural groups, which include women, the disabled, religious groups, and regional groups.

SAMPLE STATE MANDATES FOR MULTICULTURAL EDUCATION

The multicultural education activities for K–12 public schools among the states vary from having no requirements, to Phase 1, Monoethnic Courses, to Phase 4, Multicultural Education. A sampling of states that legally mandate some form of multicultural education is listed below.

> **EXHIBIT 7.1**
>
> **Phase 1: Monoethnic Courses**
>
> Originally, multicultural education was linked only to concerns about racism in schooling because African Americans demanded that schools respond to their needs and aspirations. Included in those demands were
> - textbooks that would accurately reflect African American history and culture,
> - community control of Black schools, and
> - Black teachers for African American youths.
>
> In time, American Indians and Mexican Americans made similar demands that were honored. The focus of the courses was on White racism and how Whites suppressed ethnic groups of color. Too, the assumption was that Black studies were needed only by African American students, that Asian American studies were needed only by Asian Americans, and so on.[5]
>
> The concepts espoused in Phase 1 did not bode well either for American education or for the future of the republic. If anything, "the ethnicity rage in general and Afrocentricity in particular not only divert[ed] attention from the real needs but exacerbate[d] the problems."[6]

Iowa references its requirement as *The Legal Authority: Multicultural, Nonsexist Education.* Iowa Code (Chapter 256.11).

The State Board shall promulgate rules to require that a multicultural, nonsexist approach is used by schools and school districts. The education program shall be taught from a multicultural, nonsexist approach.

The State Board shall establish a policy to ensure that school districts are free from discriminatory practices in their educational programs. In developing or revising this policy, parents, students, instructional and noninstructional staff, and community members shall be involved. In addition, each local school board shall adopt a written plan, to be evaluated and updated at least every five years, for achieving and maintaining a multicultural, nonsexist educational program. A copy of the plan shall be on file in the administrative office of the district. The plan shall include:

a. Multicultural approaches to the educational program. These shall be defined as processes which foster knowledge of, respect and appreciation for, the historical and contemporary contribu-

> **EXHIBIT 7.2**
>
> **Phase 2: Multiethnic Studies Courses**
>
> The acceptance of ethnic courses for minority groups of color prompted White ethnic groups such as Jewish Americans and Polish Americans to demand separate courses which encompassed their histories and cultures in the curriculum. As a result of the demands, schools offered multiethnic studies courses that focused on several ethnic cultures with a comparative viewpoint (e.g., The History and Culture of Minorities in the United States and Ethnic Minority Music).
>
> Although the multiethnic studies courses were less politically aligned and explored diverse points of view of ethnic groups in America, it was soon realized that multiethnic studies courses should be designed for all students and not just for those who were members of specific groups. The fundamental assumption for multiethnic studies courses was that the various ethnic groups in the United states had experiences that were both similar and different and comparisons of cultures would result in worthwhile concepts, generalizations, and theories.[7]
>
> The educational reform hoped for with multiethnic studies courses did not happen in our public schools. Barriers that contributed to the ineffectiveness of multiethnic studies courses included
>
> - negative attitudes by teachers. The use of new ethnic materials and ineffective teaching strategies made the new material ineffective and in some instances harmful.
> - recognition by teachers that ethnic studies courses alone would not and "could not enable minority students such as African Americans, Latinos, and Native Americans to achieve at levels comparable with the achievement levels of most mainstreamed White students."[8]
> - research that showed that students of color were often placed in low-academic tracks because of middle-class and Anglo-biased IQ tests.
> - language differences. Students who speak a first language other than standard Anglo-American English often fail in school.
> - negative attitudes that teachers have with students of color and students from low-income families.
>
> The result of Phase 2 was that it could *not* bring about educational reform that would enable students from various racial backgrounds and other ethnic groups to experience educational equality.[9]

tions of diverse cultural groups to society. Special emphasis shall be placed on Asian Americans, Black Americans, Hispanic Americans, American Indians, and the handicapped. The program shall provide equal opportunity for all participants regardless of race, color, age, national origin, or handicap.

b. Nonsexist approaches to the educational program. These shall be defined as processes which foster knowledge of and respect and appreciation for the historical and contemporary contributions of men and women to society. The program shall reflect the wide variety of roles open to both men and women and shall provide equal opportunity to both sexes.

EXHIBIT 7.3

Phase 3: Multiethnic Education

Multiethnic education summoned educators to develop a more unbiased educational reform, a reform that focused on the total school environment. The major thrust was to look at the entire school, rather than any one variable as the unit of change. It assumingly was a broadly conceptualized reform movement from the development of pluralistic education.[10] This pluralistic notion, however, excluded numerous groups, namely, women, religious groups, people with disabilities, and some regional groups such as Appalachian Whites.

EXHIBIT 7.4

Phase 4: Multicultural Education

Because several groups were not included in Phase 3, *Multiethnic Education*, a broader reform movement was introduced. Multicultural Education became the preferred language because the concept enabled schools to pool limited resources. Too, the new phrase, multicultural education, focused on a wider range of groups rather than to merely racial and ethnic minority groups.

Multicultural education has the support of many educators with some concerns. Many perceive that the movement may be too broad and global which thwarts the "issues of racism and discrimination, important concerns of pluralistic education in the 1960s when it emerged."[11] Others feel that the boundaries of the multicultural are now so immense that it is difficult to designate which cultural groups should be the primary focus in curriculum, publications, or conventions. "Increasingly, however, the term [multicultural education] is being used to refer to education related to race, gender, social class, exceptionality, and to the interaction of these variables."[12]

Viewed in the history of American public education, the current debate over multicultural education can be seen as the "new phrase" for the old problem on how to respond to the diversity of students. It can be said that

America is an experiment in creating a common identity for people of diverse races, religions, languages, [and] cultures. If the republic now turns away from its goal of "one people," what is its future?--disintegration of the national community, apartheid, Balkanization, tribalization?[13]

To create a common identity for people of diverse races, religions, languages, and cultures, an added approach to multicultural education must be considered. The "tips for improving multicultural education" referred to in this chapter will provide a "resolve" for many of the concerns espoused.

The plan shall also include specific goals and objectives, with implementation timelines for each component of the educational program; specific provisions for the infusion of multicultural, nonsexist concepts into each area of the curriculum developed under the provisions of subrule 12.5 (16); a description of the inservice activities planned for all staff members on multicultural, nonsexist education; and evidence of systematic input by men and women, minority groups, and the handicapped in developing and implementing the plan. In schools where no minority students are enrolled, minority group resource persons shall be utilized at least annually. A description of a periodic, ongoing system to monitor and evaluate the plan shall be included.[14]

Tennessee requires that black history and culture (49-6-1006) be taught in all its public schools.

(a) The course of instruction in all public schools should include some appropriate grade level or levels, as determined by the local board of education, courses and content designed to educate children in black history and culture and the contribution of black people to the history and development of this country and of the world. The general assembly finds that the goal of curriculum shall include the history, the heritage, the culture, the experience and ultimate destiny of all social, ethnic, gender and national groups and individuals, and that such are represented as interdependent, interactive and complimentary. The state board of education shall include multi-cultural diversity when developing frameworks and curriculum to be taught at appropriate grade levels kindergarten (K) through grade twelve (12).

(b) The commissioner of education shall annually advise all school district boards of education of the provisions of this section.

(c) The study materials used in the course of instruction authorized by this section shall follow the state board of education's guidelines concerning pornography.[15]

Wisconsin, under the Administrative Rule PI8.01(2)(h), pronounces that each school district board shall

3. Provide library facilities within the school building and make available to all pupils a current, balanced collection of books,

basic reference materials, texts, periodicals, and audiovisual materials which depicts in an accurate and unbiased way the cultural diversity and pluralistic nature of American society.[16]

Hawaii has a natural setting for multicultural education. The state's population is ethnically diverse and school populations are determined by geographic divisions rather than ethnic or cultural groups. Multicultural studies and global awareness are part of the basic education program and expected to be addressed across content and thematic areas. Multicultural studies are identified in the social studies program from K–12. For example, the K–9 curriculum contains conceptual themes devoted to culture and the secondary social studies curriculum requires students to complete courses in World History and Culture, American Problems, Anthropology, Asian Studies, Ethnic Studies, European Studies, Global Studies, and History of the Pacific. In addition, student exchange programs are carried out with cooperating countries.

Because of the diverse cultures in the state, day-to-day living offers rich experiences for students in Hawaii. Also, there are a great variety of cultural festivals and programs held throughout the year in many of the communities.[17]

Indiana requires the public schools to incorporate world culture in the social studies curriculum. Workshops in cultural diversity are conducted for teachers and administrators to make them more sensitive and aware of the needs of multiethnic students in their classrooms. The State Department of Education staff also facilitates the work of groups of Native American community members, whose purpose is to provide accurate and up-to-date information about Native American life, both past and present.[18]

Nebraska compels all school districts to submit a multicultural education program for approval by the Nebraska Department of Education. The statutory authority states that

> (1) Each school district, in consultation with State Department of Education, shall develop for incorporation into all phases of the curriculum of grades kindergarten through twelve a multicultural education program. (2) The department shall create and distribute recommended multicultural education curriculum guidelines to all school districts. Each district shall create its own

multicultural program based on such recommended guidelines. Each program shall be reviewed and, if within the guidelines, approved by the Department, and a copy of each such program shall be on file with the Department.

004 Criteria for the District Multicultural Education Program. The district multicultural education program shall:

004.01 Include studies relative to the culture, history, and contributions of African Americans, Hispanic Americans, Native Americans, and Asian Americans.

004.02 Place special emphasis on human relations and sensitivity toward all races.

004.03 Be infused into all subject areas of the core curriculum, grades K–12.

004.04 Contain a statement of the philosophy or mission of the district multicultural education program.

004.05 Contain locally developed district program goals reflecting multicultural education.

004.06 Provide learning experiences for students to obtain knowledge about and respect for the diversity and commonalities of the cultures, histories, and contributions of African Americans, Hispanic Americans, Native Americans, and Asian Americans.

004.07 Provide for staff development, including training for administrators, teachers, and support staff, which is congruent with the local district program goals developed for 004.05 which will enable them to develop an effective multicultural education program.

004.08 Include a process for selecting appropriate materials.

004.09 Provide for a process for the periodic assessment of the district multicultural education program.

004.10 Include representation by staff and community in development, implementation, and periodic assessment of a multicultural education plan. Representatives shall include the cultural diversity of the district.

004.11 Provide for an annual status report of multicultural education to the local board of education.

004.12 Incorporate multicultural education into the core curriculum, K–12, by the end of the 1994–95 school year.

004.13 Be approved by the local board of education.

005 Compliance as a Mandatory Condition for School Accreditation.
Each district shall comply with all the provisions of this Chapter as a condition for approval and accreditation to operate legally in the State of Nebraska. Failure to comply with this Chapter shall be treated as if it were a violation of a mandatory provision of 92 NAC 10 and may subject the district to loss of approval and accreditation as provided in this Chapter.[19]

The survey results[20] on K–12 multicultural education from the fifty states in the United States indicate that a majority of the states do not mandate a multicultural education curriculum. Many, however, recommend that K–12 education be multicultural.

DEMOGRAPHIC RESEARCH BASE[21]

Demographic multiculturalism is going to play a major role in accepting diversity in America. The four largest racial and ethnic minorities—African Americans, American Indians, Asians/Pacific Islanders, and Hispanics—accounted for 25 percent of the U. S. population in 1992. By 2050, these minorities may account for 47 percent of the U.S. population. The U.S. minority population is also becoming more diverse because of high rates of immigration, a younger age structure, and higher fertility among some minority groups. Because of immigration and high fertility, Hispanics are projected to be the largest U.S. minority within 20 years. Interestingly, if the American minority population lived in an independent country today, it would be the thirteenth largest country in the world—more populous than Great Britain, France, Italy, or Spain.

Defining Race and Ethnicity

An individual's race and ethnicity are socially, not scientifically, defined. In the United States, people are asked to identify their own race on government forms and surveys. In Canada, ethnicity is defined by an individual's ancestry. In other countries, religion or language distinguish the major ethnic groups.

According to the United States Census Bureau, the classifications used in population statistics comprise the four racial categories—white, African American, Asian/Pacific Islander, and American Indian/Eskimo/Aleut. A fifth "other race" category is sometimes included. Data are also collected for two ethnic categories: Hispanic and non-Hispanic. These categories conform to guidelines for government statistical reporting established by a 1978 directive from the U.S. Office of Management and Budget (OMB). The categories and definitions are as follows. For race,

- white: a person having origins in any of the original peoples of Europe, North Africa, or the Middle East
- black or African American: a person having origins in any of the black racial groups of Africa
- American Indian, Eskimo, or Aleut: a person having origins in any of the original peoples of North America and who maintains cultural identification through tribal affiliation or community recognition
- other: individuals who do not identify with any of the above categories

For ethnicity,

- Hispanic: a person of Mexican, Puerto Rican, Cuban, Central or South American, or other Spanish culture or origin, regardless of race
- non-Hispanic: persons who are not of Hispanic origin

Race and ethnic definitions overlap because Hispanics may be of any race. The overlap confuses many individuals, and many Hispanics do not identify with any of the four race categories set out in the OMB directive.

The categories and labels used in the decennial censuses shown in Figure 7.1 reflect the growing diversity of the United States population. The 1900 Census shows that the Japanese and Chinese were the only sizeable group of Asians living in the United States. In 1990, nine distinct Asian populations and catchall "other Asian/Pacific Islander" category were listed on the census questionnaire.

Census	1860	1890	1900	1970	1990
Race	White	White	White	White	White
	Black	Black	Black (Negro descendent)	Negro or Black	Black or Negro
	Mulatto[1]	Mulatto	Chinese	Japanese	Eskimo
		Quadroon[2]	Japanese	Chinese	Aleut
		Octaroon[3]	Indian	Filipino	Chinese
		Chinese		Korean	Filipino
		Japanese		Indian (Amer.)	Hawaiian
		Indian		Other	Korean
					Vietnamese
					Japanese
					Asian Indian
					Samoan
					Gaumanian
					Other API[4]
					Other race
Hispanic Origin				Mexican	Mexican or Chicano or Mexican-American
				Puerto Rican	
				Cuban	
				Central/ South American	
				Other Spanish	Puerto Rican
					Cuban
					Other Spanish/ Hispanic

[1] Three-eighths to five-eighths black
[2] One quarter black
[3] One eighth black
[4] Asian and Pacific Islander

Figure 7.1. Race and ethnic categories used in selected decennial censuses.[22]

Persons of mixed racial parentage present a challenge to the current census system. Because race is self-reported, individuals are free to choose the racial category with which they most closely identify. For example, a woman with a Chinese mother and a white father may say she is white if she identifies most closely with her white relatives. Alternatively, she may choose Chinese if she grew up speaking her mother's language and associating mainly with her mother's family. She may also select Asian on one form, white on another, which confounds the analysis of racial statistics.

A post-enumeration survey (PES) conducted after the 1990 Census found that some United States residents were reported as one race in the census and a different race in the PES. With

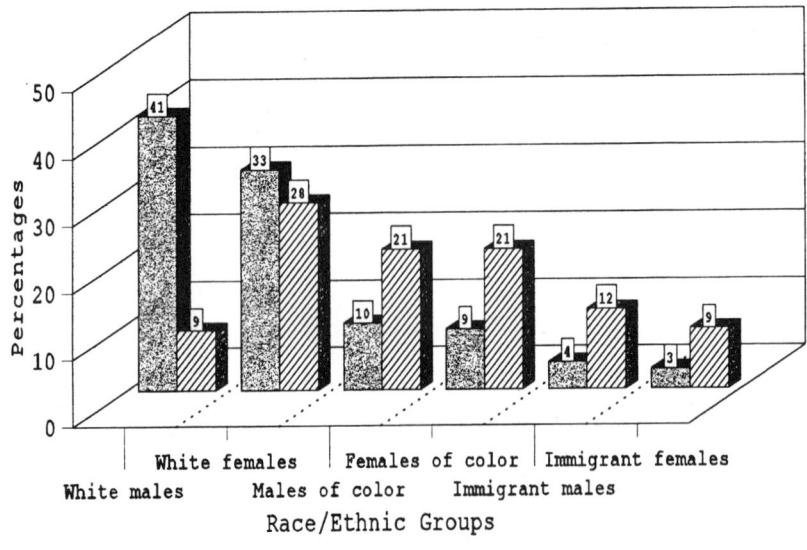

Figure 7.2. Persons entering the work force.[23]

minority births, statistics are also affected by classification changes. The National Center for Health Statistics, which records birth and death data for the United States, changed the way a newborn's race is recorded beginning with 1989. Previously, newborns were assigned a race through a complex set of rules regarding the race of the mother and father. Generally, an infant was classified as non-white if either parent was not white. Beginning with 1989, birth statistics are tabulated by the race of the infant's mother. This decreases the number of minority births because most mixed-race births are born to white mothers and non-white fathers.

Demographers predict "that by the year 2000, more than forty percent of all students in American schools will be children of color, while eighty-five percent of all teachers will be white women."[24] Another indicator of the changing mix is the ethnic composition of persons entering the work force in the United States. As illustrated in Figure 7.2, the percentage of white American workers will decrease by the year 2000 while the percentage of workers from color will increase.

As we move into the twenty-first century, the new realities of America's minority population must be addressed. The complexity and diversity of today's minority population must be recognized as we reconsider multicultural education programs and formulate new ones.

CURRICULAR BASICS FOR MULTICULTURAL EDUCATION

The United States is becoming a different society. A review of the multicultural education programs and the census projections signify that we have to redo our history and we have to redo our curriculum. Clearly, there is no template of actions at the present time that can be placed on an educational system to make multicultural education compatible with the many diverse groups. Thus, "given our nation's multicultural inevitability, schools need to help all students learn to share space with those of diverse backgrounds, prepare for a future of intergroup collaboration, and discover the commonalities that unite them regardless of differences."[25] Thus, the following guidelines are not prescriptive in nature and allow for the ever-accelerating demands our society is making to evolutionize curriculum.

Tips for Improving Multicultural Education

The basics of the multicultural education curriculum should personify a multifaceted, change-oriented approach that emphasizes equity and intergroup harmony. This emphasis should not, although it may include, be limited to

- the holding of ethnic food days, the celebration of ethnic or foreign holidays, or the commemoration of special group weeks or months
- the study of individual ethnic groups in finite, isolated units or courses
- the exclusive study of ethnic groups by members of those groups or by schools with large multiethnic populations

- the education about ethnic differences, nor is it posturing about how all people are basically alike
- reduce prejudice[26]

Rather, multicultural education should be "education that prepares the student to live, learn, and work in a pluralistic world by fostering appreciation, respect, and tolerance for people of other ethnic and cultural backgrounds."[27] Put another way, we need to transform each graduate into a multicultural person. How do we accomplish this transformation? What are the qualities that a multicultural person should have? The following curricular tips are offered to establish the needed qualities for a multiethnic future.[28]

An Understanding of Groupness

Students need to understand the importance of groups, ethnic and otherwise. Because all people belong to several groups, students should understand that group membership influences the ways a person thinks, acts, and believes, as well as the ways a person may be perceived by others.

Students should learn that while all groups have unifying elements, they also reflect internal diversity, and that group cultures are constantly changing. To be multicultural persons, students need to realize that a continually evolving knowledge of groups does provide clues to understand persons who belong to those groups. At the same time, students should learn to resist group generalizations that harden into unyielding distortions of group stereotyping.

An Understanding of Both Objective and Subjective Culture

Students need to have knowledge of the objective culture of groups that include external elements, such as art, clothing, dance, food, and music. To avoid superficiality, however, it is important that multicultural education address subjective culture—a group's values, norms, expectations, and beliefs. Because every group has historically-honed world views, schools should develop students' abilities to recognize how people of different cultures communicate their world views.

An Ability to See the Perspectives of Others

The ability to see the perspectives of others is subjective. To become multicultural persons, students must be given the opportunity in school to identify, grapple with, and understand multicultural perspectives. Multicultural education should not foster irrational acceptance of all points of view, but should encourage recognition and comprehension of multiple perspectives, even if such an understanding leads to fervent disagreement. Primarily, multicultural education should help students learn to make judgments on the basis of evidence, not reject on the basis of prejudice.

An Understanding of Our E Pluribus Unum *Heritage*

Through multicultural education, students should be given the opportunity to learn the nature and significance of the critical formative experiences of the various ethnic groups. These experiences should include both *Pluribus* experiences of individual groups and the *Unum* experiences of Americans as a whole.

The experiences should allow students to study the *Pluribus* correlations of ethnic groups to their root cultures, i.e., the significance of migration and immigration, the nature of contact with homelands, and the maintenance and modification of ethnic cultures through participation in the American experience. An understanding of those experiences will help students to consider with greater insight and sensitivity the powerful interaction between *Pluribus* and *Unum* in the present and the issues that such interaction raises for the future.

An Understanding of the Potential Contribution That Pluribus *Can Make to Society*

The multicultural education curriculum should go beyond addressing students' "roots" as a source of pride-building and intergroup understanding. It should also go beyond addressing the "problems" that different ethnic groups have faced and currently confront. It should expose students to the potential of ethnic *Pluribus*, in concert with essential societal *Unum*, as a source of national strength. If done, the multicultural person will have the wherewithal to recognize the positive power of *Pluribus* that can function hand-in-hand with cohering *Unum*.

The Capacity to Use, and Not Be Used By, the Media

Because there is a continuous operation of the media as curriculum on race, ethnicity, and foreign nations, schools should help students to learn to analyze the multicultural content of the media. Critical thinking activities will help students become more "media literate." After all, school learning does come to an end, but media learning does continue for a lifetime.

A Deeper Civic Commitment

Schools should try to develop in students a greater dedication to building a better, more equitable society. Multicultural education should be a future-oriented education. As such, it must go beyond knowledge, skills, attitudes, understanding, and sensitivity. The heart of social commitment is when people have a concern for others as well as themselves.

As noted in the first three phases of multicultural education development (see Exhibits 7.1–7.3), the multicultural education curriculum stood alone. Multicultural education curriculum cannot stand alone. Any curriculum is useful only if it is implemented in the instructional process. To have an effective multicultural education curriculum, the curriculum and instructional program must be tied together. The process includes the hidden curriculum such as teacher attitudes and expectations, grouping of students and instructional strategies, school disciplinary problems and practices, school and community relations, and classroom climates. The focus on "tips for improving multicultural education" is on process as well as on content.

Mission Statement

Multicultural education should be integrated into the curriculum in every school or school district. As such, multicultural

> **EXHIBIT 7.5**
>
> **Multicultural Education Mission**
>
> Multicultural education in the Vermillion Public School District will instill knowledge, respect, appreciation, and recognition of diversity and similarities of all people in a global society.
>
> The Vermillion Public School District will integrate multicultural education across the entire K-12 curriculum.
>
> **Multicultural Education Definition**
>
> Multicultural education recognizes diversity of culture, ability and disability, religion, family structure, gender, national and geographic origin, age, race, ethnicity, sexual orientation, socio-economic class, and language.[29]

education should operate continuously, not sporadically; it should span the curriculum from kindergarten through twelfth grade; it should cut across subject areas; and it should be implemented throughout the school year.

To implement a multicultural curriculum in a school district, it is beneficial to articulate a clear mission statement and a precise definition of multicultural education. Examples of a mission statement and a definition for multicultural education are illustrated in Exhibit 7.5.

A multicultural mission statement states the overall multicultural educational purpose of the school district. A mission statement expresses in very broad and general terms why the district endorses multicultural education. It sets the direction and creates meaning for school district educators and stakeholders. The textbook, *Outcome-Based Education: Developing Programs Through Strategic Planning*, pp. 38–40, details a step-by-step process on how to develop a mission statement.[30]

MULTICULTURAL EDUCATION ASSESSMENT

Authentic assessment for multicultural education is a process where students not only complete or demonstrate desired behaviors, but accomplish them in a real-life context. It "presents tasks that are worthwhile, significant, and meaningful—in short, authentic."[31] Authentic assessment for multicultural education constitutes more than development of better tests; it is dependent on solid classroom teaching practices and various authentic assessment tools to evaluate student behavior. The teaching practices and tools should stem from examining questions like "What are we looking for when we assess students learning multicultural education? What do we want students to know about multicultural education? What kind of classroom culture nurtures the development of multicultural education? And how can these practices be used to inform teaching and assessment?" Genuine answers to these questions will generate daily classroom teaching practices and student evaluations that drive multicultural education instruction and learning (see Endnote 32 for reference on authentic assessment).

LEARNING STYLE ASSESSMENT

The linear, sequential process of the left hemisphere dominates the curriculum and instructional process in far too many classrooms. Subsequently, right hemisphere dominant children struggle to succeed in a left hemisphere classroom environment. Because learning styles are, in large part, culturally created, assessing learning styles becomes integral to nurturing a multicultural education for each student.

Left hemisphere students, usually at the top of their reading class, can deal effectively with the abstractness of language, developing wide vocabularies of formal meanings. Conversely, the meanings for right hemisphere students are more self-centered, i.e., concrete and tied to visual and tactile symbols. This means that left hemisphere dominant learners can use words with precision to communicate meaning, while right hemisphere dominant learners have difficulty because meaning is embedded in their holistic experience. "Conveying specific meaning through language requires a separation from immediate personal experience in order to attach verbal symbols to that experience."[33] Because the right hemisphere learner specializes in direct, immediate, holistic functioning, time or abstractions such as language are not dealt with. This being so, the right hemisphere dominant learner will have difficulty using language to express explicit meaning. As opposed to the left hemisphere dominant learner who attaches language to meaning to store it in memory, the right dominant hemisphere learner stores meanings in pictures, impressions, and so on, without attaching labels to them.

It should be noted that hemispheric preference also has an effect on interpersonal style. Left hemisphere dominant learners:

- tend to relate to the teacher more objectively as a source of information
- prefer to work independently and to compete to gain individual recognition
- tend to be more task oriented and less influenced by the social environment
- [interact] with the teacher [and] are likely to be more formal and less personal in nature
- appear to be more independent of the teacher, wanting to try new tasks without the teacher's help

Right hemisphere dominant learners:

- prefer to establish a more personal and informal relationship with authority figures
- tend to respond holistically to teachers as individuals on a feeling level
- like to work with others toward a common goal, and they tend to avoid situations where they are expected to compete
- are more likely to model teacher behaviors, and to seek direction and guidance from teachers
- may be highly motivated when working individually with the teacher
- may seek social rewards rather than non-social ones[34]

Many children do not show a decided preference for one hemisphere or the other; they appear to balance the two. The research on American Indian children shows that many, but certainly not all, will probably demonstrate right hemisphere dominant learning styles.[35]

Since it is difficult to objectively assess learning styles with any degree of reliability, teachers need to broaden their teaching styles to make sure that the right hemisphere dominant learners are included. Teachers should be alert to individual students' learning styles as well as their own actions and methods in reference to their students' cultural experiences and preferred learning environments. Children need to be observed as they work. If a child appears to be having difficulty, the assignment should be altered so that he or she can use more right hemisphere strengths.[36]

American Subculture Learning Strategies

Educators need to ask, with students from diverse cultures in our classrooms, will a "single model classroom modality" fit all learners? Learning Style Inventory (LSI) research using twenty-two elements (see Exhibit 7.6) to measure cross-cultural differences in learning style differences indicates that children (grades 4–6) from "different areas of the American subculture have different patterns of preferred learning strategies."[37]

African-American and Chinese-American Children

The two groups differed significantly on fifteen of the twenty-one LSI scales. The differences were noted in the LSI elements of sound, temperature, design, motivation, responsibility/conformity, alone, variety, auditory, visual, intake, morning, late morning, mobility, parent, and teacher.[38]

African-American and Mexican-American Children

The difference between the two groups of children reached significance in twelve of the twenty-one LSI elements. The elements were light, temperature, persistence, structure, alone, variety, auditory, tactual, kinesthetic, morning, late morning, and mobility.[39]

```
          EXHIBIT 7.6
  Learning Style Inventory Elements
     • Afternoon
     • Alone
     • Auditory
     • Authority
     • Design
     • Intake
     • Kinesthetic
     • Late Morning
     • Light
     • Mobility
     • Morning
     • Motivation
     • Parent
     • Persistence
     • Responsibility/Conformity
     • Sound
     • Structure
     • Tactual
     • Teacher
     • Temperature
     • Variety
     • Visual
          [Source: See Endnote 37]
```

African-American and Greek-American Children

These two groups differed significantly on nine of the twenty-two LSI elements listed in Exhibit 7.6. The elements comprised light, motivation, responsibility/conformity, structure, alone, variety, auditory, intake, and teacher.[40]

Chinese-American and Greek-American Children

There were thirteen significant differences between the two groups on the twenty-two LSI elements. The elements consisted of sound, light, design, persistence, structure, alone, variety, auditory, tactual, kinesthetic, morning, late morning, and mobility.[41]

Chinese-American and Mexican-American Children

In only nine of the twenty-two LSI elements did the Chinese-American and Mexican-American children differ significantly.

The elements were sound, design, persistence, structure, variety, visual, tactual, intake, and late morning.[42]

Greek-American and Mexican-American Children

Greek-American and Mexican-American children had the fewest number (six) of significant differences on the LSI elements. The six of twenty-two elements that were significantly different comprise temperature, persistence, structure, auditory, visual, and morning.[43]

Research comparing the learning styles between Afro-American and Euro-American high, average, and low achievers in middle school reveals the succeeding differences.

1. Afro-American high achievers were highly teacher motivated (wanted their teacher's approval); average achievers preferred learning by listening to tapes, records, or their peers' explanations rather than directly by listening to their teacher; and low achievers were significantly more persistent than either the high or average achieving students.
2. Afro-American male high achievers required less structure than did both Afro-American female high achievers and low achievers.
3. Afro-American low-achieving boys required an authoritative teacher who provided frequent direct feedback on their performance to a greater extent than did Afro-American female low achievers.
4. Euro-American male high and average achievers preferred sound while learning; they concentrated better with music than in silence. Male middle school low achievers were less persistent than their female counterparts. However, the female high achievers, like the Afro-American male high achievers, were more teacher motivated than were Euro-American male high achievers.
5. More Euro-American than Afro-American students preferred bright light while learning.
6. Afro-American students were more teacher motivated than

were Euro-American students. This means that Afro-American students and some low achievers from the Euro-American group were more dependent on social approval and reinforcement from teachers than others.[44]

The research is replete with studies on learning styles. Educators can no longer trumpet equality for all children regardless of age, race, or religion. Ethnic and cultural differences *do* influence learning and achievement. Fortunately, many of our nation's teacher preparation institutions require pre-service educators to study both minority and majority cultures in our society and multicultural education. The standards published by the National Council for Accreditation of Teacher Education (NCATE) require teacher-education institutions to implement courses, components, and programs in multicultural education. The NCATE requirements on multicultural education were made part of the general standards in 1977 and were reissued in 1987.[45]

PARENT AND COMMUNITY RESOURCES AND SUPPORT

The problems related to multicultural education, academic achievement, student discipline, poor self-esteem, and student dropouts are concerns that schools cannot address alone. Along with the public demand for quality and accountability, these and many other education concerns warrant a partnership between the schools and the community. A "partnership" that encompasses three levels of working relationships is essential. The three levels can be viewed as a continuum:

- Cooperation is at one end, implying a simple working together toward a common goal.
- Coordination is in the middle range, entailing a sharing of resources and implying joint planning, development, and implementation of programs.
- Collaboration is at the other end, implying greater sharing and a more intensive, concerted effort including joint resource allocation and joint monitoring and evaluation.[46]

Research on parental involvement in the schools shows a positive impact on students' behavior in school, on academic achievement, and on attitudes about school and work. Further, educators themselves have identified "strengthening the parents' roles" as the one issue that should receive the highest priority.[47] Although the research indicates that parental involvement is important, the problem remains. Why? Because many of today's parents, especially single parents, have far too many obligations with family and work—"job culture has expanded at the expense of family culture,"[48] and schools or school districts have not developed a "parent partnership plan." The parent partnership plan includes a preschool partnership, a school-entry partnership, and a sustaining partnership.

Preschool Partnership

The intent of the preschool partnership is not to replace the family. Rather, the purpose is to improve a child's probability for school success. In this partnership, a Preschool PTA is established for the purpose of "building a bridge, very early, between the home and school and give helpful guidance to parents who wish to participate."[49] Parenting classes dealing with topics such as language development, how children grow, playtime, and good nutrition could be held at places convenient to parents.

An example of a Preschool PTA is Lakewood, Ohio, where eight neighborhood groups were organized involving 350 participating families. The parents got to know their neighbors and received support from each other. As one parent said, "It is important to know that you are not alone, whether you are a working mom, or a single mom, and that when you have a problem, you have someone to talk to."[50] Another parent remarked, "You borrow ideas from other parents. Some questions may seem silly, like 'How should your child respond to a bully at preschool?' But these are topics important to parents."[51]

At Louisville, Kentucky, the preschool partnership program at the Dann C. Byck Elementary School was instrumental in establishing a parent library at the school. Books, toys, and games are loaned to families in the neighborhood, and school staff members help parents negotiate time off from work to attend parenting classes. Prior to the preschool parenting classes, a majority of the kindergarten students at Byck Elementary School needed remedial help. Today, almost all of the students move on successfully to first grade.[52] Another unique feature of the Byck Elementary School preschool partnership program is that when a child is born in the neighborhood a "Byck Baby" tee-shirt, sponsored by the school-parent organization, is given to the newborn. Also, a picture of the child is proudly displayed on the school bulletin board, and the parents receive a child-care brochure.[53]

School-Entry Partnership

On the first day of school each fall, parents, guardians, or siblings usually take their 5-year-olds to school and leave after the bell rings and the teacher invites the children inside. Some parents, guardians, or older siblings stay for a short time and leave.

In the "school-entry partnership" program, "the first day of school is a time for bonding, not of separation."[54] As opposed to forming a circle on the edges, the people who brought the children to school are invited into the school and are formally welcomed into the community of learning. They, with the students, are greeted by the school principal, teachers, and school board members. The first day of school for the 5-year-olds becomes a celebration. During this celebration, goals are discussed, a school tour is arranged (new parents, guardians, or siblings should be teamed up with other parents, guardians, or siblings and students already enrolled in the school), and refreshments are served.

In Cleveland, Ohio, parents, grandparents, and guardians are invited to school on the first day, called Family Day. According to a teacher at Lincoln School in Cleveland, "Family Days are a way to move beyond the hope for parental involvement to signaling, in a concrete way, the parent's place in school."[55]

St. Ann's School in Somerville, Massachusetts, has developed a "covenant for learning." It involves all the families, and each student and parent, with the teacher, pledges to form a partnership for learning. In Grandview, Missouri, the covenant for learning has the parents pledge that they will spend 20 minutes each night to help their children with schoolwork. Reading, Ohio, introduced a city-wide covenant for learning, which not only includes the parents, but the entire community. This concept has the whole community thinking about education with a focus on the value of education.[56]

The Minneapolis, Minnesota school district introduced the Minneapolis Covenant. It includes everyone in the city, including school board members and students. In the covenant, students pledge to attend school regularly, ask for help when needed, respect other students and adults, and keep the school safe. "Parents pledge to help their children attend school on time, keep high expectations, communicate regularly with school staff, and provide a quiet space for homework."[57] In turn, school staff pledge to set high expectations, respect cultural differences, and show that they care about students.

At Forrest Park Elementary School, St. Paul, Minnesota, parents are asked to list their child's strengths and interests, along with their own goals for their child. The information gathered is used to develop a Parent-Student-Teacher Plan at the beginning of the school year. The information is helpful during parent conferences in monitoring how well school goals are being met.[58]

Sustaining the Partnership

To sustain the school-parent partnership, parents should participate in regularly scheduled conferences, as well as other informal conversations. The minimum number of parent-teacher conferences should be four times during the school year. "Currently, most parents of elementary school children meet with teachers only one to three times a year. Only ten percent meet as often as once a month."[59]

Centennial Elementary School in Tucson, Arizona, publishes a monthly newsletter with helpful hints for learning and reading at home. It sends home weekly homework packets for students in the early grades, and nightly booklets for students in grades 2 through 5. Centennial also has an interpreter attend the parent-teacher conferences for non-English speaking parents.[60] At Westwood Elementary School, Santa Clara, California, a packet containing progress reports, homework assignments, and work samples is sent home every Wednesday. Parents in the Westwood Elementary School look forward to the Wednesday packet and regard it "as my homework day."[61] The Wednesday envelope reminds students that parents know what homework is expected, and it promotes an all-around unity for the parent, the child, and the school.

A "parent center" is another innovation that can strengthen parent-school relationships. The center can be located in a comfortable room in the school where parents can gather throughout the day and mingle, informally, with other parents or with staff. Where space is limited in a school, a place can be set aside in the school library. A "parent inventory" is another technique that can be helpful to identify the skills and experience parents have and the kind of volunteer work they might wish to do. For example, Orchard School in Ridgewood, New Jersey, put together an "Encyclopedia of People" that listed parents' interests. On any given day, mothers and fathers are seen working in the library, serving as art consultants, or giving classroom talks about their jobs.[62]

To accomplish effective parent-school partnerships, a "parent coordinator" can be helpful. This could be a parent volunteer, a senior citizen, or a college student fulfilling a community service program. The responsibility of the parent coordinator includes greeting parents when they come to school, organizing parent education workshops, helping teachers with voice-mail messages, operating homework hotlines, and arranging home visits. Lowery Elementary School in Houston, Texas, for example, "uses a parent coordinator to recruit and work with parent volunteers, with remarkable results."[63] The results show that more than 600 parents have worked in the twenty-six volunteer programs, logging 13,500 clock hours of service every year. On the other hand, Whitcomb Elementary School, Richmond, Virginia, pays the parent coordinator who schedules "Lets Talk" sessions every Thursday morning. Also, there is a "Coffee with the Principal" scheduled on a monthly basis.[64]

"The message is clear. It is simply impossible to have an island of excellence in a sea of community indifference, and when parents become school partners, the results can be consequential and enduring."[65]

BENEFITS FROM PARENT-SCHOOL RELATIONSHIPS

Demonstrated research and experience have proven there are countless benefits resulting from parent and community involvement with the schools. Because there is little argument that the family is the major educational institution of a child, parents must understand they are a legitimate and integral part of the educational process. In reality, the parents, family, neighborhood, and school are seen as the major influences on the children during their premature years. Extending the parent-child relationship to the school not only creates benefits for the parents, but for the teacher and school as well.

Benefits to Parents

Parents serving as resource persons are provided with an opportunity to gain a realistic view of the classroom environment and an understanding about how the classroom climate affects their children's behavior. Parents can also learn what they can do to facilitate their children's learning at home.

Benefits to Teachers

Parents provide an opportunity for teachers to learn about the children's community and about the parents' concerns about their children. This interaction creates a team approach between parents and teachers.

Benefits to Schools

Through parental involvement, the school can be the benefactor in the form of advisory groups for curriculum development, fund raising for school projects, moral support, advocates for the school and student needs, and other activities.

Because parents are the first and foremost teachers of their children, mutually reinforced home-school programs have been identified as vital influences intimately linked with student success. The most effective schools in the United States have successfully meshed a strong bond between home and school.[66]

There is no single model for an educational partnership to fit any one community. However, "the extent of cooperation-collaboration depends on each partner's willingness to share its resources, both human and physical."[67] Planning is the key to success (see Endnote 68 for a strategic planning resource).

FEDERAL GOVERNMENT SUPPORT

Despite the constitutional silence on education, the federal government has shown considerable interest in education for American Indian and Alaskan Native children. The fact that a majority of Native American Indian children are now attending public schools has served as a catalyst for legislative intervention to provide educational opportunities for Native American students.

The Indian Education Act (IEA), passed in 1972 and amended in 1978 by Congress, established programs in recognition of the special educational and culturally related academic needs of American Indian and Alaskan Native students. The legislation for these programs was reauthorized by Congress with the Indian Education Act in 1988 and in 1994. Title IX, formerly Title IV and Title V, authorized by Public Law 103-382, makes available to school districts supplemental assistance if the districts qualify. To be eligible for a grant, the local education agency (LEA) must, among other requirements, establish a parent committee (section 9116). Further assurances of parental involvement require that the LEA reports submitted to the Secretary of the United States Department of Education must be developed in open consultation with parents of Indian children and teachers, and, if appropriate, Indian students from secondary schools, including public hearings held by the LEA to provide individuals opportunity to understand the program and make recommendations. Too, the program funded under Title IX must be developed by the LEA with the participation and written approval of a committee that is composed of, and selected by, parents of Indian children in the LEA's schools and teachers; and, if appropriate, Indian students attending secondary schools. The committee membership must be comprised of more than 50 percent parents of Indian children.

Enrollment Requirements

A local educational agency, meaning school district, is eligible for a grant for any fiscal year if the number of Indian children eligible under section 9116 [tribal affiliation] enrolled in the schools of the agency and to whom the agency provided free public education during the preceding fiscal year. There must be at least ten students, and the number of students enrolled in the educational agency must constitute not less than 25 percent of the total number enrolled in the schools of such agency. These requirements do not apply to the states of Alaska, California, and Oklahoma, or with respect to any local educational agency located on, or in the proximity to, a reservation.

Information for grant eligibility and rules and regulations pertaining to such grants considering the Indian students is made public annually by the United States Department of Education.[69] For technical assistance, six Indian Education Technical Assistance Centers (IETAC) were established to serve the states and to provide technical assistance or training (see Figure 7.3).

In addition to the Title IX program funds for American Indian and Alaskan Native youth, Johnson O'Malley (JOM) funds are also available. JOM funds are generated through the Department of the Interior and made available and contracted under Public Law 93-638, the Indian Self-Determination and Assistance Act of 1975. The purpose of the JOM funds is to provide programs that meet the special educational needs of eligible children. To meet eligibility requirements, Indian students from age 3 (by October 1) through grade 12 are eligible provided they are a member of a federally recognized tribe or are at least one-fourth degree descendent of a member. The one-fourth

CENTER	PHONE/FAX	STATES SERVED
DIRECTOR INDIAN EDUCATION TECHNICAL ASSISTANCE CENTER I ORBIS - SUITE 700 1411 K STREET, NW WASHINGTON, DC 20005	202-628-4444 1-800-621-2998 FAX 202-628-2241	AL, AR, CT, DE, FL, GA, IL, IN, KY, LA, MA, ME, MD, MI, MO, MS, NC, NH, NJ, NY, OH, PA, RI, SC, TN, VA, VT, WV, DC
DIRECTOR INDIAN EDUCATION TECHNICAL ASSISTANCE CENTER II UNITED TRIBES TECHNICAL COLLEGE 3315 UNIVERSITY DRIVE BISMARCK, ND 58504	701-258-0437 701-255-3228 1-800-932-8997 (In State) 1-800-648-3847 (Out of State) FAX 701-258-0454	IA, KS, MN, ND, NE, SD, WI
DIRECTOR INDIAN EDUCATION TECHNICAL ASSISTANCE CENTER III SCHOOL OF EDUCATION GONZAGA UNIVERSITY 302 EAST SHARP SPOKANE, WA 99258	509-328-4220 EXT. 2812 1-800-533-2554 (In State) 1-800-648-3847 (Out of State) FAX 509-484-6965	CO, ID, MT, OR, UT, WA, WY
DIRECTOR INDIAN EDUCATION TECHNICAL ASSISTANCE CENTER IV NITRC - SUITE 218 2121 SOUTH MILL AVENUE TEMPE, AZ 85282	602-967-9428 1-800-528-6425 FAX 602-921-1015	AZ, CA, HI, NM, NV
DIRECTOR INDIAN EDUCATION TECHNICAL ASSISTANCE CENTER V AIRD, INC. - SUITE 200 2424 SPRINGER DRIVE NORMAN, OK 73069	405-364-0656 1-800-422-0966 (In State) 1-800-451-2191 (Out of State) FAX 405-364-5464	OK, TX
DIRECTOR INDIAN EDUCATION TECHNICAL ASSISTANCE CENTER VI COOK INLET TRIBAL COUNCIL, INC. 670 W. FIREWEED LANE SUITE 200 ANCHORAGE, AK 99503	907-265-5970 1-800-478-0014 FAX 907-277-9071	AK

The Indian Education Technical Assistance Centers serve the states as listed and provide technical assistance and training at no cost to the LEA. When calling for technical assistance or training, please identify the nature and type of assistance needed so that you may be referred to the appropriate Center staff person.

Figure 7.3. Indian education technical assistance centers (IETAC).

degree of Indian blood requirement can be a combination of tribal affiliations. The Department of Education does not require one-fourth degree descendancy certification; however, the ED 506 Form must be signed by a parent or guardian for student eligibility.

Use of Project Funds

Title IX and Johnson O'Malley funds can be used to provide academic assistance to Native American students. Some assistance can be in the form of "study time" with tutors normally scheduled after school at a designated place. For example, the Vermillion School District in South Dakota schedules "study time" three times weekly during the academic year. A tutor pool is made up of University of South Dakota School of Education student volunteers (some are paid) to provide academic assistance to any Native American student in grades K–12. "This cooperative effort between the University of South Dakota School of Education and the Vermillion School District has been quite successful."[70]

In addition to funding academic assistance, the Title IX and JOM funds can be used for the purchase of school supplies for income-eligible students and for cultural enrichment activities that are normally offered throughout the summer months. The administrative costs for the program director or coordinator are also part of the funding formula or grant.

THE SCHOOL ADMINISTRATOR'S ROLE

The school administrator's role in multicultural education should be guided by the wisdom expressed in the words of Maya Angelou, spoken in the poem she delivered at the inauguration of President Clinton. "History, despite its wrenching pain, cannot be unlived, but if faced with courage, need not be lived again."

The school administrator must know that "history is littered with the wreck of states that tried to combine diverse ethnic or linguistic or religious groups within a single sovereignty."[71] For the school administrator, multicultural education should not just be what students are taught, but how students are taught. Therefore, it is important that an "equity pedagogy" exist in every classroom. The school administrator must ensure that his or her school or school district teach both our diversity and unity, which is based on America's founding principles. Together everyone achieves more if male and female students, exceptional students, and students who are members of diverse racial, ethnic, and cultural groups have an equal chance to achieve academically and to become productive citizens.

REVIEW ACTIVITIES

1. Define multiculturalism, and explain the differences among the four phases of multicultural education. How do these phases apply to your school district?
2. What mandates or recommendations do you have in your state? What mandates or recommendations do you have in your school? From the Sample State Mandates for Multicultural Education, list elements you can see that you have in place in your curriculum. List elements you can see that might need to be incorporated.
3. Discuss ways in which the demographic research base is affecting the learning community in your school.
4. Compare the curricular basics for multicultural education with the curriculum in your school. How does your curriculum transform your graduates into multicultural persons?
5. How has your school applied its mission statement in practice?
6. In what ways does your school accommodate learning styles? Explain why accommodating learning styles is integral to multicultural education?
7. How do parent and community resources and support enhance multicultural education? How do you build, support, and sustain a community of learners in your school?
8. What qualifications for and uses of Title IX and Johnson O'Malley (JOM) funds can you determine for your school?

ENDNOTES

1 Tiedt, P. L. and I. M. Tiedt. 1995. *Multicultural Teaching: A Handbook of Activities, Information, and Resources.* Fourth edition. Boston, MA: Allyn and Bacon, p. 10.

2 Banks, J. A. and C. A. McGee Banks. 1993. *Multicultural Education.* Second edition. Boston, MA: Allyn and Bacon, p. 1.

3 Sleeter, C. E. and C. A. Grant. 1987. "An Analysis of Multicultural Education in the United States," *Harvard Educational Review,* 57:421.

4 The content in Exhibits 7.1–7.4 are excerpts from the analytic thoughts expressed by James A. Banks in *Multiethnic Education: Theory and Practice.* Third edition. 1994. Boston: Allyn and Bacon, pp. 40–44.

5 Banks, J. A. 1994. *Multiethnic Education: Theory and Practice.* Third edition. Boston: Allyn and Bacon, pp. 40–41.

6 Schlesinger, A. M., Jr., 1991. "The Disuniting of America," *American Educator,* 15(3):29.

7 Banks, J. A. 1994. *Multiethnic Education: Theory and Practice.* Third edition. Boston: Allyn and Bacon, p. 41.

8 Ibid., pp. 41–42.

9 Ibid., p. 42.

10 Ibid., p. 42.

11 Ibid., pp. 42–43.

12 Ibid., p. 43.

13 Schlesinger, A. M., Jr., 1991. "The Disuniting of America," *American Educator,* 15(3):31.

14 The material on multicultural education requirements in the state of Iowa was submitted to the authors by the Bureau of School Administration and Accreditation, Iowa Department of Education, Des Moines, Iowa.

15 The material on multicultural education requirements in the state of Tennessee was submitted to the authors by the Department of Education, State of Tennessee, Nashville, Tennessee.

16 The material on multicultural education requirements in the state of Wisconsin was submitted to the authors by the State Department of Education, State of Wisconsin, Madison, Wisconsin.

17 The material on multicultural education requirements in the state of Hawaii was submitted to the authors by the Department of Education, State of Hawaii, Honolulu, Hawaii.

18 The material on multicultural education requirements in the state of Indiana was submitted to the authors by the Center for School Improvement and Performance, Indiana Department of Education, Indianapolis, Indiana.

19 The material on multicultural education requirements in the state of Nebraska was submitted to the authors by the Department of Education, State of Nebraska, Lincoln, Nebraska.

20 The fifty states in the United States were surveyed by the authors to determine which states mandated a K–12 multicultural education curricu-

lum. The survey results show that a majority of the states *do not* mandate multicultural education. Many of the states do, however, recommend that school districts integrate the school curriculum with multicultural education. For example, the state of Georgia does not mandate multicultural education. The state does, however, provide a "quality core curriculum" by designating the social studies program area with objectives to integrate multicultural education, K–8. An example of the suggested curriculum is as follows:

Kindergarten

Topic/Concept A: Myself, The Family, Others
- demonstrates evidence of developing a positive self-concept
- states ways in which people are alike, different
- identifies characteristics of children around the world to self and classmates (food, clothing, shelter, families, holidays)
- gives examples of how families around the world meet their needs and wants

First Grade

Topic/Concept A: The Individual, Families, Our Country
- demonstrates evidence of developing a positive self-concept
- identifies how individuals are alike and how they are different
- compares children in the U.S. with children living in other countries

Second Grade

Topic/Concept A: The Neighborhood and Community
- identifies different types of neighborhoods and the characteristics that make them different and alike
- identifies famous people of the past and present
- compares the customs of other countries to the customs practiced in the United States
- uses art, music, and literature to reflect the heritage of the American society

Third Grade

Topic/Concept A: Communities—Change and Develop
- describes cities in regard to origin, growth, and change
- discusses the history of the local community
- identifies similarities and differences between the local community and other communities
- compares the customs and lifestyles of Native Americans in the history of our country
- relates the past to the present in the study of change and continuity in human affairs

Fourth Grade

Topic/Concept A: Cultural and Geographic Regions
- describes the contributions and cultural influences of Native Americans in Georgia's history
- discusses the first European settlement founded in Georgia

- identifies Georgia's symbols and observations indicating their importance to our heritage
- identifies famous Georgians and cites accomplishments made by them

Fifth Grade

Topic/Concept A: Social Studies/Concepts U.S. History

- identifies the Indian civilizations found in America and describes the impact of the cultural contributions made by Indian tribes toward the development of the United States
- describes the period of exploration and colonization in America
- illustrates that the settlement of various groups had a significant impact on the development of the New England, Middle, and Southern Colonies in America
- describes the period of exploration and colonization of Canada
- explains how the United States and Canada are interdependent
- listens to and respects the views of others
- recognizes the right of others to hold differing positions
- formulates questions related to regions and cultures
- describes the major factors involving immigration that led to a stronger nation
- explains how the value system of a society exerts great influence on the attitudes and behavior of people

Sixth Grade

World History/Geography (Middle East, Europe, Africa—South of the Sahara)

- identifies various ethnic groups found in regions of the Middle East, Europe, and Africa—south of the Sahara, and describes impacts on the development of the regions by these groups (linguistic patterns, cultural contributions, etc.)
- traces the migrations and settlements of various groups that have had an impact on the development of each region
- traces the important historical developments of the regions of the Middle East, Europe, and Africa—south of the Sahara
- traces the important political developments of each region
- traces the important social and cultural developments of the regions
- explores the values of a society through the cultural expressions of art, music, literature, etc.

Seventh Grade

World History/Geography (Latin America, Asia, and Oceania)

- identifies various ethnic groups found in regions of Latin America, Asia, Oceania, and describes impacts on the development of the regions by these groups (linguistic patterns, cultural contributions, etc.)
- traces the migrations and settlement of various groups that have had an impact on the development of each region
- traces the important historical developments of the regions of Latin America, Asia, and Oceania
- traces the important political developments of each region
- traces the important social and cultural developments of the regions

Eighth Grade

Georgia Studies (History/Government/Geography)

- identifies the impact of European conquest on the Indian civilizations of Georgia and the impact of the Indian civilizations on the European settlers
- describes the Indian nations and tribes living in Georgia and their relationships with the English colonists
- identifies well-known and influential Georgians from the colonial era (e.g., men, women, minorities)
- analyzes sentiment in Georgia as compared with other southern states for secession from the Union
- analyzes Georgia's role in the Civil War and the impact of that war on the state and relates it to events in other states
- examines and analyzes the political, economic, and social impact of Reconstruction on Georgia and southern states
- identifies well-known and influential Georgians from Independence through Reconstruction (e.g., men, women, minorities)
- identifies well-known and influential Georgians from Reconstruction through World War II
- examines the important events and personalities in the Civil Rights Movement in Georgia
- relates the past to the present in the study of change and continuity in human affairs

In the state of Montana, the Montana School Accreditation Standards include provisions that address multicultural awareness in both student and teacher education. The Learner Access Rule (10.55.803) states that in developing and implementing processes for assessing the education needs of their students, school boards shall consider ways to

- provide learning experiences matched to students' interests, readiness, and learning style
- take into account individual and cultural diversity and differences among learners. Cultural and language differences should be viewed as valuable and enriching resources.
- nurture an understanding of the values and contributions of Montana's Native Americans and the unique needs and abilities of Native American students and other minority groups
- provide learning resources that are culturally inclusive and current
- provide opportunities for individual self-direction and decision making
- provide equal access to learning resources, including technology
- provide instructional materials that are sequential and compatible with previous and future offerings
- identify, using the school's own criteria, students who may be at risk, in need of special services or bilingual, or otherwise exceptional

To improve multicultural education, the Montana Board of Public Education established a task force to study the issue of multicultural education. The Multicultural Task Force combined efforts with the Board of Public Education's Gender Equity Task Force and developed the following goals and objectives:

- encourage educators, administrators, and community members to increase their awareness of gender and multicultural equity
- integrate gender and multicultural equity awareness into training for school district personnel and school board members

- increase the number of females and individuals from minority cultures in teaching and administrative positions
- infuse gender and multicultural equity throughout the curriculum
- provide nontraditional and multicultural role models for students

21 The research base material was selected from the government document *Population Bulletin,* Population Reference Bureau, Inc., Washington, DC. O'Hare, W. P. 1992. "America's Minorities—The Demographics of Diversity," *Population Bulletin,* 47(4):8.

22 Bureau of the Census. 1991. *Statistical Abstracts of the United States.* Washington, DC: U.S. Government.

23 Cortes, C. 1995. "Education in a Multicultural Society," *Restructuring Brief,* #9:6.

24 Bureau of the Census. 1991. *Statistical Abstracts of the United States.* Washington, DC: U.S. Government.

25 Cortes, C. 1994. "A Better Multicultural Future for Holly, Melissa, and Kai," *Instructional Leader,* 7(5):12.

26 Cortes, C. 1990. "A Curricular Basic for Our Multiethnic Future," *Doubts & Certainties,* 4(7/8):3.

27 Davidman, L. and P. T. Davidman. 1994. *Teaching with a Multicultural Perspective.* New York: Longman, p. 23.

28 The seven multicultural education qualities are suggested by Cortes, C. E. 1990. "A Curricular Basic for Our Multiethnic Future," *Doubts & Certainties,* 4(7/8):4–5.

29 The mission statement and definition for multicultural education were developed by the Vermillion Public School District, Vermillion, SD. Used with permission.

30 For a complete school district step-by-step planning model, see Boschee, F. and M. A. Baron. 1993. *Outcome-Based Education: Developing Programs Through Strategic Planning.* Lancaster, PA: Technomic Publishing Co., Inc., pp. 38–40.

31 Archbald, D. A. and F. M. Newmann. 1988. *Beyond Standardized Testing: Assessing Authentic Achievement in the Secondary Schools.* Reston, VA: National Association of Secondary School Principals, p. 1.

32 For a complete definition and process of authentic assessment, see Baron, M. and F. Boschee. 1993. *Authentic Assessment: The Key to Unlocking Student Success.* Lancaster, PA: Technomic Publishing Company, Inc.

33 Browne, D. 1986. *Learning Styles and Native Americans.* ERIC, ED 297 906, p. 11.

34 Ibid., pp. 12–13.

35 Ibid., p. 13.

36 Ibid., p. 14.

37 Dunn, R., J. Gemake, F. Jalaii, and R. Zenhausern. 1990. "Cross-Cultural Differences in Learning Styles of Elementary-Age Students From Four Ethnic Backgrounds," *Journal of Multicultural Counseling and Development,* 18:84.

38 Ibid., p. 78.

39 Ibid., pp. 78–80.

40 Ibid., pp. 80–82.
41 Ibid., pp. 80–82, 84.
42 Ibid., pp. 82–86.
43 Ibid., pp. 82, 88.
44 Jacobs, R. L. 1987. "An Investigation of the Learning Style Differences Among Afro-American and Euro-American High, Average, and Low Achievers," Doctoral diss., Peabody University, Louisiana.
45 National Council for Accreditation of Teacher Education. 1987. *Standards, Procedures, and Policies for the Accreditation of Professional Education Units.* Washington, DC.
46 Decker, L. 1994. *Home-School-Community Relations.* University of Virginia: Mid-Atlantic Center for Community Education, p. 81.
47 Boyer, E. L. 1995. *The Basic School: A Community for Learning.* Princeton, NJ: The Carnegie Foundation for the Advancement of Teaching, p. 48.
48 Ibid., p. 49.
49 Ibid., p. 51.
50 Ibid., p. 51.
51 Ibid., p. 51.
52 Ibid., p. 51–52.
53 Ibid., p. 51–52.
54 Ibid., p. 52.
55 Ibid., p. 53.
56 Ibid., p. 55.
57 Ibid., p. 55.
58 Ibid., p. 56.
59 The Carnegie Foundation for the Advancement of Teaching and the George H. Gallup International Institute, The International Schooling Project, 1994.
60 Boyer, E. L. 1995. *The Basic School: A Community for Learning.* Princeton, NJ: The Carnegie Foundation for the Advancement of Teaching, p. 57.
61 Ibid., pp. 57–58.
62 Ibid., pp. 58–59.
63 Ibid., pp. 60–61.
64 Ibid., p. 61.
65 Ibid., p. 61.
66 Material on parent and community resource support are excerpts from the *Parent Handbook.* (n.d.) Northern Plains Resource and Evaluation Center Two, Bismarck, ND.
67 Decker, L. 1994. *Home-School-Community Relations.* University of Virginia: Mid-Atlantic Center for Community Education, p. 81.
68 For a "strategic planning process," see Boschee, F. and M. A. Baron. 1993. *Outcome-Based Education: Developing Programs Through Strategic Planning.* Lancaster, PA: Technomic Publishing Company, Inc.
69 Information and application material for formula grants to local educa-

tional agencies (LEA) on *Indian education programs* are available from the U.S. Department of Education, Office of Elementary and Secondary Education, 600 Independence Avenue, SE, Washington, DC 20202-0100.

70 Satisfaction of the "study time" program with volunteer and paid tutors was expressed in the *Indian Education Programs* brochure (1996) by Kathy Prasek, Title IX and JOM Coordinator, Vermillion School District, Vermillion, SD.

71 Schlesinger, A. M., Jr. 1991. "The Disuniting of America," *American Educator,* 15(3):32.

CHAPTER 8

Student At-Risk Programs

THE term *at-risk* refers to different sets of students dependent solely upon who is applying the term to them. Some educational experts want to apply this term to only those children who have handicapping conditions; others want to focus only on those from abusive homes; others want to look only at school dropouts; still others want to focus only on those students who are at risk of being caught up in the world of alcohol and drug abuse; some want to deal only with students who have AIDS/HIV; and others want to look just at students at risk of becoming pregnant or even ending their own lives. While none of these definitions is incorrect, because all of these students above are certainly at risk, a singular more global definition needs to be utilized here to take into account as many of the above situations that students might encounter.

Because this is being written for practitioners in the field of school administration, the focus will be upon the student who is not being successful in school for a variety of reasons, but could or even should be successful. This leads us to define at-risk students as those students who, on the basis of several risk factors, are unlikely to graduate from high school and may be without the skills and self-esteem necessary to be successful in leading a fulfilling life.[1]

Regardless of why a student has been placed at risk, the results of a student dropping out of school and not graduating are high in both personal and societal costs:

- Personal income loss to those students who drop out of

school could be as high as $340,000 or higher over a lifetime.[2]
- Because of lower wages for these students, state revenues will decrease and fewer tax payments will be made.[3]
- Students who do not finish school have an unemployment rate double that of those students who graduate.[4]
- By not finishing school, the chances of incarceration for these students increases from three- to nine-fold.[5]
- The entry-level labor pool from which many businesses draw has been estimated to shrink from 25 percent in previous years to 16 percent in 1995 due to students not finishing school.[6]
- Diminished cognitive skill development reduces the options these students have in entering economic and social networks.[7]

CHARACTERISTICS OF AT-RISK STUDENTS

What then constitutes an at-risk student? From the earlier definition alone, you cannot identify just who these students are, but you are able to see some of the behaviors that they exhibit that would characterize them as being suspect to risk.

1. At-risk students usually exhibit low self-esteem, a lack of self-confidence in themselves or their work, and a lack of self-worth. They regard themselves as being in a state of helplessness and feel powerless in most situations.
2. At-risk students are avoiders. They avoid school and they avoid contact or confrontation with other students and adults. They find it easier and often more enjoyable to skip classes rather than face the reality that they are behind and do not know what is going on. School is seen as threatening to them because it is not responsive to their needs.
3. At-risk students distrust adults and the adult world in general. They view adults as the cause of the unfairness they are experiencing. Adults are deemed unresponsive to their needs and are even seen as being abusive by some students.

4. At-risk students tend to live in the present and have a very limited view of what the future will bring them. They are responsive to their own short-term successes, but do not do well with long-term projects or planning. The future to them does not hold a positive place in their lives. Because of their viewpoint, they experience a detachment from the school setting.
5. At-risk students feel that the adults they know in general have given up on them by the time they are in the middle school years. They are usually behind academically by this time, because they lack the skills in reading, writing, and math and think others view them as being dumb rather than unskilled. This leads them to feel a hopelessness about their situation at school and implants the idea that they cannot learn.
6. At-risk students generally do not do very well in regular classroom settings where the norm is a routine with long periods of sitting and listening with little variety. They are usually impatient with this type of environment and are often viewed as being disruptive because of their impatience.
7. At-risk students often can apply what is being taught in a very practical manner if this type of behavior is encouraged or even allowed. They do well with experiential-type learning situations and can usually verbalize what takes place better than they can write about it.
8. At-risk students have a hard time generally forming a link between the effort something takes and the achievement gained. Instead, they view success as just luck, or they talk about how easy the task was to begin with. They see everything as happening to them and that they have little control over what goes on in their lives. When a task is not done or done poorly, it is because the task was too hard to begin with, or they could not get the help they needed to complete the task. At-risk students generally do not assume personal responsibility and seldom learn anything from mistakes that they might make.[8]

RESEARCH ON AT-RISK STUDENTS

Schools of today attempt to maximize the learning potential

for all students through instructional opportunities in specific curricular areas. Eliminating or trying to control the risk factors that might limit the learning potential of students provides one method of maximizing this learning potential. Although few students are considered to be totally risk free with regard to factors that would cause them to drop out of high school, or face potential alcohol and drug use, or to become pregnant, or not to be successful in their lives, some students are at a much higher risk than others.[9]

There seems to be a certain portion of every school population that when studied consistently reveals a lack of the intellectual, emotional, and/or social skills necessary that would enable them to take full advantage of the educational opportunities available to them. Research points toward many identifiable factors that might lead students to thus be considered at risk. When one or more of these factors are present, they help us to identify students who are the most vulnerable or most disadvantaged and face a higher probability that a problem will occur than if the factors were absent. Figure 8.1 presents a list of factors that place students at-risk.[10]

PROGRAMS FOR DEALING WITH STUDENTS AT RISK

Understanding the characteristics and behaviors of at-risk students and the factors that might place them at risk allows us to focus on programs specifically for students in schools, such as (1) compensatory or remedial programs (Chapter 1/Title I, Head Start, and Follow Through programs that are based at the elementary school grade levels and will be dealt with here only briefly),(2) special education programs (schools have provided a continuum of services for handicapped students since passage of P.L. 94-142 in 1975 and have refined these services through later amendments and other laws), and (3) programs for general education (such as between class ability grouping and tracking, alternative schools, cooperative learning, and programs to improve teacher instructional skills). Each type of program has its own history and requirements, and each has some practical considerations that should be taken into account.

Environmental Factors
  Poverty
  Cultural barriers in:
    language, gaining
    health care, gaining
    other social services
  Living in area with:
    high unemployment
    inadequate housing
    poor schools
    high crime rate
  Minority status with:
    racial discrimination
    devalued culture in
      American society
    differing generation levels
      of assimilation
  Low educational levels
  Low societal achievement
    expectation level

Family Factors
  Alcohol or drug dependency
    by parents
  Parental abuse or neglect
    of children
  Antisocial, sexually deviant,
    or mentally ill parents
  High stress levels, including
    financial strain
  Large overcrowded family
  Unemployed/underemployed
    parents
  Parents with little education
  Socially isolate parents
  Single parent without other
    family support
  Family instability
  High level of martial conflict
  Family violence
  Divorced, separated, absent, or
    deceased parents
  Lack of family rituals
  Inadequate parenting
  Low parent-child contact
  Frequent family moves

Health, Physical, or Mental Factors
  Child of alcohol or drug
    abuser
  Less than two years between
    child and siblings
  Birth defects
  Neurological dysfunctions
  Neurochemical dysfunctions
  Neuropsychological
    vulnerabilities
  Physical handicap
  Physical/mental health
    problems
  Learning disability

Early Behavior Factors
  Aggressiveness
  Aggressiveness combined with
    shyness
  Cognitive problems
  Decreased social inhibition
  Difficult temperament
  Emotional problems
  Hypersensitivity
  Hyperactivity
  Inability to express feelings
    appropriately
  Inability to cope with stress
  Low self-esteem
  Personality shifts such as
    overreacting, ego control
  Problems with relationships

Adolescence Factors
  School failure and dropout
  Delinquency
  Violent acts
  Beginning drug and/or alcohol
    use
  Early unprotected sexual
    activity
  Teenage pregnancy
  Teen parenthood
  Unemployed or underemployed
  Mental health problems
  Suicidal behaviors/tendency

Negative Behavior and Experience Factors
  Lack of bonding (family,
    school, community)
  Rebelliousness
  Nonconformity
  Resistance to authority
  Strong need for independence
  Cultural alienation
  Fragile ego
  Feelings of failure
  Present versus future
    orientation
  Hopelessness
  Lack of self-confidence
  Low self-esteem
  Inability to form close
    positive relationships
  Vulnerability to negative peer
    pressure

Figure 8.1. Factors that place students at-risk.[10]

It is in the area of the special education and general education programs with some prevention strategies that we are going to spend the most time. Programs that have been supported by federal funding may be submitted for review to the Joint Dissemination Review Panel (JDRP) set up by the United States Department of Education to evaluate programs for possible dissemination by the National Diffusion Network (NDN). The JDRP has determined a number of the programs submitted to it to be exemplary as models for working with at-risk students. These exemplary programs have been selected, based on objective evidence of their effectiveness, and because they also provide materials and demonstration of proven practices. A few of these programs at the secondary level are shown below because of this recognition. Each program is listed by name, and a short description about it is given. Further information about these programs can be found in the Endnotes section at the end of the chapter.

- Focus Dissemination Project—a program in Hastings, Minnesota, for training secondary teachers to be able to provide alternative education for students who are disaffected or nonconforming[11]
- INTERCEPT: A Positive Alternative to Pupil Suspensions, Truancy and Dropouts—a program in Ossining, New York, whose purpose is to train secondary teachers in effective discipline procedures, classroom management skills, and instructional skills[12]
- Educational Services for School-Age Parents (ESSP)—a program in New Brunswick, New Jersey, that provides mainstreaming of regular academic subjects, a five-credit course in childcare and development, nutritional training, group and individual counseling, and an introduction to local service agencies for expectant school-age students[13]
- Cooperative Federation for Educational Experiences (Project Coffee)—an alternative occupational program in high technology in Oxford, Maine, for use with secondary students who are disaffected/alienated[14]
- Ethical Issues in Decision Making—a program in

Scarsdale, New York, that uses a theory of cognitive moral development to foster the moral growth of high school students in school governance and in ethical issues courses[15]
- Institute for Creative Education (ICE)—a sequentially ordered curriculum in Sewell, New Jersey, that teaches a creative problem-solving process in many subject areas to heterogeneously group gifted and talented classes for grades K–12[16]
- Talents Unlimited—a structured program in Mobile, Alabama, that applies a multiple-talent theory to instruction in the regular classroom[17]
- Cambridge and Somerville Program for Alcohol Rehabilitation (CASPER)—a program in Massachusetts that contains as part of its Decisions About Drinking curriculum, units for grades 3–12 designed to improve attitudes and cognitive knowledge related to alcohol use and alcoholism[18]
- Curriculum for Meeting Modern Problems (The New Model Me)—a Boston, Massachusetts, program with curricula to assist students in grades 9–12 to understand the causes and consequences of behavior. The program can be used as a course or as a supplement to existing courses[19]
- LEARNCYCLE-Responsive Teaching—an intensive training program in Seattle, Washington, designed to develop in teachers flexible, effective skills for managing and teaching mainstreamed or high-risk students[20]

PROGRAM IMPLEMENTATION AND ASSESSMENT

Why do some of these programs work and others do not? In successful programs, you normally find that an extensive set of services are offered in the program to cover the multiple needs of students. These programs and their staffs are usually flexible and allow for the individual needs of the students to be met. Successful program approaches also recognize the influence of the family as well as the surrounding socio-economic and physical environment. Services provided in these programs are pertinent, accessible to those who need them, and are easy to use. Program barriers, such as cost, culture, language, and inadequate transportation, have been minimized or eliminated. Staff associated with these programs care about students, have and take the time to provide intensive help, and are able to win trust.[21]

Any good evaluation or assessment plan uses a multifaceted approach to collecting feedback. It is best to start to assess a program when it is in progress so that changes, if they are needed, can be made more easily. This can be accomplished through the use of surveys, audits, listening sessions, taped information, developed materials, observations, questionnaires, and many other means where you can obtain feedback. The purpose is to use feedback information as a guide to seeing how the program is operating, making any adjustments or improvements to the process that the feedback calls for, and checking for success.

In order to assess whether or not an at-risk program is successful, you need to look at the entire program process from the planning phase all the way through the implementation phase. In order to do this, a fairly standard set of program guidelines are offered here.

1. *Where are we?* Administrators need to determine, first and foremost, where the school is. What are the needs and opportunities for promoting learning and reducing risk for students? This should be assessed at the community level, the school level, the classroom level, and on the individual student level.

2. *What are our goals?* Administrators must facilitate the setting of goals and objectives that are used as the guidelines for developing activities for at-risk students as well as the criteria upon which the program progress will be measured. This will necessitate bringing to the table all the policies, rules and regulations, school codes, operating procedures, and objectives under which a program may be operated.

3. *What are the activities?* Administrators must facilitate the exploration and determination of appropriate program activities for at-risk students, both planned and spontaneous, that

will be provided to assist and support students in the attainment of the program goals.

4. *What curriculum changes must be made?* Administrators must facilitate the exploration and determination of any curriculum changes that may take place by implementation of an at-risk program, which are designed to increase learning, promote positive involvement, and decrease any negative aspects of learning for at-risk students.

5. *What type of communications must we have?* Administrators must create a continuing atmosphere of communication among staff, students, parents, and the community about the goals, activities, and procedures of the at-risk program, and how input and program assessment will affect changes.

6. *What resources and staff development are necessary?* Administrators must facilitate the determination and development of plans for gathering and allocating resources, and for any staff development that will be necessary for at-risk program implementation, such as component training or weekly/monthly training sessions.

7. *What monitoring process will be used?* Administrators must facilitate the planning and implementation of a continuous monitoring process that allows for changes and modifications to take place for improvement in at-risk programs.

8. *What will be the process of evaluation?* Administrators must facilitate the determination of a process for evaluation of at-risk programs once a program has been implemented and an internal program monitoring process has indicated that plans are being carried out. Evaluation in this phase should focus on the goals and objectives of the program, how well they are being met, and what changes are taking place because of them.[22]

ROLE OF THE SCHOOL ADMINISTRATOR

The role of school administrators in this process, as alluded to above, is to provide leadership and to facilitate the implementation of an at-risk program or programs that maximize learning and minimize the conditions that deter or inhibit learning from taking place in the school. The interventions or program components advocated by administrators will depend upon the type of approach that they take and will dictate the type of solutions that they are seeking for at-risk students.

One way administrators can differentiate the types of at-risk programs for students is based on what they are to be used for. Are they to be used as therapy, accommodation, or as a preventive device? If the overall goal of the program is to try to fix the problems of at-risk students, then you would choose some type of intervention program, probably involving your counselors or social workers, or some type of remediation program to treat the problem through a therapy approach. If the overall goal is to manage and care for these students, your approach might be alternative classrooms or classes with other at-risk students where you could take an accommodating stance. This approach could moderate some of the disruptive behavior problems, but would not necessarily change the at-risk status or behaviors of the students. If the overall goal is to work with the total school and alter school practices to try to ensure success for all students, your approach could be one of trying to prevent at-riskedness now, rather than having to deal with it later.[23]

SUMMARY

The answer to the question "Which at-risk program is best for my school?" emerges from how well you as the administrator have assessed the climate of your school and the needs of the individual students. You must ask, Who have you found to be at risk? What are your expectations for improvement? Who needs to be involved in the planning and implementation of an at-risk program? Once you have gathered this preliminary data, a holistic, collaborative approach involving persons at all levels with the administrator as facilitator empowering others to be the leaders is the key to program implementation and to success.

REVIEW ACTIVITIES

1. Think of the programs in your school that were designed to meet the needs of at-risk students.

- List each of the programs and the resources being spent on them.
- Classify each program as either treatment, pacification, or prevention.
2. Assume that you are going to develop and implement an educational plan for your students who are at risk.
    - What will be the attributes of this plan that you will put into place?
    - What will be the impact on at-risk students?
    - What will be the impact on educationally advantaged students?
3. What do you believe about the factors that cause students to be at risk in your school?
4. What are the most common characteristics of at-risk students today?
5. How are the issues of dropout rates and identification of disabilities related to understanding who at-risk learners are?
6. How has the population of at-risk learners changed over the past 10 years? 20 years?

ENDNOTES

1 The definition used here was adapted from the work of Sagor, R. 1993. *At-Risk Students: Reaching and Teaching Them*, Swampscott, MA: Watersun Publishing Company, Inc., pp. 3–4.

2 Veale, J. R. 1990. *The Cost of Dropping out of School and the Productivity Benefits of Returning and Graduating. A Survey of Iowa's Alternative School Graduates from 1987 to 1989*. Des Moines, IA: Iowa Department of Education.

3 Ibid.

4 Department of Commerce, Bureau of the Census. 1989. *Statistical Abstracts of the United States, 19th Ed.* Washington, DC: U.S. GPO.

5 Veale, J. R. 1990. *The Cost of Dropping out of School and the Productivity Benefits of Returning and Graduating. A Survey of Iowa's Alternative School Graduates from 1987 to 1989*. Des Moines, IA: Iowa Department of Education.

6 Brown, R. 1985. *Reconnecting Youth: The Next Stage of Reform*. Denver, CO: Business Advisory Council, Education Commission of the States.

7 U.S. Department of Education. 1988. *Youth Indicators, 1988: Trends in the Well-Being of American Youth*. Washington, DC: U.S. GPO.

8 Sagor, R. 1993. *At-Risk Students: Reaching and Teaching Them.* Swampscott, MA: Watersun Publishing Company, Inc., pp. 11–13.
9 Peterson, R. C. 1988. "The 'At-Risk' Child," *OSAP High Risk Youth Update* 1(1,2):1–3.
10 The Factors That Put Students At Risk information is adapted from the 'Risk Factors' chart, Goplerud, E. N. 1990. "Breaking New Ground for Youth at Risk: Program Summaries." *OSAP Technical Report No. 1* (DHHS, Publication No. [ADM] 89-1658). Washington, DC: U.S. Department of Health and Human Services, p. 2.
11 For more information about the Focus Dissemination Project, contact Focus Dissemination Project, Human Resource Associates, Inc., P.O. Box 303, Hastings, MN 55033.
12 For more information about Intercept, contact Middle School, Van Cortland Ave., Ossining, NY 10562.
13 For further information concerning the ESSP program, contact New Brunswick High School, 1125 Livingston Ave., New Brunswick, NJ 08901.
14 For more information concerning Project Coffee, contact Oxford High School Annex, Main Street, Oxford, MA 01540.
15 For more information about this program, contact Scarsdale Public Schools, 45 Wayside Lane, Scarsdale, NY 10583.
16 For further information about ICE, contact Educational Information and Resource Center, Box 209, Route 4, Delsea Drive, Sewell, NJ 08080.
17 For more information about this program, contact Talents Unlimited, 1107 Arlington Street, Mobile, AL 36605.
18 For further information about CASPER, contact CASPER, 226 Highland Avenue, Somerville, MA 02143.
19 For further information about this program, contact Learning for Life/MSH. Dept. NDN, 165 Allendale Road, Boston, MA 02130.
20 For more information about Learncycle, contact Highland Public Schools, Washington State Facilitator, 15675 Ambaum Blvd., SW, Seattle, WA 98166.
21 The Why Programs Work information is adapted from the "Why They Work" chart, Goplerud, E. N. 1990. "Breaking New Ground for Youth at Risk: Program Summaries." *OSAP Technical Report No. 1* (DHHS, Publication No. [ADM] 89-1658). Washington, DC: U.S. Department of Health and Human Services, p.4.
22 Adapted from the "Components of a Comprehensive Program" in Evelyn Hunt Ogden and Vito Germinario. 1988. *The At-Risk Student: Answers for Educators.* Lancaster, PA: Technomic Publishing Company, Inc., pp. 2–4.
23 Sagor, R. 1993. *At-Risk Students: Reaching and Teaching Them.* Swampscott, MA: Watersun Publishing Company, Inc. pp. 26–27.

BIOGRAPHIES

FLOYD Boschee is an Associate Professor, Division of Educational Administration, School of Education, University of South Dakota, where he teaches and conducts research in educational leadership, supervision, and curriculum. For 18 years, he was a teacher, coach, athletic director, and assistant superintendent for curriculum and instruction. He has also served as chairman of departments of education, presented at national and international conferences, published extensively in national journals, and authored or co-authored the books, *Grouping = Growth, Effective Reading Programs: The Administrator's Role, Outcome-Based Education: Developing Programs Through Strategic Planning,* and *Authentic Assessment: The Key to Unlocking Student Success.*

Bonnie M. Beyer is an Associate Professor of Educational/Public Administration in the School of Education at the University of Michigan-Dearborn where she teaches and conducts research on the principalship, organizational leadership and theory, school law, and curriculum. Her educational experience includes 20 years of school administration in regular and special education. She has published in national journals and presented research at state and national conferences.

Jeri L. Engelking is Associate Dean and Professor, Division of Educational Administration, School of Education, University of South Dakota, where he is a college administrator and teaches and conducts research in educational leadership, multimedia computer technology, and school law. For 13 years, he was a teacher, coach, athletic director, and building level and district level public school administrator. He has also served as the Director of Graduate Studies for the School of Education, published extensively in national journals, and presented at numerous international and national conferences.

Marlys Ann Boschee is an Associate Professor, Division of Curriculum and Instruction, School of Education, University of South Dakota, where she teaches reading methods courses and is an academic advisor for education majors. She began her career as a teacher in a one-room rural school and was an elementary teacher, grades 1 through 6, for several years prior to completing her master's and doctorate degrees in school administration and curriculum and instruction. She has published in national journals, presented at state and national conferences, and co-authored the book, *Effective Reading Programs: The Administrator's Role*.

INDEX

ADAMS, M. J., 156
ALCORN, M. D., 157
ALEXANDER, P. A., 78, 79, 80
ALEXANDER, M. D., 44, 191
ALEXANDER, K., 44, 191
America 2000, 41
American Psychiatric Association
   diagnostic criteria, 23
Americans with Disabilities Act, 6, 16
AMUNDSON, K., 158
ANDERSON, T. R., 158
ARCHBALD, D. A., 254
Area Redevelopment Act, 198
Aspira of New York, Inc. v. Board of City of New York, 167
At-risk students, 207
   abusive behavior, 257, 258
   administrator's role, 265
   characteristics, 258
   definition, 257
   factors, 261
   programs, 260
      assessment, 264
      implementation, 263
      research, 260
Athens, 49
Attention Deficit Disorder, 23
Attention Deficit-Hyperactivity Disorder, 23
AU, K., 156
Autism, 21

Babylonians, 49
BAGHBAN, M., 156
BANKS, C. A.
BANKS, J. A., 250
BARON, M. A., 254, 255
BERGMAN, J. L., 157
BERNSTEIN, C. D., 44
BEYER-HOUDA, B., 192
Bilingual education, 159
   administrator's role, 186
   aides, 175
   black English, 167
   career counseling, 179
   challenges, 160
   chronology of legislation, 170
   description, 159
   English as a second language, 180
   enhancement, 184
   family culture, 185
   financial assistance, 171, 177
   guidelines, 168
   historical background, 162, 163
   immigration policies, 159
   implementation grants, 172, 173
   innovation, 184
   instructional programs, 178
   intensified instruction, 183
   international communication, 160
   language proficiency, 179
   level appropriate, 171

Bilingual education, *(continued)*
  limited English proficiency, 159
  local educational agency, 176
  paraprofessionals, 175
  parent involvement, 185
    support, 185
  program development, 172, 173
  program scope, 163
  projects
    enhancements, 174
    school-wide, 175
    system-wide, 175
  purposes, 161
  standard English, 167
  supplemental programs, 174
  technology, 183
  Title VI, 159, 165, 166, 169
  Title VII, 161, 163, 171
  transitional program, 181
    maintenance, 182
    two-way, 182
Bilingual Education Act, 164, 166, 171, 176, 178, 179, 183, 185, 186, 188
Binet, Alfred, 52
Binet-Simon Intelligence Test, 52
BISH, C. E., 80
BLOOM, B., 60
BOSCHEE, F., 156, 157, 254, 255
BOSCHEE, M. A., 157
BOYCE, B., 46
BOYER, E. L., 255
BRODINSKY, B., 158
Brown v. Board of Education, 4, 7, 165, 170
Bureau of Adult Vocational and Technical Education, 200
BROWN, R., 267
BROWNE, D., 254
BURNS, P. C., 158
BURRELLO, L. C., 45

CAMBRON-MCCABE, N. H., 191
Career education, 196
  definition, 197
  implications, 197

Career Education Incentive Act, 200
Career Preparation Education Reform Act, 195, 199, 210, 214
Carl D. Perkins Career Preparation Education Reform Act, 199, 210
Carl D. Perkins Vocational Education Act, 195, 198, 199
  supported activities, 195
CASSIDY, J., 81
Castaneda v. Pickard, 168
  guidelines, 169
CATTELL, J. MCK., 52
Charlemagne, 50
Ch'ing Dynasty, 50
Cisneros v. Corpus Christi, 165
Civil Rights Act, 159
CLARK, B., 81
CLENDENING, C., 79, 80, 81
COLEMAN, M. R., 82
COMER, J. P., 106, 158
CORTES, C., 254
CRANNEY, A. G., 155
CULLINAN, D., 45
CURRAN, F. X., 43, 44
CUSHENBERRY, D. C., 155, 158

Daniel, R. R. v. State Board of Education, 37
DAVIDMAN, L., 254
DAVIDMAN, P. T., 254
DAVIS, R., 79, 80, 81
Deaf-blind, 21
DECKER, L., 255
DEHANN, R., 79, 80
DELISLE, J., 81
DEWALT, M. K., 43
Diana v. State Board of Education, 4, 7
DUNKLEE, D. R., 191
DUNN, R., 254
DYER, P. C., 157

Education for All Handicapped Children Act, 1, 2, 3, 6, 7

Education of the Handicapped
    Amendments, The, 6, 7
Educational equity, 4
Educational Services for School-Age
    Parents, 262, 268
Elementary and Secondary
    Education Act, 4, 7, 59, 60,
    83, 198
EPSTEIN, M. H., 45
Equal Educational Opportunities
    Act, 159, 168
Ethical issues in decision making,
    262
Eurocentric view, 217
EVANS, R. N., 214

FARSTRUP, A. E., 156
FEELEY, J. T., 156
FISCHER, L., 44, 191
FLIEGLER, L. A., 80
FOSTER, A. H., 82
Free appropriate public education,
    8
FREHILL, M., 81
FRYE, J. J., 157

GALLAGHER, J. J., 78, 81, 82
GALLAGHER, S. A., 82
GALTON, F., 51
GARDNER, J., 59
GASPARD, N. J., 46
GEIGLE, R. M., 78
GEMAKE, J., 254
George-Barden Act, 198
George-Dean Act, 198
George-Ellzey Act, 198
George-Reed Act, 198
Geraud v. Schrader, 165
GERMINARIO, V., 268
GETZELS, J., 59
Gifted and Talented Children's
    Education Act, 62
Gifted education, 47
    ability areas, 47
    administrator's role, 75
    common myths, 48
    definition, 63, 66, 67

funding, 67–69
"g" factor, 54
historical background, 48
    2000 B.C. to 500 A.D., 49
    500 A.D. to 1800, 50
    1800 to 1950, 51
    1950s, 56
    1960s, 59
    1970s, 60
    1980s, 64
impact, 57
legal base, 67–71
percentage gifted, 47
program assessment, 74
program implementation, 73–74
program options, 72–73
Public Law 91-230, 60
Public Law 93-380, 61
Public Law 95-561, 62
"s" factor, 54
sacrificing investment, 64
seven primary mental abilities,
    55
state mandates, 68, 69
    Alabama, 70
    Connecticut, 71
    Nebraska, 71
    Wyoming, 69
Goals 2000: Educate America Act,
    92, 201
    components, 94
GOODLAD, J. I., 44, 46
GOPLERUD, E. N., 268
GOVE, M. K., 155, 156
GRANT, C. A., 250
GUILFORD, J. P., 57
GUNNING, T. G., 155, 156, 157

HAIRSTON, J. B., 191
HAMILTON, R. R., 191
HANSON, R., 158
HARING, N. G., 45
HARRIS, P., 155
HATA, D., 215
HAVIGHURST, R., 79, 80
HAYES, B. L., 157
Hearing impaired, 20

HEDGE, M. N., 45
HILDRETH, G., 79
HILL, P. T., 106
HILLER, R., 190
Hobson v. Hanson, 4, 7
HODGKINSON, H., 158
HOLLINGWORTH, L., 54
HONEYMAN, D. S., 44
HORTON, J. L., 46
HOYT, K. B., 214
HULL, D., 214

IMBER, M., 191
Inclusion, 36
    continuum of services 39, 40
    social value, 37
    successful inclusion, 38
    transition services, 38
Improving America's Schools Act,
    84, 98, 175
Indian Education Act, 245
    enrollment requirements, 246
Indian Self-Determination and
    Assistance Act, 246
    technical assistance centers, 247
Individualized Education Program,
    9
Individuals with Disabilities
    Education Act, 2, 4, 6, 7, 8,
    38

JACKSON, D., 80, 81
JACKSON, P., 59
JACOBS, R. L., 255
JALAII, F., 254
Japanese Tokugawa Society, 51
JAVITS, J. K., 82
JEFFREY, J., 158
Job Training Partnership Act, 202
Johann Comenius, 51
JOHNSON, L. G., 157
JOHNSON, N., 81
JOHNSON, T. P., 43
Joint Dissemination Review Panel,
    262
JONES, L. L., 156
Jose P. v. Ambach, 167

KELLETT, C., 215
KELLY, C., 191
KEMERER, F. R., 191
KENNEDY, J. F., 78
KINDER, J. S., 157
King Nebuchadnezzar, 49
KIRBY, D., 78, 79, 81
KIRP, D. L., 191
KITANO, M., 78, 79, 81
KLINE, L., 158
KRATHWOHL, D. R., 60
KUNKEL, A., 46

Larry P. v. Riles, 7
Law v. Nichols, 165, 168
Learning disability, 17
Learning styles, 234–239
Least restrictive environment, 11
LEVIN, B., 191
LOVITT, T. C., 44, 46

MACKIN, E. F., 214
MAMARAS, J., 215
MANGUM, G. L., 214
Manpower Development and
    Training Act, 198
MARLAND, S. P., 80, 82, 197, 214
MASLOW, A., 57
MASON, J., 158
MASON, J. M., 156
MATTIA, P. D., 43, 44
MCALOON, N. M., 158
MCCARTHY, M. M., 191
MCCORMICK, L., 45
MCDONNELL, L. M., 106
Mehmet the Conqueror, 50
Migrant education, 98
    parent involvement, 100
    program development, 98
MILLER, J. S., 155
MILNE, B., 78
Morgan v. Kerrigan, 167
MORSE, B., 215
MUIA, J. A., 78, 79, 80
Multicultural education, 217
    administrator's role, 248
    assessment, 233

benefits, 244
children of color, 228
curriculum, 218, 229
definition, 217
funding, 245, 248
historical background, 218
minorities, 225
mission statement, 233
parent center, 243
post-enumeration survey, 227
preschool partnership, 240
race/ethnic categories, 227
resources, 239
  community, 239
  parents, 240
school-entry partnership, 241
state mandates, 218
  Georgia, 251
  Hawaii, 223
  Indiana, 223
  Iowa, 219
  Nebraska, 223
  Tennessee, 222
work force, 228
Multiple disabilities, 19

National Advisory Council on Career Education, 200
National Apprenticeship Act, 198
National Association for Retarded Citizens, 7
National Coalition of Title I/Chapter 1 Parents, 101
National Defense Education Act, 58, 198
National Institute of Education, 200
National Parent Center, 101
Natonabah v. Board of Education of Gallup-McKinley County School District, 165
NERI, P., 215
NEWMANN, F. M., 254

Office of Career Education, 200

Office of Educational Research and Improvement, 214
OGDEN, E. H., 268
Omnibus Trade and Competitiveness Act, 199
Orthopedically impaired, 20
OSBORN, A. F., 57
OSBORN, A. G., Jr., 43

Palace school, 50
PARNELL, D., 214
Pennsylvania Association for Retarded Citizens v. Commonwealth of Pennsylvania, 4, 7
PETERSON, R. C., 268
PIKULSKI, J. J., 157
PINNELL, G. S., 157
Plato, 49
PRASEK, K., 256
Preschool PTA, 240

Reading
  ability, 107
  administrator's role, 150
    moral obligation, 154
    solution, 151
    spectacular changes, 150
  approaches, 116
    basal, 119
    individualized prescriptive, 117
    language experience, 121
    literature-based, 121
  choosing books, 123
  early experiences, 146
    educational, elementary, 148
    educational, secondary, 148
    reading, 147
  historical background, 108
    Hornbook, 108
    McGuffey Reader, 110
    New England Primer, 109
  parental support, 149
  preventive programs, 124
    Boulder Project, The, 131
    Early Intervention in Reading, 129

Reading, preventive programs
      (continued)
   Reading Recovery, 125
   Students Achieving
      Independent Learning, 135
   Success For All Program, 133
   Winston-Salem Project, The,
      134
   program assessment, 152,
   program implementation, 136
      informal inventories, 137
      interest inventories, 138
   reading skills, 143–144
   research, 112
   secondary school, 145
      building motivation, 143
   selecting teachers, 140
   state requirements, 110, 112
      Alabama, 111
      Connecticut, 111
      Hawaii, 111
      Idaho, 111
      Mississippi, 111
      Missouri, 111
   teacher skills, 142
   theories and models, 113
      bottom-up, 114
      interactive, 116
      top-down, 115
Regular Education Initiative, 5, 7
Rehabilitation Act, 2
RENZULLI, J., 81
REUTTER, E. E., Jr., 191
RIGGS, G. G., 78
Rio v. Reed, 167
ROE, B. D., 158
ROSS, O. P., 82

SADKER, D. M., 155
SADKER, M. P., 155
SAGE, D. D., 45
SAGOR, R., 267, 268
SAMUELS, S. J., 156
SCHIMMEL, D., 191
SCHLESINGER, A. M., Jr., 250, 256
School-to-Work Opportunities Act,
   201

SCHOOP, R. J., 191
SCHUNERT, J. R., 157
SERGIOVANNI, T., 46
Serious emotional disturbance, 18
Serna v. Portales Municipal Schools,
   167
SHEARER, B. A., 157
SHORT, R. A., 157
SHRYBMAN, J. A., 44, 46
SIEGEL, D. F., 158
SLEETER, C. E., 250
Smith-Bankhead Act, 198
Smith-Hughes Act, 197
SOMERFIELD, M., 155
SORENSON, G. P., 44
Sparta, 49
Special Education
   administrator's role, 42
      challenges, 2, 3, 16
      visionary leadership, 42
   definition, 2, 6, 9
   disability classifications, 17–24
   due process, 10
   funding, 11
      building level expenditures,
         14
      capital expense, 15
      formulas, 13
      local distribution, 12
   historical background, 1–3
      Public Law 94-142, 1, 2, 6
      Public Law 101-476, 2, 6
   least restrictive environment,
      11
   legal base, 3
      children with disabilities, 6
      civil rights protection, 6
      educational equity, 5
      legal advocates, 3
      obligations, 16
      Public Law 93-380, 5
      Public Law 93-516, 5
      Public Law 99-457, 6
      rights of children with
         disabilities, 8
      Section 504 of the
         Rehabilitation Act, 3, 15

sequence of legislation for the handicapped, 7
Title 34 of the Code of Federal Regulations, 6
Meetings and hearings, 24
  annual review, 29
  assessment, 27
  identification and placement, 26
  multidisciplinary conference, 27
  pre-referral intervention, 25
  staffing, 30–31
  student rights, 32
  three-year reevaluation, 32
non-discriminatory evaluation, 11
programs and services, 33
  curriculum development, 34
  Individual Education Plan, 33
  instructional support, 35
  staff development, 36
related services, 10
Speech and language impairment, 18
Sputnik, 56, 58
STANDERFORD, S., 106
Stanford-Binet Test of Intelligence, 53
STANLEY, P., 215
STEIN, M., 81
STEWART, D., 189
STOODT, B. D., 158
STRICLAND, D. S., 156
STULLER, J., 81
Suleiman the Magnificent, 50
SWASSING, R., 79, 80
SZPORER, M., 157

Tang Dynasty, 50
TANNENBAUM, A., 80
TAYLOR, B. M., 157
TAYLOR, D., 155
TAYLOR, I. A., 57
Tech-prep education, 196
  articulation agreement, 196
  programs, 199
  purpose, 196
TEITELBAUM, H., 190
TERMAN, L. M., 53, 79
THOMPSON, D. C., 44
TIEDT, I. M., 250
TIEDT, P. L., 250
Title I, 83
  add-on programs, 99
  administrator's role, 101, 103
    competency areas, 102
    interpersonal skills, 102
  beyond federal regulations, 98
  eligibility, 89
    criteria, 90
  extended day programs, 99
  funding, 91, 95,
    first year, 96
  historical background, 83–84
  language skills, 99
  migrant education, 85, 98
  parental involvement, 96, 100
  program development, 97, 98
  program requirements, 90
  pull-out programs, 99
  purpose of, 83
  school district requirements, 87
  send-in programs, 99
  service plan, 93
  staff training, 100
  state requirements, 85
  survival skills, 99
traumatic brain injury, 22
Teachers of English to Speakers-of Other Languages, 181
TORBE, M., 155
TORRANCE, E. P., 59
TOVEY, D. R., 157
TOYNBEE, R., 60
TRACHTENBURG, P., 155, 156
Turkish Empire, 50

United States Census Bureau, 226
United States Department of Education, 47

United States Office of Gifted and
  Talented Education, 61, 64
United States Office of
  Management and Budget,
  226
United States v. Texas, 165

VACCA, J. L., 155, 156
VACCA, R. T., 155, 156
VAN GEEL, T., 191
VEALE, J. R., 267
Visually impaired, 20
  terms, 20
Vocational education, 195, 197
  funding, 198
  governance, 198
  purpose, 195
Vocational Rehabilitation Act, 5, 7,
  198

WALLAS, G., 55
WARD, C., 155
WEPNER, B., 156
WHITEHEAD, B. M., 157
WILL, M. C., 44
WITTY, P., 80
WOOD, J. W., 43, 44
WOOD, R. C., 44

YUDOF, M. G., 191

ZENHAUSERN, R., 254